RECOGNITIONS

JULIUS EVOLA

RECOGNITIONS

STUDIES ON MEN AND PROBLEMS FROM THE PERSPECTIVE OF THE RIGHT

TRANSLATED BY JOHN BRUCE LEONARD

ARKTOS
LONDON 2017

Published in 2017 by Arktos Media Ltd.

www.arktos.com

Printed in the United Kingdom.

Originally published as *Ricognizioni. Uomini e problemi.* Italy, 1974.

TRANSLATION	John Bruce Leonard
EDITOR	Melissa Mészáros
COVER	Tor Westman
LAYOUT	Daniel Friberg
ISBN	978-1-912079-18-6 (Softcover)
	978-1-912079-17-9 (Hardback)
	978-1-912079-16-2 (Ebook)

CONTENTS

TRANSLATOR'S FORWARD

Recognitions is Evola's last book. That honor is usually, and in a way justly, accorded to *Ride the Tiger*, as this was the last book of unitary theme which Evola penned with the intention of publishing *as* a book. The present work rather has the character of a collection of various essays from Evola's last years. Nonetheless, it would be a mistake to consider this volume as being but a posthumous assemblage of the author's minor writings. Evola was alive when this book was published; it was indeed issued as the fifteenth number of a special series from the publishing house *Edizioni Mediterranee* called *Orizzonti dello spirito*, a series which Evola himself founded and personally directed almost until his death. The work in every way bears Evola's imprimatur, and it deserves to be regarded as his final *opus*—not only for his personal oversight of its arrangement and publication, but also for its quality and its abiding pertinence.

Judging by its tone and its content, it is credible that Evola himself was aware that this should be his final literary effort, that he organized it as his final testament, his last word on the work of a lifetime. With the surety of a master's hand, he touches on most of the major themes that he made his own in the course of a rich, varied, and productive writing career. From esotericism to his exceptionally even-handed verdicts on modern and classic literary figures; from his investigations into the secret history of Antiquity to his relentlessly trenchant critiques of "current events" in politics and society; from his political Traditionalism to his metaphysical spiritualism, *Recognitions* is almost

as wide-ranging as Evola himself. One emerges from this book as a
diver who has delved, without the aid of any equipment, deep into the
currents of some life-filled ocean—amazed that he should have seen
so much and been carried so profoundly in so brief a time, almost, as
it were, in a single breath.

For this reason, *Recognitions* makes for an excellent introduction
to Evola's thought. It can profitably be read from front to back as a
survey of Evola's final judgements on any number of present or past
philosophical, historical, and spiritual figures and currents; but it can
also be browsed at pleasure and according to one's taste, beginning
from those essays which treat of specific "men and problems" in which
one is particularly interested. Each essay is naturally self-contained
and can be read independently of its context; but at the same time,
each essay is the product of Evola's remarkably integrated and organically interconnected ideas, so that the entire volume, though it be a
compilation, nonetheless possesses a decided rhythmic and philosophical integrity. This makes for a certain richness which is unusual
in compendia of this kind, and the diligent reader will certainly find
that *Recognitions* bears reading and rereading.

I have referenced the *pertinence* of this book for our contemporary
plight. Though the world has changed dramatically in the almost
half-century since Evola's death, the problems that Evola most directly
confronts are every bit as relevant today as they were in his time. The
esoteric problems are, of course, perennial; so far as the political questions go, they have but extremified in the passage of the years. Nothing
about our contemporary straits should have much surprised Evola.
The organized chaos of the "Fifth Estate" whose advent he proclaims in
Chapter 3 has done nothing but expand in influence. We have all of us
danced, to some extent or other, the frenetic dance of the "Tarantula's
Bite" of Chapter 8. The great forces which Western materialism has unleashed in the Orient, which Evola describes with such succinct skill in
Chapter 11, perchance stand now upon the brink of flooding out upon

the world. The question, considered in Chapter 23, of whether or not this West today has its idea, is more urgent than ever. And the "culture of the Right," the "historiography of the Right" of the final chapters of this volume, are yet in need of the united work of our present generations. Indeed, looking at the world today, one is hard-pressed to find any contemporary current which Evola did not predict, and at least touch upon, precisely in the present essays.

The reader might of course propose certain issues of gravity which are not mentioned in the present volume. Yet this book precisely, as indeed all of Evola's work, can offer us something even more precious than the direct address of this or that specific problem; it can prepare us *in spirit* for all problems, for catastrophe itself; it can teach us the heights. Today, as much as the day it was first published, it is an inimitable resource for "recognition" of the times, and of ourselves within, and without, the times.

Note on the Title

Recognitions rings strangely in the English ear; but *Ricognizioni* is no less peculiar in the Italian. I have therefore not altered the title, as is sometimes done when foreign titles do not render well in secondary languages. I take it for granted that the name in all its peculiarity was selected quite deliberately.

"Recognition" means first and foremost to recognize the *face* of someone—which means, by an older etymology, the *persona*, the *personality*, problem which occupies Evola deeply in the course of these essays, and particularly in those which are dedicated to the analysis of specific human beings or their work. Secondarily, "recognition" means to recognize merit or demerit, to rightly judge of the quality and the temperament of "men and problems"; thus we say, for instance, that such and such a man or action has been "recognized" with such and such an award. The title therefore indicates the importance of *rank*, of being able to perceive and adjudicate the quality of the characteristic figures of our time, and to locate them in an overall vision and hierarchy, according to the clear standards of the Right and the Tradition. Many of the essays herein are therefore naturally dedicated to correcting *errors* of recognition—critiquing figures who are in urgent need of critique from the perspective of the Right, such as Giovanni Gentile, Giovanni Papini, and Pope Rancalli. Others are dedicated to recalling to our esteem congenial and important figures who are nigh-forgotten or underestimated—figures certainly of the rank of Joseph de Maistre and René Guénon, but also lesser known names like Vilfredo Pareto and Werner Sombart, statesmen like Metternich, and names from a distant antiquity like Epicurus and Emperor Julian. Others yet are dedicated to sorting out problems upon which the Right has evidenced some degree of confusion or dithering, as the questions of "work" and of Masonry.

Finally, and most fundamentally, there is the innermost sense of recognition: not indeed the recognition of the ideas and rank of others, but *the recognition of our own ideas, the rank of our own souls and spirits.* Evola's investigations here serve principally to prepare the way for a new "orientation," to use one of Evola's favorite words; they serve to direct us toward the heights, even as "metal immediately *feels* the magnet, discovers the magnet and orients itself and moves irresistibly toward it" (Chapter 6), and guide us to our proper place in a hierarchy dedicated to those heights. The "contrary of a revolution" which Evola hoped to prepare (and indeed, as multiple passages from this work attest, which he never ceased working toward and believing to be possible) can only begin *within* the men of the Right, in an internal "revolution from the heights" precisely *contrary* to that process of spiritual degeneration which he describes so hauntingly in his analysis of "The Problem of Decadence."

As he himself put it with his imperious elegance, "Today there is truly a great need for people who do not chatter, nor 'write,' nor argue, but who begin with *being*" (Chapter 38). *Recognitions* is nothing if not a call to precisely *that* kind of beginning—a call from a man who, more than almost any other of our sickly, materialistic, externally obsessed modern times, lived in precisely such a way, and never wearied of directing himself toward being and toward the heights.

For all these reasons, *Recognitions* is thus a profound work of "pedagogy," a work dedicated to forcing the best members of our present generation to *recognize themselves*. Its structure, its content, its form, are all ideal for orienting these men and bringing them to awareness of the scope of the grave tasks now before those of us who would renew the Tradition. And for this reason the publication of this volume in English translation comes not a moment too soon.

Note on the translation

I have attempted everywhere to render Evola's prose more Anglo-Saxon, but nowhere more pedestrian. Where Evola has preferred abstruse or arcane vocabulary, I have sought its equivalent in English. Nor have I tried to disentangle his elaborate Latinate sentence structure, save as I have felt that this was required by the obligations of good English prose. I have nowhere attempted to normalize his idiosyncratic expressions, when these are equally curious in the original Italian—as when, for instance, he states that the philosopher Benedetto Croce opposed fascism on account of his "personal equation," rather than from any consistent ideological motivation. Likewise I have preserved (save in very few cases where this would have proved confusing) his almost exclusive narration in the first-person plural, even when this formality seems odd; the reader who finds this ubiquitous "we" aloof or haughty is invited to peruse Chapter 15 of the present volume. Certain passages in this volume are technically exacting—for instance, the entire chapter on Michelstaedter. I have not sought to render these passages any more accessible, for I have not forgotten the teaching of the ancients, which is surely never neglected by Evola, that reading, too, can have its "initiatory" aspect. I have wished to preserve Evola's difficulty in the spirit of Evola himself—a man who was by birth, by temperament, and by destiny an aristocrat, and who wrote under no other sign.

If anyone should find the challenging quality of the writing herein to be obnoxious or exclusivist, he is invited to take his protest before the Baron himself, whose spirit, we may dare pray, yet "deigns to glance down upon the affairs of us mortals" from those heights to which it has doubtless ascended.

— John Bruce Leonard

1. ON THE "NEW HUMANISM"

Taken in a broad sense, the term "humanism" is perhaps the aptest characterization of the principle orientation and the ultimate grounding of the civilization of the modern era. Indeed one can generally designate as humanism that shift which has made man as man the center of the vision of life, of activity, and of values. As is known, this orientation commenced in the West in the Renaissance period; it was associated with the first surfacing of a profane science of nature, with the bursting forth of a special kind of artistic creativity, with alterations of custom, and with a particular line of study which took its bearings from antiquity. Its general watchword was the overcoming of the dark Medieval Period, the revelation of life, the discovery of Man and of his "dignity" and "liberty," and the opening of those roads that lead toward dominion of the world.

So far as the paramount feature of this humanism goes, René Guénon's statement applies to the movement as a whole: man severed himself from heaven with the excuse of conquering the earth.[1] In more concrete terms one can say that the alteration consisted in the shift

---

1 René Guénon (1886-1951) was a French writer, one of the paramount defenders and explicators of the idea of Tradition. He was highly regarded by Evola, with whom he kept a long correspondence. In Guénon's quest for a living tradition of initiation, he moved to Cairo in 1930, where he remained until his death. He was the author of some thirty books on the occult sciences, spiritualism, symbology, and the plight of the West. Guénon is referenced throughout *Recognitions*, but see in particular Chapter 35 which is dedicated to him.

of the center of being, from that which represents the dimension of transcendence in man to that which is purely human, in a one-sided, abnormal, finally teratological development of the latter to the detriment of the former, and even unto the atrophy and the silencing of the former: whereas it was precisely this aspect—the dimension of transcendence—which characterized the true dignity of man.

Humanism in the current sense of the term should be considered only as a particular phenomenon in a vaster whole—as a line of study in the art and letters of antiquity. One must underline however the "tendency" in all such studies: the antiquity they kept particularly in view was that part of antiquity which appeared more or less congenial to the new climate. The sacral and metaphysical aspects of antiquity, the symbolic contents and "non-human" evocators present in many works of ancient art—all of this was more or less neglected; a recovery or "rediscovery" of everything in antiquity which had significance for what may be called a "traditional" vision of the world is practically nonexistent in the erudite humanism of the Renaissance period. In this humanism, rather, the ideals of a simple "culture" began to take shape—a "culture" associated for a time with the idea of a "formation of the personality." Put in such terms, this "culture" could evidently encompass nothing other than a partial or peripheral domain.

It is on this plane of "culture" and "human personality" that "humanism" would reappear some centuries on in the so-called neohumanism defended by Wilhelm von Humboldt[2] and others. And here we are presented with a highly characteristic situation. Following a natural concatenation of causes and effects, he who "severed himself from heaven with the excuse of conquering the earth" had to pay the piper for his conquest, to the extent that technology and industrialization took form in the new profane science of nature. The price was

---

2   Humboldt (1767-1835) was a Prussian diplomat and an intellectual, remembered principally for his contributions to linguistics and education. His Enlightenment-style defense of freedom and "self-cultivation" influenced Schiller and Marcuse.

the enslavement of man to productive work, following the decline of traditional craftsmanship. Neo-humanism was marked chiefly by an attempted reaction against this revolution: it defended the values of pure "culture," which was the foundation for the formation of the personality, against the first intrusions of the world of labor. And the needs it formulated continued to be affirmed by those who considered the new civilization not as a *Kultur* but as a *Zivilisation*.[3] These last are the German terms which Spengler used to characterize his opposition to a spurious and material kind of civilization, for he held such civilization to be deleterious to the values of personality and of the spirit. Unfortunately, such values rarely meant anything more than *precisely* the simple world of "culture" and of "thought," whose outer boundary was seen to lie in philosophical speculation. Literature, thought, and philosophy against natural, technological, and industrial science— such has been the stance of neo-humanism.

That is fleeting and precarious enough a position, confronted with those trends obedient to the so-called "meaning of history," which has signified nothing else than the realization, at an augmented pace, of a complete "terrestrialization" of man and the liquidation of whatever could yet count as his vestigial personality in the face of the collective and the "social," the standardized, the uniformistically unified. And so almost at once a defection arose in the neo-humanistic camp. In Germany, one understood by "classic humanism" the position defended by Humboldt; but this humanism was countered by a neo-

---

3 The two possible forms of society according to Oswald Spengler. The first, *Kultur*, might be described as embodying the virile youth of a society, vital and spiritually valid; the second, *Zivilisation*, represents a kind of ossification of *Kultur*, the intellectualistic and decrepit conclusion of *Kultur* in empty formalism and stagnant skepticism. Evola touches on this distinction again in Chapter 6 below. Spengler (1880-1936) was a German historian best known for his book *The Decline of the West*, a two-volume work in which he outlined his theory that the "Faustian Civilization" of the West has entered into its winter, its terminal decline.

humanism of writers and pedagogues in the writings of men such as T. Litt and E. Spranger.[4] These last sought through specious arguments to eliminate the antithesis affirmed by Humboldtian humanism, and to demonstrate that applying oneself to nature, inserting man into the modern world of work and technology, technical-professional training, and so on and so forth, are but so many means for an "up-to-date" formation of the true personality. But theirs at bottom were nothing but feeble voices compared with the more brazen and concrete forms of ideology which most fully embraced the "meaning of history." The term "humanism," in full conformity with the wider sense given to it at the beginning of these notes, was taken up again by Marxism and by Soviet communism, which presumed to represent and to realize "integral humanism," a "new humanism," by stigmatizing as a parasitical form and an idle bourgeois and individualistic digression everything to which the previous "aristocratic humanism of culture" might have returned. The "humanism of work" is yet another formula of our days, and it indicates the descent in level[5] of the needs on the part of those who had claimed to celebrate the "discovery of man," his dignity, the "infinity" of his spirit: it is all nothing but rhetoric which has finally been replaced by the cult of that work animal called collectivized man. Truly, it is enough to make the Olympians smile, if they yet deign to glance down upon the affairs of us mortals...

Even in Italy, manifestations of this same orientation have unfortunately not been lacking, in the work of certain intellectuals of our land.

---

4   Theodore Litt (1880-1962), German phenomenologist and educator. Eduard Spranger (1882-1963) was a German psychologist, whose *Types of Men* (1914) made a notable contribution to personality theory with his six "value attitudes" as the description of ideal types of personalities.

5   This is an important concept in Evola, and one to which he returns time and again. "Descent in level" or "elevation in level" is taken to indicate the inner, spiritual change of an individual, in his movement toward or away from the heights.

To give a sense of the sphere in which these intellectuals move, we would like to mention a book which happened to fall into our hands. Its author is Ugo Spirito, and its title is—none other—*The New Humanism*. Ugo Spirito is an old acquaintance of ours, and a disciple of Gentilian "actualism."[6] Spirito later deviated somewhat from his Master, above all in certain politico-social applications of his doctrine, which already anticipated his subsequent "opening to the left." Indeed it was Spirito together with Arnaldo Volpicelli[7] who, at the Convention of Corporative Studies held in Ferrara in 1932,[8] defended a vaguely communist interpretation of fascist corporatism (the nationalized

---

6   "Actualism" is the idealistic philosophy of Giovanni Gentile (1875-1944), the neo-Hegelian intellectual of the Fascist Period. Gentile was a principle intellectual and political figure during Mussolini's rule, and remained a rigorous proponent of the fascist regime throughout all its vicissitudes. He even came to be known as the "philosopher of fascism," though this last epithet is contested by Evola in the chapter of the present volume dedicated to Gentile (Chapter 34 below). "Actualism" emphasized the primacy of the "pure act" of thinking, so much so that this act is seen to produce the world of phenomena itself—another idea which Evola critiques below.

7   Intellectual (1898-1962) of the Fascist Period and student of Giovanni Gentile. Together with Ugo Spirito, he directed the journal *Nuovi studi di diritto, economia e politica* (New Studies in Law, Economy, and Politics).

8   The Second Conference on Trade Unionist and Corporatist Studies, which was the scene of a heated debate between the "privatistic" and the "publicistic" visions of the fascist state—a kind of reflection in miniature of the wider debate between liberal capitalism and socialism. Arnoldo Volpicelli and Ugo Spirito were the major, and certainly the most vocal, defenders of the "publicistic" or corporatist position, which argued the individual must be subsumed under the collective, and that every individual within the fascist state must be considered as an organ thereof. A direct quotation from Spirito's contribution to that conference indicates the spirit of his ideas: "Capital passes from the shareholders to the workers, who become the owners of the corporation." This conference was as heated in its fallout as it had been in its content, leading to a lengthy debate in the years following on the nature and organization of the fascist state. The "violent reactions" of which Evola speaks came in this post-conference period.

"proprietary corporation") reflecting the thesis that communism was but an "impatient corporatism," a corporatism that proceeds too hastily—meaning that there were no substantial differences between the ideas of fascism and communism, that at bottom one dealt solely with different times or different techniques for the realization of the same objective. This thesis provoked violent reactions on the part of those who had a sense of the higher values of the fascist movement (we remind ourselves of an excellent little polemical by Guido Cavallucci: *Is Fascism on the Road to Moscow?*[9]).

Subsequent developments demonstrated however that the disciple here anticipated the Master, because in Gentile himself an analogous leftist line of thought soon followed, when he proclaimed a so-called "humanism of work." This was supposed to surpass the previous "humanism of culture," which by that time had been judged inadequate and outdated.

Speaking of which, a curious inversion of attitudes could be observed in the "two brothers of discord" of that ideological camp, both exponents of Italian neo-Hegelianism: Croce[10] and Gentile.

---

9   There is not much information available on Guido Cavallucci. We learn from the *Path of Cinnabar* that he was a friend of Evola's, and served a time as the president of the *Unione Monarchica Italiana*, an organization founded in 1944 and dedicated to the defense, and subsequently the restoration, of the Italian monarchy. The book referenced here is difficult to find even in Italian, and has never been translated into English.

10   Benedetto Croce (1866-1952), celebrated Italian statesman, art critic, and philosopher, developer of an idealistic historicism. Although Croce began by hailing the advent of the fascist regime, he later distanced himself from it, and finally transformed into one of its most vocal critics after the political murder of Giacomo Matteotti by a fascist group—a watershed event in the early years of the Fascist Period which many of the regime's critics attempted to trace back to Mussolini himself. (Mussolini's involvement in the murder is still debated.) Croce was tolerated by the fascist regime, notwithstanding his blatant and open censure of the same, and remained a Senator during the Fascist Period.

Commencing from a liberalism of the right, Croce, after several preliminary studies of the ideologies of Marxism and communism, maintained a consistently negative attitude toward them. If in the end he sided against fascism, this was due more to his personal equation than to a true adherence to his originating theories. According to these theories, the category of the political was neatly detached from that of the ethical, so much so that Croce had recognized the right of a "strong State," had rejected every "abstract moralism" in politics, had spoken with irony of the "Goddess Justice" and the "Goddess Humanity." Immediately after the First World War he sided against the forces of subversion, recognizing that it was not through discussion that they might be finally sorted out. Croce at that time stigmatized the lack of authority in the State, as fascism had done from the first. But then Croce discovered that the "meaning of history" (the famous "meaning of history" in all and everything) stood beneath the sign of a sort of freedom which the fascist regime could not permit, and he passed over to determined anti-fascist opposition.

Except that in Croce, as in Gentile, there is an incongruity—owing, no doubt, to purely personal factors—in the doctrinal premise shared by both of these "absolute historicists." In point of fact absolute historicism negates every difference between "be" and "ought to be," which amounts to saying that absolute historicism sees, in whatever realizes itself historically, the measure of all that is just, rational, all that has a right to exist. For this reason, Croce should have recognized the legitimacy of fascism, given that it had won the game, and should have banished every attitude of capricious opposition to the realm of those fancies which these philosophers call "abstract will" and "abstract moralism."[11] Gentile, distancing himself from Croce and adhering to the victorious fascist regime, was more consistent, at least in the 20s, but not after: when the course of the Second World War provoked the crisis of

---

11   For more on these ideas, see Chapter 34 below.

fascism, and it became clear that fascism was falling irremediably to the losing side—that the "meaning of historical" had shifted to the opposing side, to the Allies, because they were winning—Gentile, as an absolute historicist, should have changed flags. Instead nobly he did not, and it cost him his life.[12] First, however, almost as if to exhibit the latest developments in the "meaning of history," he announced the aforementioned "humanism of work" in his book, *The Genesis and Structure of Society* (1943). Regarding this book, his disciple Ugo Spirito had this to say: "It is perhaps his most beautiful book... in which all of Gentile's speculation is gathered in the form of futuristic necessity. In this book one finds the theory of what can without doubt be defined as Gentile's *communism* [sic—the italics are Spirito's]. Communism, in fact, seems to him to be the regime of the future, a regime which cannot be achieved, in his opinion, by immediate revolution, but which, even if through slow evolution, ought to represent the end we seek to realize"—which corresponds exactly to the devious tactic used by the communists in what are still democratic countries, keeping their final strategic objective ever firmly in place. They have acted this way above all in Italy, where they have been sponsored by our moronic and irresponsible politicos.

This is the framework in which the revolutionary "new humanism" took form in Spirito's book—a humanism which was also supposed to be "scientific," the liquidator of that cultural and individualistic humanism of Renaissance origin, and therefore also that of the nineteenth century.

But let us return to Spirito to see more clearly what this hoped-for new humanism might consist of, apart from its communistic or communistical orientation. In truth, Spirito's book is composed of scattered writings which first appeared elsewhere, and only a few of these have true relevance to his theme.

---

12 Gentile was murdered 15 April, 1944, by members of a communist partisan group, who approached his car under the pretext of asking him for directions, and proceeded to shoot him to death when he rolled down his window.

Here once again the problem of the antithesis between philosophy and science is taken up—an antithesis which is supposed to have given origin "to the traditional concept of culture." But already this point of departure is invalidated by the fact that it takes its movement from two terms which are nothing other than the products of a process of disassociation from, and degradation of, something anterior and superior to both.

It is in this sense that both terms must indeed be considered: on the one hand, simple, rootless philosophical speculation, the work of a merely human reason which has become the extreme application of itself, and on the other that knowledge which is related exclusively to the world of those phenomena which present themselves to sensorial experience, and which are organized by science of the modern kind— the same science which has imposed the belief that no other form of knowledge is either possible or conceivable.

To be sure, Spirito makes reference "to a third form of knowing that preceded philosophical knowing itself, even before scientific knowing," but here one treats but of a passing and irrelevant allusion, and Spirito knows no better than to refer this "third form" to "religion" as it is vulgarly conceived—as a simple system of faith assailed by doubt, which was indeed succeeded by the phase of philosophy and "metaphysics" (in the degraded sense given to this term by contemporary philosophy). In reality, the true point of reference should have been constituted just as it was in those civilizations that we are in the habit of calling "traditional"; that is to say, not of simple religion, faith or devotion, but of a single formative, in a certain sense transcendental, force which was active in the various domains of human knowledge, human action and human existence, and which gave place to an all-embracing and general order, at once organic and hierarchical.

But the problems considered by Ugo Spirito lack the sense of such horizons, and so prove to be completely out of sync; and the path congenially chosen to get to the bottom of them leads one ever *lower*. Indeed, in the last analysis his solution—an antithesis between philosophical thought and science—is obtained through the virtual suppression of the first term. Spirito, who was already convinced that in the "actualist" Gentilian philosophy "all the history of Western thought is summarized" (!!!), now makes a negative survey of what comprises contemporary philosophical thought: in his opinion, nothing can be found in it but "spurious philosophies." He is not altogether mistaken in this, even if certain positive points escape him—points which are offered from a special, not entirely philosophical, point of view, by existentialism and so-called "phenomenology." But, on the whole, today one can effectively speak of a process of internal self-dissolution in philosophy; philosophy has been left behind by other orientations and other interests of modern man, in the same way that the simple cultural and literary ideal of humanism appears now to be taken largely for granted.

Spirito takes up an old argument (used already by Kant to justify the assumption of his critical philosophy): that is, the multifarious discordant variety of philosophical systems in manifest antithesis to the univocality, the general consensus and the certainty, that exist in the scientific field. Thus the situation appears to be critical, for two reasons: if one is not to end up in pure negation—if one recognizes, as a matter of principle, an insuppressible metaphysical need—there is no alternative but to seek the satisfaction of this need within the sphere of science itself. In the second place, there are some who admit that "however grand the world of science and technology might be, there exists another world beyond it, which is really the world of values; science in relation to that world can serve as nothing other than a tool, as a means of achieving ideals which are not themselves scientific." Well enough: but even this same position must be overcome; it must be demonstrated that the world of science and technology already contains values of an ethical and spiritual rank.

Spirito believes he can sort out both these points, and for this reason his new humanism assumes an openly scientistic character.[13]

As regards the first point, Spirito informs us that there is no need to seek a synthesis between "metaphysics" and modern science, because modern science already contains a metaphysics. What would this metaphysics be? Surely not that which corresponds to certain impromptu speculative whimsies of certain true scientists today, who, so soon as they leave their specialist domain, display only the most touching ingenuity and bootlessness. It would consist rather in this: that the scientist, after being firmly settled on the ground of "facts" and "reality," believes *a priori* in the intelligibility of these things, and, elaborating his scientific knowledge with its laws and its determinisms, demonstrates the *"rationality of the real"*—which in science certainly takes as "its formulation and its effective realization the immanentist Hegelian metaphysics" (put simply, the metaphysics behind the famous principle, "All that is real is rational and all that is rational is real"[14]). Now, this means ignoring completely all the principles of scientific epistemology—the nature both of the procedures and of the "knowledge" of modern science. After the failure of the so-called "natural philosophies" of Schelling[15] and also of Hegel himself (to

---

13 Italian: *caratteri apertamente scientisti*. The word *scientisto* here is a neologism, and is used by Evola to indicate the questionable extensions of scientific thought to inappropriate realms. This term will be translated by the equivalent English neologism "scientistic" throughout.

14 This from a remark of Hegel in his *Elements of the Philosophy of Right*. The same comment was later analyzed by Engels (in his article "Ludwig Feuerbach and the End of Classical German Philosophy," first published in 1886 in *Die Neue Zeit*), and was found by Engels to justify revolution.

15 Friedrich Schelling (1775-1854), German philosopher of the German idealist tradition. His *Naturphilosophie*, to which Evola here makes reference, sought to show how the ideal emerges from the real. His influence has been comparatively negligible, which might explain Evola's speaking of the "failure" of his philosophy.

whom however one must acknowledge at least the merit of having seen the true task), one should not speak of "rationality" at all in the entire harvest of modern science—at least unless one wishes to completely distort the meaning of the word.

In the first place, all scientific procedures, even the most abstract and theoretical, have a practical and pragmatic character, and it seems that Spirito does not have the slightest suspicion of what was written already long ago, not by the improvised critics of science, but by men competent in the field, starting with Poincaré, Duhem, Brunschvicg, Meyerson, etc., up until the most modern, up until Heisenberg himself.[16] Even beyond the fact that what has justly been called "the scientific superstition of the fact" has by now been overcome, science cannot demonstrate the "rationality" of natural phenomena but only their "mathematizability," which is to say their susceptibility to being ordered using mathematical formula, assuming that—and this is important—one considers only those aspects of these phenomena which lend themselves to mathematics, and neglects the other aspects (for example, the so-called "secondary

---

16   Jules Henri Poincaré (1854-1912), French philosopher and practitioner of science and mathematics who is regarded as one of the forerunners in chaos theory, along with multiple contributions he made to physics. Pierre Duhem (1861-1916), French physicist and mathematician, whose contributions include several in the field of thermodynamics. Léon Brunschvicg (1869-1944), French idealistic philosopher who dedicated several of his studies to science and mathematics. Émile Meyerson (1859-1933), Polish-born French chemist and philosopher of science whose work later inspired the paradigm interpretation of scientific research defended most famously by Thomas Kuhn. Werner Heisenberg (1901-1976) was a noted German theoretical physicist best remembered for his development of the enigmatic "uncertainty principle" in quantum mechanics.

qualities"[17]). The system of modern science has a merely "hypothetic-deductive" character; it entails a progressive unification of relations, while presupposing always certain data which remain absolutely impenetrable, which are simply observed and documented. If one takes any single formula from the science of nature—even up to the famous Einsteinian equation regarding matter and energy, or the law of the discontinuous production of "quanta"—one can always ask: why in *this* way, and not in another? — and the scientist cannot respond, for he finds himself before the irrational, before something purely "given."

Croce had every reason to call scientific concepts "pseudo-concepts": they totally lack "noetic,"[18] which is to say cognitive, character. They are pure practical instruments, "working hypotheses," and scien-

---

17 The distinction between primary and secondary qualities has been a recurrent theme of modern thought, starting from Galileo and Descartes. John Locke dwelt long on it. Primary qualities are thought to be objective and to exist independent of any observer; they include qualities like extension and weight. Secondary qualities are thought to be subjective and to rely on sensations; they include qualities like color and taste. Primary qualities are the proper objects of scientific research; secondary qualities can only be approached through primary qualities (color understood, for instance, as a function of light waves).

18 "Noetic" is from the Ancient Greek νόος, meaning generally "mind or intellect," though it is sometimes translated with the word "spirit." This was an exceptionally importance concept in classical Greek philosophy, and was considered by many Greek philosophers as fundamental to the very quest for wisdom itself. Plato in particular presented "nous" as the ability to perceive truth, even independently of sense perception. "Noetic" in this context would thus mean having the quality of "nous," that special quality of the mind which enables the human being to grasp the truth. Evola's critique of science here is a deep one. It is related to the fact that science, unlike metaphysics, does not seek out first principles; and for this reason, no truly noetic explanation of phenomena can be given, but only an improvised and merely practical one. Science, as opposed to higher ways of thinking, cannot ever explain "why in this way, and not in another?"

tific honesty consists in being ready to abandon them and change them
so soon as any previously unobserved or poorly observed phenomenon
intercedes to spoil the party. The single goal is the maximum practical
(meaning experimental and technical) grasp of phenomenal reality. In
general, every schoolchild knows that a merely "statistical" character
is to be ascribed to all the laws of science; they possess the character
of "probability" alone. They are defined on the basis of the quantitative
addition of more or less permanent phenomena, not on the basis of a
logical and rational nexus—and this, not to mention some of the more
recent theories regarding "improbability," formulated on the basis of
research which has sought to penetrate into the deepest layers of "reality." No, it is clear that there is no "metaphysics" of modern science.

All this as regards the science of nature in the proper sense. But
there is also the affirmation of Spirito, on the other hand, that the
Delphic "know thyself" by now "converts itself into the consciousness of a subject who has become the object of scientific research,"
for which one no longer need turn to a spiritual master who might
direct us toward the world of contemplation, of the *gnosis*[19] or of high
ascesis, but instead to our physiologist, our neurologist, our biologist,
our psychoanalyst and so forth. And not only: but in the scheme of
the new humanism this consciousness, once entrusted to a sacred and
initiatory center, would no longer be an individual task, but would
become something collective, given the increasingly collective character of modern scientific research. So far as all this goes, we believe

---

19   "Gnosis" is from the Ancient Greek, γνῶσις meaning "knowledge." The term
      was absorbed into Gnosticism, a spiritualistic tradition which takes its origins
      from the Jewish Torah, early Christianity, and Platonism. It sought an immediate
      contact with the divine and the realization of the divine within the individual.
      Ascesis comes from the same root as our "ascetic," the Ancient Greek ἄσκησις,
      meaning "a discipline." Ascesis represents a practice or regime of life meant to
      prepare for spiritual awakening through purification, training, and discipline of
      the mind and the body.

every comment would sour. Let us only observe that that man who, as we said at the beginning of this writing, is forced to hush up and to systematically obscure the dimension of transcendence, of the "being" in himself, by throwing himself into "history" and into "progress," will in many cases reduce himself truly into a being which can quite adequately and exclusively be understood by the same profane sciences indicated by Spirito.

As for this last point—namely, that the world of science and technology is not merely the ordered material means toward ends transcending science, but rather that it satisfies also ethical and spiritual needs and provides a solution for the problem of ends—as far as this goes, let us listen to what the apostle of the new humanism has to say: "diverse political ideologies, religions, and philosophies have so far divided men and peoples, putting them at odds with each other. Science and technology on the other hand everywhere establish unity and consensus." Moreover, the new media of communication, speed, the press, the radio, television, the cinema, and so on, carry us out of our closed worlds, ever more uniting minds and customs and broadening horizons.

Thus one proceeds toward unity and unification—and this is supposed to be the ethical potential and the message of science and technology, its indication of a higher human ideal. Here too, the equivocation could be no greater, and one cannot help but rest stupefied. It is merely an exterior unification that science and technology have brought, and its counterpart is an internal emptying, an uprooting, an assault on everything of quality and against true difference and personality; it means merely standardization, the world of quantity and of the masses, estranging every higher interest ever more, and bringing about all the modern facilities[20] and all the anesthetics and narcotics fabricated to conceal the void from today's individual, to hide his lack of every true

---

20 Evola uses the English word "facilities."

sense of existence. It is the complete inversion of the true, traditional ideal of humanity, since unity is not destructive only if it is realized at the zenith, hierarchically, through well-defined articulations and differentiations. And Spirito takes up once more the forbidden scientistic utopias of the nineteenth century,[21] attributing to science the power to eliminate every profounder motivation, be it higher or lower, irrational or demonic, of human activity, to carry us to a state in which all exist in harmony and collaboration—even as we presume is the case with the scientists themselves. This, moreover, will never be possible without a "washing" of minds and of souls in the grand style, which Spirito basically concedes when he says that there are obstacles to the realization of what he takes to be the ideal condition; if there is not yet "the possibility to believe in this tomorrow," then "we will not seek the reason certainly in the world of science but in the world of politics, of religion, of metaphysics," where "contrasts of traditions, of history, of mentality" subsist. Therefore, by an inference of logic—*tabula rasa*,[22] away with it all.

---

21   Probable reference to the ideas of such men as Henri de Saint-Simon (1760-1825), Charles Fourier (1772-1837), Edward Bellamy (1850-1898), and of organizations such as the Fabian Society. Saint-Simon was born a count, but later and most democratically renounced his title. He called for an industrial society ruled by the working class, and saw science as the road to the realization of this idea. His ideas influenced the prominent anarchist Pierre-Joseph Proudhon, and also Marx and Engels. Fourier envisioned a socialistic society without property, and proposed a utopistic society based on the principle of labor. (Dostoevsky powerfully critiques Fourier's ideas at many points in *Notes from an Underground Man* and *Demons*.) Bellamy, an American, wrote a novel called *Looking Backward* which foresaw the emergence of a socialist society through the technical development and sophistication of industrialism. The Fabians held a similar view. In the present connection, it is interesting to note that all of these ideas and movements connected the idea of *science* with the idea of *socialism*, even as Marx himself did.

22   Latin: "blank slate." The term is associated with the Enlightenment, and most famously with John Locke, though he himself never used it. He held that the human being is born without any mental content, and that all knowledge and all mental structures derive from experience.

Behold, therefore, the horizons of the new humanism with which Spirito would like to award us: "the humanism of work," and scientism along with it; a general levelling, a gray and emptied unification of humanity. What is left for us to say? This fervent adherent of the "actualism" which celebrated the "indomitable creativity of the absolute spirit" has in the end conformed perfectly to the "meaning of history." *Pour la bonne bouche,*[23] we will close with these two direct quotations from the book in question: "Above all beyond the Iron Curtain, and in particular in the Chinese experience, which is almost entirely free from Western traditions, we can already see the precursory signs of the society of tomorrow." "The education and the scholastic organization of the future should be shaped to this new humanistic ideal."

---

23 French: "saving the best til last," or "in closing." Lit., "for a good mouthful."

2. REVOLUTION FROM THE HEIGHTS

Urgency has become one of the general characteristics of recent times—the thrust and the action of a rupture starting from *below*, and in function of the low, exercised upon existing structures. And this corresponds to the only proper and legitimate meaning of the term "subversion."

This situation takes as its evident presupposition the crisis of the whole of the structures involved, be these politico-social or cultural and intellectual structures. Thus it accompanies a process against the modern world, against bourgeois society and capitalism, against an order which has been reduced to an externally checked disorder, against forms of existence which have become devoid of every higher, dehumanizing, creative meaning—or, to use a term which today is commonly abused, of "alienation."

The revolt against all these aspects of a problematic civilization can be legitimate. But that which characterizes recent times is the dearth of every rectifying, liberating, or restorative action *from the heights*; this often necessary initiative and action of rupture is allowed to commence precisely from below, where this "below" is understood both as a reference to inferior social tiers, as well as to inferior values. Thus the almost inevitable consequence is the shifting of the center of gravity toward a level which stands yet lower than that of these crisis-ridden structures which have become almost empty of every vital content.

In the politico-social field the phenomenon presents such definite forms that it is almost superfluous to linger on them. No one is so myopic as to fail to understand, by now, what the famous "social justice," for example, really means. It is in no way true justice, the distributive justice of the *suum cuique*,[24] based on a principle of inequality, and already defended by the classics beginning with Aristotle and Cicero. It is rather a partisan pseudo-justice, at the exclusive service of the interests of the lowest classes, the so-called "workers," and at the expense of all others. It exists under the sign of myths that serve only to pave the way little by little for the ascent of the leftist forces in the State.

Against this action commencing from below—which by now is exceptionally organized and almost unstemmable, and which is tied to that humbug notion that one can find the man of nature, health, generosity, and so on, only in the lower classes, so that therefore the ultimate end of the subversive movement should be a new, effective "humanism"—against this action there is almost no one who is capable of reacting with energy. The principle of reaction ought to be this: that one can denounce the errors, the defects, the degeneration of a system—that one can be, for example, decisively against the bourgeoisie and against capitalism—only by commencing from a plane situated above it, not below it. One should react, that is, not in the name of "proletarian" so-called "social" or collectivist values, but rather in the name of aristocratic, qualitative and spiritual ones: that which could bring about a yet more radical rectifying action, if only men could be

---

24 Latin: "to each his own," meaning classically that each member of the commonweal should receive that which is fit to him by his nature and his quality. As a philosophical precept it traces its origins to Plato and in particular to the *Republic* (Cf. Book 4, 443a). The Latin phrase comes from Cicero (see *De Rerum Natura*, Book III, 38). It is strictly related to the idea of "distributive justice" which Evola here references, and which was one of Aristotle's political themes (see *Nichomachean Ethics*, Book III, 9.1280a7–22). Aristotle understood by distributive justice "giving the equal to equals, and the unequal to unequals," concept connected strictly with the idea of merit, and tied to the aristocratic regime which Aristotle often calls the best regime.

found who are truly up to the heights,[25] and who are armed with suf-ficient authority and power, so as to prevent or to smash, by a *revolution from the heights*, any such velleity or principle of revolution from below.

Unfortunately, however, one sees ever more clearly how far such perspectives lie beyond the intellectual horizons of our contemporaries. One can ascertain rather how even those who presume to battle against the "established disorder" of the modern world by raising indictments (which are by now obvious and almost taken for granted) against the current society, and putting forth even the values of personality and of Christianity, do not hide their elective affinities for the lower, for the "demands" of the low, and for the pseudo-humanism of the left, and demonstrating precisely as much intolerance and incomprehension for every possible solution which takes the form of a system resting on a principle of authority and sovereignty, of true order and true justice. As typical examples, we can indicate Maritain and Mounier, but also a traditionalist like L. Ziegler.[26]

---

25 Italian: *all'altezza*, meaning of a quality suitable to confront a given situation or problem. The phrase occurs frequently in Evola, and will be translated "up to the heights" throughout the present volume.

26 Jacques Maritain (1882-1973) was a French intellectual who converted to Catholicism. He was one of the drafters of the Universal Declaration of Human Rights, and an advocate for "Integral Humanism," which attempted to derive the premises for a complete humanism from the Christian doctrines of the Church. He was influential with the Christian Democratic movement, one of the groups predominantly involved in reforming Italy into a democratic state after the War. Emmanuel Mounier (1905-1950), too, was a French intellectual, the thinker behind the idea of "personalism," a form of humanism which em-phasizes human responsibility in the unfolding of history. This idea greatly influenced the later Catholic Worker movement. Leopold Ziegler (1881-1958) was a German idealistic thinker and upholder of traditionalism who might be distinguished from such proponents of the tradition as Evola and René Guénon by his unequivocal embrace of Christianity. This seems to have led him to a certain interpretation of tradition in an egalitarian and universalist key; there is certainly nothing "aristocratic" about his traditionalism.

It is most interesting to recognize the solidarity of this orientation with others which are perceptible in properly cultural spheres. Are not the so-called "neo-realism"[27] and other similar tendencies characterized precisely by their abusively presenting as "real" only those meanest, most miserable, equivocal, and often filthiest and vulgarest aspects of existence? While the remainder supposedly has nothing to do with what is authentic, sincere, and "real"?

A yet more significant case, which indicates the vast range of action in the diffusion of the tendency in these words, is to be found in psychoanalysis and modern irrationalism.[28] These embark from a critique, in itself legitimate, of the fetishism of "reason" and of abstract intellectualism, and of the superstructures of the conscious *I*. But from

---

27   The Italian Neorealist movement was complex and multi-faceted, and included such otherwise unrelated works as Carlo Levi's *Christ Stopped at Eboli*, Italo Calvino's *The Path to the Nest of Spiders*, and Cesare Pavese's *The Prison* in literature, and Vittorio De Sica's *Bicycle Thieves* and Lucchino Visconti's *Senso* in cinema. One of the themes to all these figures was a decided opposition to fascism and a thoroughgoing, pseudo-communistic concern for the plight of the poor and the working class. They tend to focus on the events of ordinary life, particularly among the lower classes and the downtrodden, and emphasize the brutal and the ugly elements therein. As but an example of the trend—many of the cinematic exemplars of this movement used "real people" in the place of trained actors for their films in order to give their work a feeling of raw authenticity.

28   Psychoanalysis, which originated in the work of Freud in the nineteenth century, often tends to view the human being as the unwitting servant of those subconscious or unconscious drives in his psyche, of which he has no awareness save peripherally, and over which he has no control. Evola never tires of pointing out the inadequacy and one-sidedness of this view, and its tendency to draw men toward what is lowest in them. Irrationalism as a philosophical movement is not unrelated to the viewpoint of psychoanalysis; it too accentuates the instinctual and the passionate as being of greater primacy and efficacy than the rational. It draws partial inspiration from the German philosophers Schopenhauer and Nietzsche, but also to the American pragmatists Charles Sanders Peirce and William James, and it is connected to existentialism.

this, they proceed immediately to an opening of man, not toward the high, but toward the base. Against the "rational," they asserted the worth of the simply irrational, of "life"; against consciousness, the unconscious, wherein one usually wished to see the motive force of the psyche. Thus here too the result was regression, a translation of the center of human gravity toward what is low. The cause is analogous to that which we indicated in the politico-social field: one acts as if outside of the "rational" and the abuse of the rational, there existed only the sub-rational (the unconscious, the vital, the instinctive, etc.), and not also the *super-rational*—as attested by everything in the history of societies connected to true human greatness.

Analogous considerations could be brought forth to indicate similar parallels in contemporary cultural phenomena—for example, existentialism and the many varieties of so-called neo-spiritualism. We cannot linger on all this. Let it suffice that we have briefly demonstrated in an entire group of phenomena an identical tendency, as well as what these in their very presence unfortunately indicate regarding the visage of the times: namely, the non-existence, today, of anyone who takes a stand, and who knows how to act, not from the base, but from the heights, in all realms.

3. THE ADVENT OF THE "FIFTH ESTATE"[29]

It is an indisputable merit of Marxist historiography that it attempts to identify a general guiding directive in history which unfolds in precise phases. This historiography considers the entirety of events on which the other historiographies usually bring all their attention to bear—war, national revolutions, developments and mutations of one kind or another—as unessential, as secondary and episodic, compared to the movement as a whole.

Almost no attempt of the kind has been made by the opposing side, that is, by the Right. Naturally the Marxist interpretation of the "meaning of history" (as a concatenation of economic determinisms

---

29   Italian: *il Quinto Stato.* The Estates were Medieval social orders applicable broadly to the whole of society. The First Estate was comprised of the clergy, the Second of the nobles, and the Third of the burghers. The French Revolution was famously taken to be the revolt of the Third Estate, and this theme was later adopted by Marxism, which held that the movement from the first two Estates to the Third was but a prelude to the final overthrow of the bourgeoisie by the proletariat, or the Fourth Estate, in the socialist revolutions. Through the usage of Edmund Burke and Thomas Carlyle, the "Fourth Estate" in English is most commonly taken to refer to the press. This is, however, a peculiarity of English, and originally, the Fourth Estate simply indicated those portions of society which lay outside the framework of the three Estates of the Realm. It applies most directly therefore to the commoners and the rural classes, and this is clearly the meaning it takes in both Marx and in Evola, as can be clearly seen in the present chapter. In what follows, the Fourth Estate should never be understood as referring to the press.

which will lead fatalistically to the dominion of the so-called working class) should be trenchantly rejected; but it should be rejected by placing oneself methodologically on the same level: that is, by recognizing the necessity of framing historical events in a schema which is no less broad—albeit one which sounds in a rather different key and conforms to higher perspectives, not the coarse and primitive ones of historical materialism.

Piero Operti[30] has recalled the general conception on which one might base an anti-Marxist historiography. This conception has been sketched, with significant agreement and contemporaneity, by several traditionalist writers: in the first place by René Guénon, then by V. Vezzani and H. Berl,[31] partially even by Spengler himself (whose considerations however were limited to the developments and individual cycles of civilizations), to say nothing of the contribution that we ourselves have made to this matter.[32] The subject which we would like to treat in the present chapter is the phenomenon of the "advent of the Fifth State." To understand this, we must first of all give a brief account of the conception just mentioned, which hinges on the idea of a regression or a descent of political power, of the type of civilization, and, in general, of the predominant values, along those four planes

---

30   Italian historian (1896-1975) who was a decorated volunteer soldier during World War I. He was a follower of Croce and was suspended from his teaching post during the Fascist Period for his anti-fascist positions. However, unlike many of those who resisted the fascist regime, he was as strongly opposed to the communists, and was generally taken to be a man of the Right. His opposition to both the principle political powers of the day earned him few friends, and he has been more or less marginalized since the War.

31   Vittorino Vezzani (1885-1955) was a spiritualist and a contributor to various journals of esotericism and occultism. He wrote on mysticism in the Indian and Christian traditions and on metaphysics. Heinrich Berl (1896-1953), who also wrote under the pseudonym Heinrich Lott, was a German writer, journalist, and musicologist. Evola considers one of his books in the present chapter.

32   See in particular *Revolt Against the Modern World* and *Men Among the Ruins.*

which every complete, and, we can even say, "normal" social organization encompasses in a hierarchical system. At the summit of this organization stood the masters vested with spiritual authority; then came the warrior aristocracy; in third place the propertied burghers and whoever concentrated their interests on the economic plane (the "merchants," the Hindu *vaiçya*[33] caste); and finally came the workers, the "people."

Now, it is quite clear that in the history known to us this pyramid has crumbled, and we have seen a descent from one to the next of these four levels. From a civilization characterized by the sacred, in which the master[34] or the ruling class exercised a higher right based predominately on a spiritual foundation and "divine right," we passed to societies supported solely by the warrior aristocracy; a phase which closed with the cycle of the great European dynasties. With the French Revolution, democracy, liberalism, and industrialism it was the Third Estate to *de facto* assume the power as a capitalistic and plutocratic burgher class, and the effective masters became now the lords of money, the various "kings" of coal, of steel, of oil, etc. The socialist and proletariat movements, which ended with communism and Sovietism, are prelude to the occurrence of the last layer, the Fourth Estate, which wants to undermine the civilization of the Third Estate (in principle, it is in this light that one should really understand the conflict between "Orient" and "Occident," between the communistic States and the

---

33 Or the *Vaishya*, the caste of merchants, money-lenders, and property owners. Originally the caste was comprised of farmers and traders, but it grew into something distantly analogous to our middle class.

34 The Italian is *capo*, which could most literally be translated as "head," in the same sense that we speak of "heads of state." It is also often used to mean something like our "boss." Evola often uses this term to refer to historical periods in which the latter English term would be frankly inappropriate, and the former would be awkward. I have therefore chosen to render it "master" in what I hope is the spirit of Evola's intent, and it will be so rendered throughout.

United States, together with their satellites) and to guarantee itself world dominion: the Fourth Estate against that which remains in the world of the Third Estate.

From the point of view of the Right, it is in these terms that the "meaning of history" presents itself—only, in point of fact, we ought rather to called it the *meaninglessness* of history. But does this regressive process stop at the Fourth Estate? Between the two world wars, a singular little book appeared, whose author, H. Berl, went a step further. The book was called *The Advent of the Fifth Estate* (*Die Heraufkunst des Fünsten Standes*). Apart from its theoretic contents and its interpretation of history in the regressive key, it was saturate with strong emotional charges. Berl had written it in a sanatorium, as if in a delirium (he himself said that "there is fever in every page"). Leaving this aside together with several of his exaggerations, the thesis he sustained is not without interest for whomever wishes to come to terms with certain aspects of our times.

According to Berl, the descent in history will not stop with the Fourth Estate—that is, with the collectivized Marxist and communist world. It will rather tend to perpetuate itself in the emergence of a Fifth Estate. What would this Fifth Estate be? Here we must refer above all to the idea that every organization comprises two principle elements: the forces of order on one side, the forces of chaos on the other. Organization emerges from a formative action which binds and restrains the latter forces within determinate structures (wherein they can manifest themselves creatively, as dynamic factors). And when a cycle approaches its terminus, this elemental substratum, the sub-personal background and one could almost say Goethian "demonic"[35] which in the traditional civilizations was brought to heel, kept in check and elevated by a superior law, and by the natural prestige

---

35   Probable reference to Goethe's *Faust*, in which the Devil calls himself the spirit of negation: "I am the spirit which ever negates!" he proclaims when he introduces himself to Faust.

which invested the spiritual, heroic, and aristocratic values and their representatives—this substratum tends to return to its free state, to act in a destructive way, to gain the upper hand. This is the boundary: it corresponds to the advent of the Fifth State.

In every "revolutionary" phenomenon as such there is always an emergence of this amorphous substrate, which is more or less contained in the successive developments; but in the first phase it is always characterized by something wild, by the pleasure in destruction and subversion, by a regression of the individual into the collective, by the "devils of the collective." The pages written by Joseph de Maistre[36] on the French Revolution are of perennial value in this respect. On the other hand, the Fourth Estate can be conceived of generally as the anti-State, if by the State one speaks in the traditional sense, as a super-elevated reality and as the incarnation of an idea and a higher ordering power. Berl believed he had recognized in the modern phenomenon the symptoms of an organized and endemic delinquency, the prime typical example being American gangsterism. Its characteristic feature in recent times is therefore precisely the feature of "organization." Paradoxically, one could say that here "chaos organizes." Indeed, the same forces often hide also in the political systems created by the Fourth Estate, by communism and Marxism, because by a natural law of gravitation, a given stage, in the process of falling, commonly ends up by opening itself to that which belongs to a yet lower level.

---

36 Maistre (1753-1821) was a French philosopher, writer, lawyer, and diplomat. He is best remembered (particularly among traditionalist circles) for his trenchant defense of monarchical authority; more broadly he is taken, together with Edmund Burke, as one of the inspirational figures behind contemporary conservatism. He was a Catholic, a defender of Papal authority even in temporal matters, and a firm and unremitting opponent of the Enlightenment. Evola's reference here to Maistre's pages on the French Revolution is to *Considerations on France*. For more on Maistre, see Chapter 31 of the present work.

In this context we should consider not only what has relevance to the political and social plane, but also what regards the very personality, the destruction of personality. Throughout history there have always been cruelty and atrocities, but the characteristic element which might be diagnosed in the latest times are rationally studied, sinister methods of degradation intended to reduce the beings to whom they are applied to automated puppets, to degrade them in their own eyes (a number of valid considerations on this point, albeit with tendentiously one-sided references, have been carried out by the Catholic existentialist Gabriel Marcel[37]). One is reminded of certain processes behind the scenes of the Iron Curtain, and of a certain regime of concentration and "re-education" camps. The attack is brought against that "form" in the outstanding sense—"personality." The two planes are naturally different, but the convergence of their direction, their "signature," is well recognizable.

From the time that Berl's book came out, phenomena have been delineated in the modern world in other fields which could in part be traced back to the "emergences" he noted. Certain aspects of the so-called "generation of revolt," for instance, are worth mentioning. Revolt can be legitimate when it is brought against a civilization in which almost nothing has a higher justification any longer, a civilization which has become hollow and absurd, one which, mechanized and standardized, tends toward the sub-personal in an amorphous world of quantity. But when one treats of "rebels without flags"; when revolt is, so to speak, an end in and of itself, everything else being pretext; when it is accompanied by an unleashing, by primitivism, by abandonment in what is elementary in an inferior sense (sex, negro jazz, inebriation, gratuitous and often criminal violence, complacent exaltation of the

---

37   Marcel (1889-1973) was a French intellectual, playwright, and music critic. He converted to Catholicism in 1929, and though he was known as an existential-ist, he refused to be associated with Sartre. His book *Man against Mass Society* discusses the present theme.

vulgar and the anarchic)—then it is not a stretch to establish a certain connection between these phenomena and others, which on different planes attest the action of the forces of chaos emerging from below, following the ever more visible cracks in the extant order, seizing possession of the storm-tossed and the traumatized among modern men.

Let us resist ceding to the temptation of indicating other concomitant phenomena which likewise attest, though from another side, an assault against the personality. For instance, what else does psychoanalysis represent if not an opening of that diaphragm which often providentially closes off a sub-personal subsoil, and one constituted moreover by obscure forces? What does it represent, if not the inversion through which this subsoil is presented as the primary element of man, as the true motive force of the psyche? One easily perceives the similarity between these phenomena and the rise of whatever in the ideology of the left is presented as an ascent on the social and historical plane—an ascent into the very higher political structures which are thereby swept away and divested. This invites comparison with the assault brought against what ancient thought called *egemonikon*,[38] that is the sovereign in man, which is today reduced equally to a mere superstructure.

However, the ideas here briefly explicated might have a greater interest for us in the properly social and existential aspects of these phenomena connected to the true "meaning of history," or else to anticipatory symptoms pertaining to the logic of this meaning. One must be on guard against exaggerations and against every "apocalyptic" view of the world; but many things in this context should force everyone to reflect, even those who are still sedated by the myths of progressivist democracy—indeed, even those who reveal themselves incapable of gleaning the rigid nexus of cause and effect within the present secular

---

38 Greek, ἡγεμονικόν: "the authoritative or ruling part of the soul or universe" idea which figured prominently in Stoic philosophy. Our English word "hegemony" comes from the same root.

course of events. The four-part descent in level of civilization and of social organizations is a reality; likewise is the emergence, upon the point of reaching the final step, of the nether forces, the forces of chaos, which in a certain sense cannot be said to belong to the properly human world, and which can perhaps best be comprehended by the formula of the advent of the Fifth Estate.

4. THE STATE AND WORK

No orientation to the Right is conceivable without taking a decided stand against the myth of "work" and of the "worker," and against the aberrant culmination of this myth in latest times which is constituted by the concept of the "Workers' State."

It is needless to say that by Right we mean, as always, the true Right—not the economic and capitalistic Right, which are the easy target for subversive forces, but rather the Right defined by political, hierarchical, qualitative, aristocratic, and traditional values, custodian of the idea of the true State.

Someone might object that such a Right does not exist in the game of extant political forces in Italy, perhaps even in Europe. But even in the currents that are at least called "national," the profound degradation inherent in the myth of the worker ought to be felt and ought to give rise to a natural reaction. Instead, too often, one indulges an equivocation which carries one inevitably to acquiescence to the vernacular and the ideology of the opposing side. But that is how matters stand today. To refrain from burning incense before the working class, to perceive that the quintessence of every non-retrograde and non-"reactionary" politics is servitude to that same working class and slavish obedience to its ever more impertinent "demands"—this seems indeed to surpass the modicum of physical and moral courage at the disposal of the better part of those who administer our politics today.

Moreover, recently indulgence in the aforementioned ideologies appears even in the margin of nationalistic currents. The concept of the "Workers' State," though embellished for the occasion with the added qualification "nationalist," was lately proposed for study and discussion by the younger milieu. On another plane, this was introduced as symbolizing the "revolutionary" attitude, quite as if the presently reigning Constitution did not begin with the solemn proclamation that Italy "is a republic founded on work"[39]—for which it is clear that the asserted "revolutionary" demand can be understood only along the radical lines precisely of Marxism, socialism and communism (movements in which the myth of work and of the Workers' State truly finds itself at home), not through a rejection of the system now in force, or of a revolution which might be reconstructive and restorative of the natural hierarchy of values and of dignities.

Frankly speaking, it is almost tedious for us to revisit such matters. Our own stance dates back to the already distant year of 1934, when the first edition of our *Revolt Against the Modern World*[40] was issued, and from then on we have never tired of denouncing ideologies of this kind. It is true that even in the Fascist Period, in certain syndicalist and "pancorporative" circles, one glimpsed analogous tendencies, but these remained ever marginal and inoperative. Mussolini always refused to conceive of the Fascist State as

---

39 In the Italian: *L'Italia e' una Repubblica democratica, fondata sul lavoro.* This is indeed the opening line of the Italian Constitution: "Fundamental Principles," Article 1.

40 Evola's magisterial overview of Traditionalism. Evola considers the civilizations of past and present in their structure, their means and their aims, and offers a thoroughgoing critique of modernity from the perspective of a by-now long distant traditionalist form of spiritual civilization. *Revolt Against the Modern World* is considered by many to be Evola's *magnum opus*.

a mere Workers' State;[41] he affirmed the primacy of the political, he affirmed values higher than economic ones; he conceived of the very corporations that organized and disciplined the forces of labor and production as means, not ends.

Nor did he, near the end of the Fascist Period, follow the distortion contained in Giovanni Gentile's formulation of so-called "humanism of work" with its backdrop of the "meaning of history"—all of which was interpreted precisely in the manner of leftist ideologies. By this view, after the emancipation of the human spirit which was "celebrated" in the Renaissance and in the humanism of that time, the liberal revolution represented a second conquest in the same direction; but its latest progress will be the "humanism of work" together with the "ethic of work," that is, the recognition of the spirituality and dignity of work, etc. etc. The convergence of these ideas with the Marxist philosophy of history could not be clearer, and this Gentilian "humanism" paired off with the "true humanism" of Marx and Lenin, along with everything that one reads in the Soviet constitution about work understood not as a duty imposed sadistically on everyone, but rather as an "honor."[42]

On the other hand, one knows of all the tendencies toward an "enlightened" and no longer retrograde Catholicism which today hold to a similar line, by singing the praises of the "ascent of the working class." The stages of human progress, according to the Catholic Maritain, are exactly the same as those conceived by Gentile. The culmination

---

41 Cf. Section 8 of Mussolini's "Doctrine of Fascism," published as the entry for "Fascism" in the Italian Encyclopedia of 1932: "Fascism stands against socialism, which petrifies all historical movement into class struggle, ignoring that statal unity which binds the classes into a single economic and moral reality." This is one of the few documents in which Mussolini committed his doctrine to writing. The passage was ghost-written by Giovanni Gentile (for Gentile, see note 6 to Chapter 1 above, and Chapter 34 below).

42 In Article 14 of the Soviet Constitution of 1977, labor is called the "source of the well-being of the people" and "the prime vital need of every Soviet citizen." It is called a "matter of honour" in Article 60.

of history, for all such thinkers, is the "civilization of work" and the mysticism of the "worker," this new subject of history, this new taboo and sacrosanct being, whom no one must dare to touch.

It is needless to say that from the traditional point of view the stages of this presumed progress correspond rigorously with those of a gradual degradation and inversion—one which, moreover, has struck out also against ideals, values, predominant vocations, and, in general, against civilization itself. Indeed it is obvious that passing from civilizations that gravitate toward spiritual and transcendent values to civilizations whose center is constituted wholly by the values, albeit the worthy values, belonging to a warrior aristocracy, and, from this, to a capitalistic and industrial civilization based on economy, material organization, and money and profit, and, at last, the final shift toward a society having for its center and its myth pure work and the worker—it is obvious that this process cannot be conceived otherwise than as a process of regression.

The generalization of the meaning of the word "work" is characteristic of the final phase of this regression. It can signify only one thing: the tendency to conceive every activity under the sign of those inferior activities to which alone one can correctly apply the term "work." It degrades all activities and brings them back to the same common denominator. This is what happens, for example, when one begins to speak of "intellectual workers," of "workers of muscle and mind," wherein is concealed the absurdity of a conception of society and a state based exclusively on "work" and on "workers." Such an abuse must be denounced. It must be affirmed that work is work, and nothing more. It is nonsense to apply the term "worker"—not to mention "laborer"—to the inventor, to the artist-creator, to the thinker, to the warlord, to the diplomat, to the priest, to the scientist, even to the great organizer and captain of industry. The activity of all these men cannot be defined as "work," nor can they be included in any way in the "working class." Indeed, we would not even call "worker" the peasant, at least insofar as he is not some paid hand, but rather remains faithful to the earth and farms according to the tradition, and takes an interest in this which does not exhaust itself in the pure idea of proceeds. (Today such a type of peasant, in conformity with "social progress," is on the point of vanishing.)

It cannot be contested, however, that parallel to the above-mentioned abusive generalization of the word "work," we have seen in recent times a degradation which in certain sectors confirms that generalization. Not a few activities which up until yesterday had quite another character are in fact now becoming "work." For instance one could well call "work," in the more brutal sense of the term, certain forms of sports and of sportive training.

Today the Catholics happily forget the fact that according to the Biblical tradition (to which, on the other hand, they hold so strongly when protesting against birth control) work was conceived in strict connection with the fall of man and as a kind of atonement, thus as nothing which one can glorify. It is known that classical antiquity attributed a negative value to work in its proper and legitimate, meaning material, sense: *labor*[43] could be equated almost with suffering and with

---

43 Not to be confused with the English word, *labor* is Latin, meaning "work" but also "toil, exertion, effort," and even more pointedly, "suffering, hardship, distress"; for which it, like the English equivalent, is connected also to childbirth. (Interestingly, the Italian word *lavoro* has lost the latter connotation.) As Evola indicates, the verb *laborare* means primarily "to suffer" or "to be ill, to be in distress," *for which* it comes to mean "to work." *Laborare ex capite*, which Evola considers presently, means literally "to suffer from the head." *Otium*, from which we derive our comparatively rare English word "otiose," means "leisure" in the older sense of that word—that is, not "leisure" in the sense of "idleness," but "leisure" in the sense of that state of peace, ease, calm, often interior, which is required for certain higher activities. *Negotium*, which has later taken on in many languages an almost positive connotation related to economic activities (consider the English "negotiate" or the Italian *negozio*), in its origin meant, like *labor*, "pain, trouble, distress" and only subsequently meant business, a job.

punishment, and the verb *laborare* signified "to suffer"—*laborare ex capite* in Latin means, for example, to suffer a headache. Reciprocally, the term *otium*, in antithesis to *labor* and *negotium*, often was used by the classics to designate, not idleness but time dedicated to non-material, intellectual activities, to studies, to literature to speculation and the like; while *otium sacrum* figured even in religious and ascetic terminology, and was associated with contemplative activity. Here we cannot resist the temptation of citing a Spanish proverb: *el hombre que trabaja pierde un tiempo muy precioso*, that is "the man who works (in the proper sense) loses most precious time." To lose this precious time—precious because it can be better used—might be a necessity, a sad necessity. *But the fundamental point ought to be the refusal to make such necessity into a virtue, or to exalt a society in which this has become the keystone.*

In every sane and normal vision of life, work must be considered a simple means of sustenance in the case of beings who are not qualified to perform an activity of a higher kind. To work as an end in and of itself, and beyond that which is required for one's own sustenance, is an aberration—and precisely the "worker" ought to understand this: the "work ethic," the "humanism of work," "work as honor" and all the rest of this blathering are naught but means of mystification, so as to better weld the chains that bind the "worker" to the mechanism of "production," which has almost become an autonomous process. Already on another occasion we have cited this anecdote: in an Asian country a European entrepreneur, having noted the scarce diligence of the natives in their work, decided to double their wages. The consequence was that the natives immediately began to work half as many hours as before, given that they now thereby earned as much as they needed. If the climate of "social progress," of overreaching one's proper condition at all costs, of artificially multiplying one's needs, did not make such an attitude appear deprecable, precisely the prevalence of this attitude in normalized inferior social strata (and also in superior ones) would be one of the most efficacious means to stop the "gigantic unleashing," that is the economy, the productive paroxysm which is becoming the destiny of "civilized" humanity.

Returning a moment to classical antiquity, beyond *otium* in the sense here clarified, another term was held as antithesis to *labor: opus*,[44] "a work." Properly speaking, one applied *labor* to the slave alone, while the free man accomplished "works," whence the Latin term *opifex* which evidently in this connection cannot be translated by "worker" in the modern sense. Now, Spengler has indicated a most significant mutation when he observed that while modern man tends to "labor" even when he "produces a work"—that is, when he creates, acts, accomplishes—traditional man gave the higher character of "work" even to that which could be, in a certain sense, a job. Moreover, this qualitative character was maintained up until yesterday in the realm of traditional artisanship. The paradox is that in the exaltation of work and the tendency to reduce the State to a mere Workers' State, work is ever more discredited, it has lost and has had to lose in exceedingly wide sectors its personal and qualitative character as "a work," so far as to sink ever lower along the scale of activities worthy of a free man, which are exercised not for pure necessity or merely for the prospect of gain.

In correlation to this, we have seen the degradation of the type of the "worker" who becomes a "conscientious member" of the "working class," a "seller of work" organized in the trade unions, who thinks solely in terms of "salary," of "claims" and of "interest" without any regard for the common good, without obeying any disinterested and noble motive, nor any values of fidelity, dedication, and intimate adhe-

---

44 This word is to some extent preserved in English, as for instance when we speak of a writer's *opus magnum*. *Opifex* means literally "workman," but as Evola points out this is inadequate; the Romans would not have applied this idea of work, for instance, to any manual laborer. It has closer connections rather to our notion of "artist," in certain exclusive senses of that word.

sion. (It is even difficult to imagine that this might be yet possible, surrounded, as we are, by a senseless, mechanical, anodyne system.) It is precisely on account of this base level of work and of the worker of today that one proclaims the "Workers' State" and speaks of the "social nation which is realized in the Workers' State, that synthesis of the ideals of the new generation [!!!]."

In terms of its doctrine, it is obvious that the Worker's State is the pure and simple negation of the traditional concept of the State. The regressive character of those developments which Marxist historiography wishes to present as progress is evident, if one considers the model which bit by bit has been chosen for the State. When, at the twilight of those civilizations based on spiritual and aristocratic values, effective power passed into the hands of the capitalistic and mercantile bourgeois, the foundation of the state was brought back precisely to the principles of that caste, which is to say, to the *contract* (contractualism, the "social contract")—a concept which naturally implicates material advantage and excludes every truly ethical factor and every organic nexus. "Governing" thus has become synonymous with "managing," as in a business or a private administration—and it is not in the least surprising that in the United States one speaks, not of "government," but of "administration" (the Eisenhower administration, the Kennedy administration). Then we descended lower yet: the model is no longer that of the company or the society created by contract, but rather even that of the socialized and rationalized factory. This is the level to which the concept of the "Workers' State" ideally belongs.

A sure guide for judging political forms is given by the conception of the hierarchy of various faculties in any man worthy of this name—by the natural analogy existing between individual being and that grand organism which is the State. The entire extension, the quantitative development which material activities, "work," production, economy might have in a certain type of civilization, should not impede the clear, constant recognition of their hierarchical place, corresponding precisely to that of the material functions of an individual organism, remaining ever at the service of a higher life. Only under this condition can a normal order exist. The true State incarnates those principles, those powers, those functions that in man correspond to the central and sovereign element, destined to give a higher meaning to life, to direct the purely naturalistic and physical sphere toward transcendant ends, experiences, and tensions. If one denies to the State the autonomy proper to a super-elevated power and authority, one negates its very essence, and nothing will remain of it but a caricature, something mechanistic, disanimate, opaque, superimposed on a collective existence which is itself no less empty. The primacy given politically to "society" (we have just indicated the analogy between such a concept and that of "society" in the commercial and business sense) is the first stage of this negation. The later phase is certainly that characterized by the "Workers' State," with the individual thought of merely as the "worker citizen." As we said, it takes as its model the factory under a socialized and collectivized regime.

It is not necessary to say that the addition of the word "national"— "national Workers' State"—is but pure mendacious tinsel. "Work" in the modern sense has nothing of "national" character, it has no fatherland; stripped of its qualitative and technified particularities, it is everywhere the same, and peoples, races, and even genders bring about no true differences in it. But if with the epithet "national" one wished to indicate the nation as a super-ordered end, it is evident that one would have to commence by restoring a higher meaning to the concept of nation, one inseparable from the ideal of the true State: a meaning which naturally cannot come to the nation from the world of work, such a world being merely a means. For which the use of that hybrid formula—"national Workers' State"—betrays unambiguously the incapacity to think in a clear manner, an incapacity which, moreover, succumbs—consciously or unconsciously—to the influence and the ideologies of the left and of the "working class."

As one sees, there is in any case an equivocation which leaves the door open to the adversary. One should finally have the courage to think all these problems through to the depths, without confusion, calling things by their right name. Let us therefore repeat that work is work, and nothing more. The working class is only an inferior part of the whole (today, qualitatively, more than ever—for the reasons we have indicated). The incomparable proliferation which this idea has had in the world of today, given the present material type of our civilization, and the possibility of exercising subversive and often openly extortionary pressures, does not in any way change the subordinate meaning proper to it in a normal hierarchy. Neither "work" nor "workers" can have any place in the higher and most essential degrees of this hierarchy. If we wish to provide indications for useful reflection and discussion amongst that still-healthy part of today's youth, it is on the basis of this view that we must provide them. There are already enough "openings to the left" elsewhere; one does not need to set oneself to competing also on the "national" front—even if one's intent remains merely "prophylactic," as is the asserted pretext in the unhappy adventure of the current "center-left."[45] The appeal to intellectual courage and to a true revolutionary spirit (more precisely:

---

45 The "center-left" to which Evola here refers was that founded in 1963 by Aldo Moro. It might be considered a "prophylactic" movement insofar as it led to a fragmentation of the forces of the left into the communist-socialist camp on the one hand, and the more moderate "organic center-left" on the other. This "center-left" went on to attempt a coalition with the relatively conservative Democratic Christians in the 70s in a political maneuver known as the "historical compromise." The success of all these measures can be seen in the fact that Aldo Moro was kidnapped and murdered by exponents of the Red Brigade, a revolutionary communist organization. The "historical compromise" was thereby compromised; and nothing further came of it, if not a continual expansion of the power of the communist forces into the field of politics, to the detriment of Italian conservative parties.

counter-revolutionary, because the true revolution today can only be a revolt against the political and ideological system ruled by the ideas here stigmatized)—such an appeal today is truly a categorical need.

5. BIOLOGICAL YOUTH AND POLITICAL YOUTH

One of the questions which is often resubmitted to the milieu of the Right, is the relation of the new generation with the previous—the "revolutionary" youth in its relations with the men and with the ideas of the Fascist Period. In point of fact there are some who believe they here recognize a phenomenon ascertainable also more generally: the new generation no longer understands the previous; the accelerated rhythm of events has interposed between the one and the other an ideological distance much greater than that which in other times normally separated them.

Nevertheless one detects in this formulation a certain superficiality and bias. And indeed, are these concepts of "youth," of the new generation of the "revolutionary vocation," really bereft of ambiguity?

We must commence from a specification of the plane on which these notions stand: whether one is speaking of the biological plane or rather of a higher plane, as can well be supposed in our own case. If one wants to consider these things spiritually, one must take care, because there are situations in which these values might be inverted, as for instance in what concerns the "new," the young, that which has come latest. Thus if we generally consider the generations that succeed each other within a given cycle of civilizations, we can even enunciate a paradox in the cases mentioned, because that which stands at the origins should be called truly young, while the latest generations, the chronologically younger, would be the older, the senescent, the crepuscular, even if their mere infantility and prurience can sometimes be erroneously taken as signs of youth. To cite an example, the so-called "youth" of the North-American races, with their "new world" and their primitivism, reveals precisely the infantility proper not to "young" generations but to the last generations, to those that one finds retrogressively toward the end of a cycle—the cycle of Western civilization in general.

We mention this because something analogous applies also to a more concrete sphere. Looking inward for a moment—can we truly call young (apart from in a biological and censual sense) an unfortunately quite considerable portion of Italian "youths" today? That indifferent and agnostic youth, engrossed in materialism and petty hedonism, incapable of any kind of leap, incapable of holding to any kind of a line, invigorated at most by a football match or by the Tour of Italy? We would sooner call this "youth" dead before it has even been born. Whoever today does not let himself go, whoever lives an idea, whoever knows how to keep himself upright on his feet, and scorns whatever is feeble, oblique, distorted, vile—such a one is infinitely "younger," whatever his age may be, than *that* portion of today's "youth."

It is precisely along these lines that we must understand what is young in a not merely biological sense, and this must be defined as their common denominator, in order to overcome artificial antitheses. If we had to indicate the fundamental character of youth understood in this higher sense, we would say it is defined by the *will for the unconditional*. Indeed, the entirety of idealism in a positive sense can be reduced to a similar factor; also every kind of courage, of leap, of creative initiative, every attitude which brings one resolutely to new positions, every holding of one's own person in little account. In particular true youth has, physically speaking, the almost paradoxical disposition of a growing life which, rather than being attached to itself, knows how to squander itself, so that it can hold even its own death to be of no account.

We should distinguish between the most elementary phase, in which the qualities here indicated manifest themselves only in spontaneous, disordered and transitory form, often as a fire in the straw, and the phase in which they are confirmed and stabilized. The first is frequently the condition of the true youth who then bit by bit "normalizes," "gets his head on straight," convincing himself that "idealism is one thing, life another," abdicating his will for the unconditional. Such a youth thus reveals in the end its primarily physical basis. The second case occurs instead in that man who has had to confront trials, hard trials, and has overcome these trials without succumbing.

All of this holds both in the interior realm as well as in the political. And with this we can return to the problem from which we commenced. What *is* this generation of yesterday which the generation of today can no longer comprehend? In reality one is but the recurrence[46] of the other: even yesterday (after the First World War) there was a "generation of the front lines"; even yesterday intolerable political, social, and moral conditions arose, and the premises of the fascist movement were formed, out of an impatience, an idealism, and a virilism fused together through a life of peril and combat. Today things present themselves again in the same terms; only today there is the circumstance of a still harder trial—a "generation of the front lines" which has survived not a victory, but a defeat and a decomposition.

Put in these terms it seems there should be only a fundamental continuity between these two generations. This continuity of a "youth" which is not biological but political ceases only when one begins to speak of the men of yesterday who lost their way when fascism came

---

46 Evola here uses the term *ricorso*, which might be understood in the sense of Giambattista Vico's philosophy of history. Vico held that history consists of "*corsi e ricorsi*," which might best be translated as "occurrences and recurrences." The recurrences, one might say, are spiritually identical but formally diverse repetitions of one and the same event or historical manifestation. For more on Vico, see note 140 to Chapter 13 below.

to power, who were not any longer capable of maintaining their intransigence, their will for the unconditional, their radicalism, but who sold their primogeniture for a plate of lentils, or for this or that semi-bureaucratic appointment in the scene of a deplorable, cinematic "hierarchy" and a new conformism.

It would however be truly unjust to weave a blackshirt out of every thread,[47] and to fail to recognize that in fascism there were men who kept their feet, though they were often hindered in every way by this or that unofficial gang. The reunion of these men with the new wave, with the new youth and the new "generation of the front lines," ought to be natural, on account of their congeniality: even as one and the same stream, in overcoming some obstruction and blockage, regains its course.[48]

Let one more point be mentioned. It is not always easy—particularly in the case of the Italians, the Mediterraneans—to grant oneself an autonomous value. Many feel the need to agitate in order to feel their individuality, their own importance; they must counterpoise themselves at all costs to something or to someone. It is in this light that we must judge certain aspects of the "revolutionary vocation," as well as a certain individualism of the "youth," when it seeks everywhere to differentiate itself, and indiscriminately espouses new ideas simply because they are new. At the bottom of this, there is often, however, simply an "inferiority complex": just the need to matter in some indirect way, through antithesis and contrast, since one does not feel

---

47 The Italian idiom is *fare di ogni erba un fascio,* or "to make a bundle out of every blade of grass." The equivalent in English would be "to make a mountain out of a molehill," but obviously in the present case there is a play on words, given that *fascio* is the etymological root also of the word "fascism" itself: the bundle of rods, *fasces* in Latin, which represented the commonweal formed from the unity of individuals into a whole. I have attempted perhaps awkwardly to preserve this play on words in the rendering "weave a blackshirt out of every thread."

48 Italian: *corso.* See note 46.

confident enough in oneself alone. This is an attitude that the political youth of today, and not simply the biological youth, should correct. The highest ambition should not be to become a revolutionary at all costs, but rather to be the exponent of a tradition, the bearer of a transmitted strength which must be nourished and increased in everything which might guarantee it an inflexible direction. The same holds also in the domain of ideas, and one of the proofs of one's interior freshness is understanding that the right ideas stand above every contingency, and that with them the true personality acquires value: not in a confused revolutionary impulse, not in a preconceived mistrust of the past, not in a disorderly dynamism which only betrays the lack of a true internal form. Without drawing any particular deductions from this—for this is not the place—we can easily recognize here that feature of the political youth of today which is drawing up as a general attitude, so that, through a unification of forces, it can pursue a precise political ideal: the ideal of the true organic State.

6. THE PROBLEM OF DECADENCE

Whoever rejects the myth of progressivism and of evolutionism, which is nowadays generally taken for granted; whoever, through an interpretation deriving from higher values of at least the most recent history, comes to ascertain that regression is the meaning of this history—such a one shall find himself standing before the "problem of decadence." If evolution rests on a logical impossibility—since more cannot derive from less, nor the superior from the inferior—an analogous difficulty seems to introduce itself in any attempt to explain this modern regression. How is it possible that the superior might degenerate, that a given level of spirituality and of civilization might be lost?

The solution would not be difficult if one could rest content with simple analogies: the healthy man might grow ill; the virtuous can become vicious; by a natural law, which arouses surprise in no one, every organism, after its birth, its development, and the fullness of its life, grows old, grows weak, dies. But this is an observation, not an explanation—even supposing that between the two orders there exists a complete analogy, which is dubious enough given that one is dealing here with civilizations and politico-social organizations, in which human will and human liberty play a very different role than in the naturalistic phenomena we have mentioned.

However, this objection comes up against the theory of Oswald Spengler, who employs precisely the analogy offered by these organic facts. He assumes that, just as each organism, each civilization has its dawn, its phase of full unfolding, then an autumnal aging, a sclerosis, and, finally, death and dissolution.

The cycle proceeds from the originating organic, spiritual and heroic forms of what Spengler calls *Kultur*, to the materialized, inorganic, massified and disanimated forms of what he calls *Zivilisation*. Such a theory repeats in part another theory of traditional character regarding the so-called "cyclical laws." These refer, moreover, to a considerably vaster realm, one might even say a metaphysical realm, which is capable of carrying us a little deeper in the analysis of our problem. It offers, effectively, the beginning of an explanation as to why one must here refer to the manifestation of a force which little by little exhausts itself—just as the pumping force of a piston (to use a banal but meet image), which provokes an expansive movement that gradually slows and recedes unless a new input arrives (an input which would give rise, in our case, to a new cycle). We must specify that on the plane of human reality the form in question should be understood as a superior organizing force which binds the inferior forces, imprinting them with form. When the originating tension weakens these lower forces release and gradually gain the upper hand, making way for phenomena of a disintegrating character.

This view appears to be relevant for that specific framework within which we would like to limit the problem of decadence. Its point of departure, similar in part to Spengler's, is a dualism of the types of civilization, and consequently also of State. On one hand there are the traditional civilizations, differing amongst themselves in form and in everything contingent, but identical in their principle: these are civilizations in which spiritual and super-individual forces and values constitute the axis and the supreme point of reference for the general organization, for the formation and for the justification of every subordinate reality.

On the other hand there is civilization of the modern type, identical to anti-tradition, built of merely human, terrestrial, individualistic and collectivistic works and factors; it is the complete development of everything that a life disassociated from overlife might attain. And decadence appears as the meaning of history, due to the fact that one ascertains in this history the failure of civilizations of the traditional kind, and the ever more precise, general, planetary advent of a new common civilization of the "modern" kind.

The specific problem, therefore, is how such a thing is possible. Let us restrict the field of our inquiry yet again; let us consider that which has real bearing on hierarchical structure and on the principle of authority, since, at bottom, this constitutes the key to everything else. In the case of traditional hierarchies and of that formative action which we have just introduced in reference to cyclical laws, we must contest the idea that the fundamental and exclusive factor of these hierarchies was a species of imposition, of direct control and violent dominion, on the part of those who at least believed themselves superior over that which was inferior. One must grant an essential weight to spiritual action. Thus traditionally one could speak of "acting without acting," one used the symbolism of the "unmoved mover" (in the Aristotelian sense)[49] and of the "pole"—the immutable axis around which every ordering motion of the subject forces is performed. The "Olympian" attribute of true authority and sovereignty was underlined, its way of directly affirming itself, not by violence but by presence. At times, finally, the image of the magnet was used, which, as we shall see, provides the key to all the problems presently under examination. The conception of

---

49 The "unmoved mover" (Greek: ὁ οὐ κινούμενος κινεῖ) was conceived by Aristotle as being the prime cause of the cosmos. It is the originator of causality, but itself is not subject to causality. In the *Metaphysics* it is identified with the divinity which contemplates itself. Aristotle considered this the necessary ultimate consequence of the principle that "nothing comes from nothing." For more, see Aristotle, Book VIII of the *Physics* and Book XII of the *Metaphysics*. Evola gives considerable attention to all of these problems in the first part of *Revolt Against the Modern World*. (See especially Chapter 3.)

the violent origin of every hierarchical and civil order, which is dear to the historiography and the ideology of the left, should be rejected, being as it is primitive, false, or at least incomplete.

In general it is absurd to believe that the representatives of a true spiritual authority and of the tradition, who had some direct interest in creating and maintaining those hierarchical relations by virtue of which they could appear even visibly as the masters, set about running after men to grab them and to tie each one to his post. Not simply submission, but adhesion and recognition on the part of the inferior are rather the fundamental basis of every normal and traditional hierarchy. It is not the superior who has need of the inferior, but the inferior who has need of the superior; it is not the master that has need of the minion, it is the minion that has need of a master.

The essence of hierarchy is to be found in the fact that in certain beings there lives, in the form of presence and of actuated reality, that which exists in others only as confused aspiration, as presentiment, as tendency; for this, the latter are fatally attracted by the former, naturally subordinate themselves to the former, subordinating themselves less to something exterior than to their own truest "I." Here we can find the secret of every readiness in sacrifice, every lucid heroism, every free virile devotion within the world of the ancient hierarchies—and, on the other hand, we can find here also the origin of a prestige, of an authority, of a calm potency and of an influence, which not even the best-armed tyrant could ever guarantee to himself.

The recognition of this fact sheds a different light not only on the problem of decadence but also on the possibility, in general, of every subversive revolution. Has one not perhaps heard it repeated that, if a revolution triumphs, it is sign that the ancient masters were enfeebled and the ancient ruling classes were degenerate? That might be true, but it is *ex parte*. One should certainly keep such an idea in mind, for example, wherever there are wild dogs at the chain which end up biting someone: this evidently would prove that the hands which hold these animals firm are not, or are no longer, strong enough. But things stand otherwise if one contests the exclusively violent origin of the true State, when the point of departure is that hierarchy whose most essential foundation we have just now indicated. Such a hierarchy can be overthrown in one case alone: when the individual degenerates, when he uses his fundamental liberty to deprive his life of every higher reference and to constitute himself to himself almost as if he were a lump of flesh. Then the points of contact are fatally interrupted, the tension slackens which unified the traditional organization and made the political process into the counterpart of a process of elevation and of integration of the single individual, of the realization of latent higher possibilities; then every force vacillates in its orbit, and finally—perhaps after a vain attempt to substitute the lost tradition with rationalistic or utilitarian constructs—flies free. The apices might even remain pure and intact on high, but the rest, which hung before as if suspended from them, shall now be like an avalanche. With a motion at first imperceptible, then growing in speed, it loses its stability and precipitates down, to the bottom, to the leveling of the valleys: liberalism, socialism, collectivism *en masse*, communism.

This is the mystery of decadence in the restricted compass to which we have limited our reflections; this is the mystery of every subversive revolution. The revolutionary commences by killing the hierarchy in himself, mutilating in himself those possibilities which correspond to the interior foundation of order—and he then proceeds to demolish the order outside himself as well. Without a preliminary interior destruction no revolution—in the sense of anti-hierarchical and anti-traditional subversion—can be possible. And since this preliminary phase escapes the notice of the superficial observer and of the myope who does not know how to see or evaluate anything but "facts," so one is accustomed to considering revolutions as irrational phenomena, or to explaining them exclusively by material or social considerations, which in any normal civilization have never been anything but secondary and subordinate.

When the Catholic mythology, speaking of the primordial fall of man and the very "revolt of the angels,"[50] relates all this to freedom of the will, at bottom this carries us back to the same explanatory principle. One treats of the fearful power inherent in man to use his liberty toward spiritual destruction, toward repulsion of all that which might guarantee him a higher dignity. This is a metaphysical decision; and the current which snakes throughout history in the various forms of the anti-traditional, revolutionary, individualistic, humanistic, secularistic, and in the end "modern" spirit, is nothing but the manifestation, and so to speak the phenomenology, of this decision. This decision is the primary effective and determinate cause in the mystery of decadence and of the destruction of the traditional.

In comprehending this, we are near to penetrating the sense of ancient traditions, whose nature is sufficiently enigmatic, relative to those masters who, in a certain sense, still exist, not ever having ceased to be, and who can be rediscovered (they themselves, or else their

---

50   References to the expulsion of Adam and Eve from the Garden of Eden (See the Old Testament, Genesis 3) and the fall of Lucifer from Heaven, originating from Lucifer's attempt to overthrow the throne of God with a contingent of angels, and resulting in the casting down of the rebels into hell. The Biblical basis for this tale is somewhat slight. See Isaiah 14:12-17 and 2 Enoch 29:3. The Catholic Encyclopedia entry for "Devil" contains the following: "The authoritative teaching of the Church on this topic is set forth in the decrees of the Fourth Lateran Council (cap. i, 'Firmiter credimus'), wherein, after saying that God in the beginning had created together two creatures, the spiritual and the corporeal, that is to say the angelic and the earthly, and lastly man, who was made of both spirit and body, the council continues:

'Diabolus enim et alii dæmones a Deo quidem naturâ creati sunt boni, sed ipsi per se facti sunt mali.' ('the Devil and the other demons were created by God good in their nature but they by themselves have made themselves evil.')"
Cf. also Milton, *Paradise Lost*, Book I.

"abodes") by means of actions described in various ways but always symbolically; the search for them is equivalent in fact to reintegrating oneself, creating a given attitude, whose virtue is analogous to those essential qualities by which a given metal immediately *feels* (so to speak) the magnet, discovers the magnet and orients itself and moves irresistibly toward it. We limit ourselves to this hint, for whomever wishes to develop it.

But looking to our present times a profound pessimism arises in this connection. Even were such true masters to appear today, they would not be recognized unless they concealed their quality, and presented themselves essentially as a species of demagogues and agitators of social myths. It is for this too that the epoch of the monarchies has closed, when previously, while order subsisted, even a simple symbol might have sufficed; it was not necessary that he who incarnated this symbol was always up to its height.

7. THE INVERSION OF SYMBOLS

Contrary to what the disciples of the myth of progress believe, the revolutionary movements of the modern epoch, far from representing something positive which has given life to autonomous and original forms, have essentially agitated for inversion, subversion, usurpation and degradation of the principles, the forms, and the traditional symbols of the precedent regimes and civilizations. This could be easily illustrated with typical examples taken from various spheres, commencing from a consideration of the "immortal principles" of the French Revolution itself. But for now we wish only to linger on consideration of certain terms and certain characteristic symbols.

Before anything, let us take the *color red*. This color, which has become the emblem of subversion, previously, as purple, had recurring connection with the regal and imperial function—connection not unrelated to the sacred character recognized in it. The tradition can carry us as far back as classical antiquity, where this color, in its correspondence with fire conceived as the highest of all the elements (that which, according to the Ancients, was the substance of the highest heaven, for which this heaven was called empyrean[51]), is associated

---

51   From Ancient Greek ἔμπυρος, "in the flame." According to ancient cosmology the empyrean represented the heaven above heaven, which was made of fire. This theme was taken up also in ancient philosophy. Aristotle conceived of the cosmos as composed of spheres, the fourth and penultimate of which was the lunar sphere of fire; see Aristotle, *Metaphysics* 1073b1–1074a13. Heraclitus held that fire was the fundamental element of all things; see Fragments 30 and 90.

also with triumphal symbolism. In the Roman rite of "triumph," whose character was more religious than military, the emperor, the victor, not only dressed in purple, but originally dyed himself in the same color, so as to represent Jove, the king of the gods, who was thought to have acted through the emperor's person, and thus to be the true artificer of the victory. It is superfluous to cite examples of successive traditions which regarded red as the color of regality: in Catholicism itself the "purple" is sign of the "princes of the Church."[52] Here and now we see this same color degraded in the red Marxist flag and in the red star of the Soviets.

Or let us take the very word "revolution." Few are aware of the perversion of this word's proper original sense in its modern usage. Revolution in the primary sense does not mean subversion and revolt, but really even the opposite—that is, return to a point of departure and ordinary motion around a center, for which in astronomical language the revolution of a star is precisely the movement it accomplishes in gravitating around a center, thus obstructing that centrifugal force by way of which it might lose itself in infinity.

But this concept plays an important part in the doctrine and in the symbolism of regality. The symbolism of the pole had a nearly universal character as applied to the Sovereign, the fixed and stable point around which the various politico-social activities are ordered. Here is a characteristic saying of the tradition of the extreme Orient: "He who reigns by virtue of Heaven (or divine mandate) resembles the polar star: he rests firm in his place, but all the other stars direct themselves around him."[53] In the near Orient the term *Qutb*, "pole," designated not only the sovereign but more generally him who gives

---

52   The "princes of the Church" are the cardinals, whose robes are scarlet during periods of conclave. References are sometimes made to "the scarlet" in speaking of the Catholic orders as a whole.

53   Quotation from Confucius' *Analects*, 2.1.

law and is the head of the tradition of a given historical period.[54] It might also be noted that the royal and imperial insignia of the scepter originally had no other meaning. The scepter incorporates the concept of "axis," analogy to the concept of the "pole." And this is the essential attribute of regality, the basis of the very idea of "order." When this is real, there exists always something stolid in a political organism, despite every agitation or turmoil owing to historical contingencies: in this connection one might use the image of the hinges of a door, which rest immobile and hold the door fast even when it slams shut.

"Revolution" in the modern sense, together with all that it has created, is rather like the unhinging of the door, the opposite of the traditional meaning of the term: the social and political forces loosen from their natural orbit, *decline,* know no longer nor center nor any order, other than a badly and temporarily stemmed disorder.

We have made reference to the star of the Soviets, the star with five points.[55] Analogous considerations can be made for this star. We will limit ourselves to recalling that such a sign—the so-called "pentagram"—even after the Renaissance counted as an esoteric symbol of the "microcosm," that is, of man conceived of as the image of the world and of God, dominator of all the elements thanks to his dignity and his supernatural destination. So too in the legends and the stories of magic

---

54 Particularly in the Sufi tradition, in which this word Qutb is taken to indicate the perfect human being. The word Qutb has also astronomical significance. Spiritually, it is taken to represent the axis extending from God to the spiritual leader on Earth. Such spiritual leaders are secret and unknown to the world. For more on these ideas, see the first chapters of Evola's *Revolt Against the Modern World*, especially Chapter 3.

55 The red star which famously accompanies the sickle in Soviet regalia. The red is supposed to represent the blood of exploited workers, and the five points are sometimes taken to represent the five fingers of the worker's hand, though other interpretations have also been offered. This same star appears in yellow in the Chinese flag.

(one recalls Goethe's *Faust*)[56] this star appears as the consecrated sign which is obeyed by spirits and elements. And so, through a process of degradation which it would be interesting to follow in its phases, the pentagram star, from that symbol of man as spiritually integrated being and supernaturally sovereign, has come to be the symbol of man terrestrialized and collectivized, of the world of the proletariat masses aiming at the dominion of the world in the sign of a messianism which itself is inverted, atheistic, destructive of every higher value and of every human dignity.

This degradation of symbols is, for every attentive overview, an extremely significant and eloquent sign of the times.

---

56 Johann Wolfgang von Goethe (1749-1832) was one of the most important German cultural figures of all time. His work is famously broad-ranging, from poetry to novels to criticism to scientific investigations. Nietzsche called *Conversations with Goethe*, the biographical record of Johann Peter Eckermann's contact with Goethe, the best of German books. Goethe is probably most famous, however, for his two-part dramatic poem *Faust*, to which Evola makes reference here; Faust imprisons the Devil with the use of a pentagram (only to be subsequently fooled by the Devil into letting him free again). See *Faust*, Part I, 1385-1405.

8. THE TARANTULA'S BITE[57]

Story has it that in the land of an ancient civilization far from Europe, an American expedition, bemoaning the poor competitivity of the native inhabitants who had been recruited for work, believed a suitable means could be found for spurring them on: the Americans doubled the hourly pay. Failure: following this raise, the better part of the workers came to work only half the hours of before. Since the natives held that the original reward was sufficient for the natural needs of their life, they now thought it altogether absurd that they should have to seek more for themselves than that which, on the basis of the new criterion, sufficed for the procuring of those needs.

This is the antithesis of what we have recently begun to call Stakhanovism.[58] This anecdote might act as a testing stone for two

---

57 According to an old Italian tradition, the bite of the tarantula leads to a condition of hysteria and extreme agitation bordering, by certain accounts, on madness. Accordingly the name *tarantism* was given to this condition, and it was a common condition in the south of Italy in the sixteenth and seventeenth centuries. The *tarantella* dance takes its origin from this sickness, first because those who were gripped by tarantism felt a desperate need for frenetic physical activity, and later because this very need was formalized into a form of dance which was held to be therapeutic for the disease. In the present case, the furious contemporary desire to work, to be productive, to engage in commercial activity, is likened to this old malady.

58 After Alexey Stakhanov, a Russian miner who became renowned throughout Soviet Russia for his remarkable stamina. He set the world record for coal mining, reportedly mining 227 tons of coal in one day. This record was later disputed by some who believed he had been aided by the Soviet authorities themselves in order to produce propaganda for the workers, but Stakhanov's name remains to this day crystallized in the Italian language in the term *staconovista*, meaning a man of tireless work ethic.

worlds, two mindsets, two civilizations, by which one of them might be judged sane and normal, and the other deviant and psychotic.

In referring to a non-European mentality, let no one adduce any commonplaces here, regarding the inertia and the indolence of these races, as compared with the "active" and "dynamic" Western ones. In this, as in other spheres, such objections have no *raison d'être*: it suffices to detach oneself a moment from "modern" civilization to perceive *also in us*, in the West, the same conceptions of life, the same attitude, the same esteem of lucre and of work.

Before the advent in Europe of what has officially and significantly been called "mercantile economy" (significantly, because one knows in what account the traditional social hierarchy held the "merchant" and the lender of money), out of which modern capitalism would rapidly develop, it was the fundamental criterion of economy that exterior goods must be subject to a certain measure, that the pursuit of wealth should be excused and licit only as it served to guarantee a subsistence corresponding to one's state. Subsistence economy counted as the normal economy. This was also the Thomistic conception and later on even the Lutheran conception.[59] It was essential that the single individual recognized that he belonged to a given group, that there existed determinate a fixed or limited framework within which he might develop his possibilities, realize his vocation, tend toward a partial, specific perfection. The same thing held in the ancient corporative ethics, wherein the values of personality and quality were emphasized,

---

59 For the Thomistic conception, see *Summa Theologica*, II-II Q. 66. For example, he says in Article 2, "A more peaceful state is ensured to man if each one is contented with his own." For Luther's view, see his tract *On Trade and Usury*. Toward the beginning of this work he says, "Therefore some of the merchants, too, have been awakened, and have become aware that in their trading many a wicked trick and hurtful financial practice is in use, and it must be feared that the word of Ecclesiasticus applies here and that 'merchants can hardly be without sin.'" (Translation Charles M. Jacobs.)

and wherein, in any case, the quantity of work was ever a function of a determinate level of natural needs. In general, the concept of progress in those times was applied to an essentially interior plane; it did not indicate leaving one's station to seek lucre and to multiply the quantity of one's work in order to reach an exterior economic and social position which did not belong to one.

All of these, however, were once perfectly Western viewpoints—the viewpoints of European man, when he was yet sane, not yet bitten by the tarantula, not yet thrall of the insane agitation and the hypnosis of the "economy," which would conduct him into the disorder, the crises and the paroxysms of the current civilization. And today one trumpets this or that system, one seeks this or that palliative—but no one brings the question back to its origin. To recognize that even in economy the primary factors are spiritual factors, that a change of attitude, a true *metanoia*,[60] is the only efficacious means if one would still conceive of halting the slide—this goes beyond the intellect of our technicians, who have by now gathered to proclaim in unison that "economy is destiny."[61]

But we already know where the road shall lead us upon which man betrays himself, subverts every just hierarchy of values and of interests, concentrates himself on exteriorities, and the quest for gain, "produc-

---

60 From the Ancient Greek μετάνοια, "changing one's mind" (lit. "beyond the mind"). This is a prominent Biblical theme, and is generally translated by the word "repentance." Its original meaning, probably also among the Christians, was a change of heart, a spiritual conversion; and this is clearly the meaning it takes on in Evola's use.

61 These were the words originally of Walter Rathenau (1867-1922), a Jewish German statesman and diplomat during the Weimer Republic. He was the signee of the Treaty of Rapallo, by which Russia and Germany renounced their territorial claims after World War I, leading to increased trade between the two. For his signature to this document, and for his intellectual ideas, which tended toward socialism, Rathenau was held to be a revolutionary in some circles, and he was assassinated in 1922 by the right-wing Organization Consul.

tion," and economic factors in general form the predominant motive of his soul. Perhaps Sombart[62] better than anyone has analyzed the entire process. It culminates fatally in those forms of high industrial capitalism in which one is condemned to run without rest, leading to an unlimited expansion of production, because every stop would signify immediately retreat, often being forced out and crushed. Whence comes that chain of economic processes which seize the great entrepreneur body and soul, shackling him more totally than the last of his laborers, even as the stream becomes almost autonomous and drags behind it thousands of beings, finally dictating laws to entire peoples and governments. *Fiat productio, pereat homo*—precisely as Sombart had already written.[63]

The which reveals, by the way, the backstage work of "liberation" and of American aid in the world. We stand at the fourth of Truman's points[64]—the same Truman who, brimming over with disinterested love, wishes " the improvement and growth of underdeveloped areas" of the earth: in other words: carrying to its term the new barbaric

---

62 Werner Sombart (1863-1941), a German economist and sociologist. He began as a student of Marxist thought (Engels said he was the only German professor to have understood Marx) but by the end of his life had approached the National-Socialism of the Nazis. Throughout his career he was known for his intrepid consideration of the role that race plays in society. His early connections to Marxism and his later connections to Nazism have sadly blackened his memory, and, as Evola states in Chapter 25 (where he considers certain aspects of Sombart's thought in greater depth), Sombart "is an author worthy of more study than we generally give him."

63 Latin: "Let there be production, though man should perish." Taken from Sombart's *Der Bourgeois* (1913), yet to be translated into English.

64 From President Truman's famous "Point Four Program," as announced in his inaugural address of January 20, 1949. (The subsequent citations in this chapter are also taken from that address.) This program was purportedly a foreign policy of aiding underdeveloped countries and encouraging their growth and industrial progress. As Evola points out here, it is unlikely that the motivations behind this program were really so altruistic.

invasions, the brutalization in economic trivia even of those countries which by a happy confluence of circumstances are yet preserved from the bite of the tarantula, are yet preserved in a traditional tenor of life, are yet withheld from that economic and "productive" exploitation which carries us to the bitter end of every possibility for man for nature. The system of the Americans, *mutatis mutandis*, persists in these commercial companies, which carry cannons along with them in order to "persuade" whomever has no interest whatsoever in commerce...

That ethic epitomized in the principle *"abstine et substine"*[65] was a Western one; so was its betrayal in a conception of life which, instead of maintaining need within natural limits toward the pursuit of that which is truly worthy of human striving, takes for its ideal instead the growth and the artificial multiplication of need itself, and also of the means to satisfy this need, with no regard for the growing slavery this must constitute first for the single individual and then for the collective, in accordance with an ineluctable law. No one should marvel that on such a basis there can be no stability, that everything must crumble and the so-called "social question," already prejudged from the start by impossible premises, must intensify to the very point which is desired by communism and Bolshevism...

Moreover, things have gone so far today that any different viewpoint appears "anachronistic," "anti-historical." Beautiful, priceless words! But if ever one were to return to normality, it would become clear that, so far as the individual goes, there is no exterior, "economic" growth worth its price; there is no growth whose seductions one

---

65   Latin: "endure and abstain," often translated "bear and forebear." It was a saying of the Greek Stoic Epictetus (c. AD 50-135). Epictetus was born a slave, and his main work, *The Discourses*, is formed of the statements he made to his pupis, which were transcribed and compiled by his student Arrian. *Abstine et substine* in many ways epitomizes the Stoic philosophy which later had such influence over Roman civilization: to tolerate the ills that come upon us and to refrain from forming attachments to things over which we have no control.

must not absolutely resist, when the counterpart of letting oneself be seduced is the essential crippling of one's liberty. No price is sufficient to recompense the loss of free space, free breath, such as permit one to find oneself and the being in oneself, and to reach what is possible for one to reach, beyond the conditioned sphere of matter and of the needs of ordinary life.

Nor do matters stand any differently for nations, especially when their resources are limited. Here "autarchy" is an ethical principle, because that which has weight on the scale of values must be identical both for a single individual and for a State. Better to renounce the phantasm of an illusory betterment of the general conditions and to adopt, wherever it is necessary, a system of "austerity,"[66] which does not yoke itself to the wagon of foreign interests, which does not let itself become embroiled in the global processes of a hegemony and an economic productivity cast into the void. For such processes, in the end, when they find nothing more to grasp on to, will turn against those same individuals who have woken them to life.

Nothing less than this becomes evident to whomever reflects on the "moral" implicit in the simple anecdote recounted at the beginning of this essay. Two worlds, two mindsets, two destinies. Against the "tarantula's bite" stand all those who yet remember just activity, right effort, what is worthy of pursuit, and fidelity to themselves. Only they are the "realizers," the beings who truly stand on their feet.

---

66 Evola here uses the English word "austerity." Quotation marks are Evola's.

9. ROME AND THE SIBYLLINE BOOKS

In any consideration of the secret history of Ancient Rome, the examination of the so-called *Sibylline Books*[67] constitutes a task whose importance cannot be overstated. To become aware of this, naturally, one requires adequate principles, and in the first place one must hearken back to the idea that the constitution of the Roman world was not homogeneous: contrary forces crossed and collided within it. Though it drew enigmatically from civilizations and races that were essentially part of the Pelasgian pre-Aryan Mediterranean cycle,[68] Rome came to manifest an opposite principle. In Rome, the virile,

---

67 The most pertinent information regarding these books is contained in the present chapter. The Sibylline Books were texts used as an oracle toward the resolving of particular crisis during both the Roman Republic and Empire. As Evola explains, the original books were destroyed in a fire, and were replaced with a most suspect compendium of texts of dubious origin.

68 The Pelasgians, according to Greek mythology, were the descendants of Pelasgus, who was according to certain versions of the myth the first man. There have been a number of historical figures of this name, but Evola is certainly referring to the early inhabitants of the Aegean Sea region, from whom the Greeks adopted the worship of many of their deities, including Zeus and Hephaestus, though the Pelasgians themselves worshiped a Mother Goddess. They were held to be responsible also for the introduction of the alphabet and numerous forms of learning and architecture. The Pelasgians were thought to be the ancestors of the Etruscans, who were subsequently totally assimilated into the earliest Roman society—hence the racial influence in Rome which, according to Evola, strove against the Aryan solar element.

Apollinian and solar element opposed itself, in various forms, to that of the promiscuous-feminine, telluric, lunar element of the previous world—an element which, in the end, had succeeded in overwhelming Olympic and heroic Hellas itself. Only this overview permits one to comprehend the profound sense of all the most important upheavals in the ancient life and history of Rome. That which was specifically Roman in Rome was constituted by an incessant battle of the virile and solar principle of the *Imperium* against an obscure substratum of ethnic, religious, and also mystical elements, wherein the presence of a strong Semitic-Pelasgian component is incontestable, and in which the telluric-lunar cult of the great Goddess Mothers of nature played an exceedingly important part. This battle had alternating epochs. The pre-Roman element, subjugated at an early time, successively enjoyed a revival in subtler forms, and in strict dependency with cults and forms of life which were decidedly Asiatic-Meridional. It is in this ensemble that one must study the essence and the influence of the *Sibylline Books* in Ancient Rome: they constitute an extremely important conduit for the subterranean action of corrosion and of denaturalization of the Aryan Roman world in its last phase—at that point, that is, in which the counteroffensive felt itself near to its dreamed goal.[69] Not only the generic element of Asiatic-Semitic decomposition there enters significantly and almost nakedly in play, but also another, properly and consciously Judaic element.

The tradition refers the origin of the *Sibylline Books* to a female figure and to the king of a foreign dynasty: the texts are offered by

---

69 [Evola's footnote.] The systematic framework of this interpretation of the Roman Period, which had its best expression in J.J. Bachofen (cf. *The Myth of the Occident and the Orient*), can be found by the reader in the second part of our work: *Revolt Against the Modern World*. [For more on Bachofen, see note 429 to Chapter 38 below. —*Trans.*]

an old woman to Tarquinius Superbus,[70] that is to the last dominant
figure of the Roman Priscian[71] epoch to derive from the pre-Roman
and Pelasgian lineage of the Etruscans. These books were collected in
the temple of Capitoline Jove itself.[72] Entrusted to a special college—the
duumviri who subsequently transformed into the *quindecimviri sacris
faciundis*[73]—they became a species of oracle from which the Senate
requested counsel. In 83 they were lost in the fire that destroyed the
Campidoglio. Their reconstruction was attempted through research

---

70 Lucius Tarquinius Superbus (535-509 BCE), the seventh and final king of Rome.
He was a direct descendant of Lucius Tarquinius Priscus (see subsequent note)
and he was known for his overweening pride (hence the epithet *superbus*, meaning "proud or arrogant"). He was overthrown in by Lucius Junius Brutus in
509, who founded the Roman Republic. The old woman here mentioned is the
so-called Cumaean Sibyl, and the legend has it that she offered the king nine
books of prophecy, asking high price for them. When he would not pay, she
burned three of them, offering him the remaining six at the same price. Once
more he refused, and once more she burned three. He accepted her last offer of
the remaining three at the original price, and these became the Sybilline Books
which were kept in the Temple of Jupiter. It is most characteristic of Evola
to refer to Tarquinius' dynasty as "foreign": Tarquinius was descended of an
Etruscan line, which according to the present analysis would link him decisively
to the "pre-Aryan Mediterranean cycle" to which Evola alludes above.

71 That is, the epoch associated with the fifth king of Rome, Lucius Tarquinius
Priscus, or Tarquin the Elder (616-579 BCE). Tarquin the Elder was known to
flaunt many of the fashions of the Etruscans, particularly in military affairs, but
also to some extent in religious practices; he may have introduced sacrificial
rites following Etruscan practices.

72 The Temple of Jupiter, the most important temple of Ancient Rome, was built
on Capitoline Hill. It was destroyed in a series of fires, and with it a portion of
the original Sibylline Books.

73 Latin. *Duumviri*: "two men"; *quindecimviri sacris faciundis*: "fifteen men of sacred duties." The *duumviri* were joint magistrates who attended in particular to
juridical matters, including the administration of justice. Their duties included
care and consultation of the Sibylline Books. The fifteen later adopted these last
duties in particular.

into the best known sacred places of the Sibylline religion, and the new text became the object of successive revisions. Naturally, in this new phase, it must have been rather easy to infiltrate these texts through the more or less spurious material that was collected. The texts were kept exceedingly secret. Only the college hitherto named could see them and directly consult them. As we know from the horrible death of M. Atilius,[74] communicating anything of them to outsiders was considered a misdeed, and brought an inexorable punishment.

If we leave aside those books commonly called the *Hebrew Sibylline Books*[75] (*Orac. Sibyll.*, III, IV, V), we know nothing specific about the content of the *Sibylline Books*: we know only certain effects that they produced, which however can furnish us the essence of the matter. The material, "objective" basis of an "oracle," is in fact that which is least important to it. This material is indeed nothing but a basis, a support: it is an instrument which, in special circumstances, permits certain "influences" to express themselves, even as, on another level, various phenomena are brought about by the presence of a medium or by a

---

74 Marcus Atilius (or Acilius), birth and death unknown. He was appointed by Tarquinius Superbus as one of the first *duumviri*, but he was caught copying the Sibylline Books, in consequence of which transgression he was sewn into a sack and cast into the sea.

75 Also known as books 3-5 of the Sibylline Oracles. The original Sibylline Books were burned by Flavius Stilicho (359-408), the half-Roman half-Vandal general who rose to power in the Western Roman Empire around the turn of the fifth century. He evidently believed the Books were being used to undermine his rule, and so disposed of them accordingly. The Sibylline Oracles refer instead to a collection of poetic and prophetic utterances put into the mouth of the Sibylline oracle. They were likely written by numerous authors, and include a confused hodgepodge of ideas stemming from Christian, Roman, Greek, and Jewish sources. Books 3-5 are thought to have been produced by Jewish authors in Alexandria, hence their name in Italian: *i Libri Sibillini Ebraici*, or the Hebrew Sibylline Books. Their origins are obscure, their authors unknown, and it is moreover believed that they were tampered with after their writing, receiving amendment and additions.

state of trance. Thus, when considering the first *Sibylline Books*, it is less interesting to know what formulae and sayings they might have contained, than that "line of thought" which betrays itself through a series of responses which issued from them, often through various case-by-case interpretations of identical texts. It is this line of thought which permits us to know with exactitude the true nature of the influence connected to the oracle.

Now, we see that this oracle almost always acted so as to distance Rome from its traditions, and to introduce exotic and modifying elements, cults which subversively catered to the plebs above all—that is, to the element which in Rome was maintained by an unconscious coalescence with the precedent Italo-Pelasgian civilization, as opposed to its solar and Aryan core. Used ever to calm the people in moments of danger, of calamity, and of uncertainty, the *Sibylline Books* and their responses should have indicated the aptest means to guarantee the benevolence and complicity of divine powers from on high. Yet never did the responses have as consequence the reinforcement of the Roman people in its antique traditions or in the cults which most characterized its sacral patriciate; they always ordered the introduction or adaptation of exotic divinities, whose relation to the cycle of pre- and anti-Roman civilizations of the Mother is, in the vast majority of cases, exceedingly visible.

The contents of one of the oldest Sibylline responses, which dates to 399,[76] on the occasion of a plague, can be considered as an overall symbol of the sense of the denaturing that gradually began its work. The oracle wanted the Romans to introduce the *lectisternium* and the *supplicatio*[77] correlated to this. The *supplicatio* consisted in kneeling

---

76   See Livy, *The History of Rome*, Book V.13.

77   *Lectisternium* is Latin, from *lectum sternere*: "to spread on a couch." The *lectisternium* were thus propitiatory meals offered to the gods and goddesses, originally accompanied by a seven day festival during which, according to Livy, quarrels were stopped and prisoners were released. *Supplicatio* is the Latin word for "supplication."

or prostrating oneself before the divinities, embracing or kissing their knees or their feet. As much as this rite might seem normal, or at the least only a little excessive, to whomever is inured to the forms of religion which replaced ancient paganism, nonetheless this usance was unknown to the ancient Roman: he knew no Semitic servility before the divine. He prayed, invoked, and sacrificed manfully, on his feet. This is already an index of a profound transformation, of the passage from one mentality to another.

In 258, Demeter, Dionysus and Kore[78] were introduced into Rome by the *Sibylline Books*. This is the first great phase of the spiritual offensive: it conducted the two great terrestrial Goddesses of nature with their orgiastic companion, symbol of every confusion and anti-virile mysticism, into the world that Priscian Rome had built through its destruction by arms of races and power centers which themselves had already incarnated finished, spiritually-infused forms. In 249, ever through the will of the *Sibylline Books*, Dis Pater and Proserpina,[79] that is precisely the nether-telluric divinities, the most typical personifications of that which opposes Olympic and Apollonian ideals, entered Rome. These were followed, in 217, by an Aphroditic divinity, Venus Erycina,[80] and finally, in 205, in the most critical moment of the Punic Wars, we see enter, so to speak, the Matriarch of this entire cycle, she who could call herself the personification of the entire

---

78 *Demeter*: Greek goddess of agriculture and the harvest, sister of Zeus. *Dionysus*, also known as *Bacchus*: pre-Gracian God introduced into Greece in the seventh century BCE, he is the god of wine, vintage, madness and fertility. *Kore*, also known as *Persephone*: queen of the underworld, daughter of Zeus and Demeter and wife of Hades.

79 *Dis Pater*, later identified with *Pluto* (Roman) or *Hades* (Greek): originally a god of subterranean riches, fertility, and mines. *Proserpina*: fertility goddess, daughter of Ceres, and parallel in many ways to Persephone. The central myth regarding Proserpina is her abduction by the god of the underworld.

80 The Roman equivalent of Aphrodite, the goddess of love, sex, beauty, desire, and victory.

Pelasgian-Asiatic and pre-Roman spirit—Cybele, the Magna Mater.[81] All these divinities were entirely unknown to the Romans: and if the plebs, regalvanized in its most spurious substrate, was seized by an often frantic enthusiasm for them, the senate and the patriciate in the initial days did not fail to show their repugnance and their awareness of peril. Whence the strange incongruity that while Rome with every pomp went to take the simulacrum of Cybele from Pessinus,[82] yet it prohibited the Roman citizens from taking part in this goddess' ceremonies and orgiastic festivals, which were presided over by Frigian eunuch priests. But, naturally, this resistance was but brief in its duration. It had the same destiny as the prohibition against Dionysism and Pythagorism. And again in 140 the *Sibylline Books* introduced yet another figure from the terrestrial feminine cycle, Venus Verticordia or Aphrodite Apostrophia.[83]

The collective transformation leading to all this, had already been noted by Livy (XXV, 1) who, referring to the period around the year 213, wrote verbatim, "Religious forms, the better part of them come from abroad, so agitated the citizenry, that either men or the gods seemed of a sudden altered. The Roman rites were by then abolished not only in their secret forms or in the domestic cult, but also in public; and in the Capitoline Forum there was a crowd of women who neither sacrificed nor prayed any longer according to the tradition of the fatherland." So

---

81 Cybele, also known as Ida, was a Phrygian goddess whose name probably derives from *mountain*: originally, she was the Mother of the Mountain. Her cult was introduced in Greece between the sixth and the fourth centuries BCE, and she was associated strongly with Dionysus.

82 A Phrygian city which had been a center of the early cult of Cybele. The Romans sacked it in 204 BCE, and stole the large black stone there which was thought to be the image of Cybele.

83 Another variant of the goddess of love. *Verticordia* from Latin: "changer of hearts." *Apostrophia* from Ancient Greek: "she who turns away." Evola provides the following reference here: Cf. Geffcken: *Die Oracula Sibyllina*, Leipzig, 1902.

it was that, the more widely Roman power extended itself, the very forces it conquered abroad began to wage a second war on an invisible plane, through this work of corrosion and denaturalization—war in which these forces brought ever more visible and resounding successes.

We arrive thus at the period of the so-called *Hebrew Sibylline Books*, which appear to have been compiled between the first and the third centuries. A goodly part of their text is known to us. Schührer[84] uses the expression "Jewish propaganda under a pagan mask (*jüdische Propaganda unter heidnischer Maske*)" with respect to them—opinion which is shared by a Jewish scholar, Alberto Pincherle,[85] who recognized in these texts an explosion of Jewish hatred against the Italic races and against Rome. A maneuver of mystification is here repeated in a more tangible and indisputable form—one that already the ancient oracles had applied insofar as they sought to justify themselves, through the Sibyls, by means of Apollo. Through the relations of the Sibylline religion with the Apollonian cult—relations which are anything but limpid—the oracles, which had been introduced into Rome by the Etruscan king, snatched up, so to speak, a higher title of authority, by pampering the Apollonian vocation of the Roman race. And this until the time of Augustus, who, feeling himself to be the initiator of a new Apollinian and solar era, ordered the revision of the Sibylline texts so as to extrapolate from them all spurious passages. Naturally, matters proceeded quite differently, and the tree made itself known by its fruit:

---

84 Emil Schührer (1844-1910), German protestant theologian who made diligent study of the Jewish influences in the time of Jesus. Evola here provides reference to Schührer's major work *A History of the Jewish People in the Time of Christ*, and gives the following specification in the Leipzig German edition of 1909: v. III, p. 533 *et seq.*

85 Pincherle (1894-1979, not to be confused with the Italian author Alberto Moravia, who was also born Alberto Pincherle) was a historian and scholar of Christianity. Evola provides the following reference: *Gli Oracoli Sibillini giudaici*, Roma, 1922, p. XVI.

that oracle introduced precisely the most anti-solar series of divinities into Rome. The same alibi was attempted by these new *Sibylline Books*: here one finds a pure Judaism which dresses its ideas up to make them seem like the authentic prophecy of an exceedingly ancient pagan Sibyl, so as to obtain a corresponding credence in Rome. Whereupon one arrives at the incredible paradox, that many in the Roman milieu took this very tradition of apocalyptic images as wisdom, when it was exclusively the expression of Jewish hatred against the Romulean city and against the Italic peoples.

These oracles can be conceived of as a pendant of the Johannine Apocalypse.[86] But the Apocalypse, in the Christian religion, was interpreted on a universalistic, symbolic, and teleogical plane, so that the Jewish thesis, which originally stood at the center, was almost erased. In the *Sibylline Oracles* this thesis instead remained in its original state. The prophecy of the pseudo-Sibyl was turned against the races of the Gentiles: it predicts the vendetta that Asia will bring against Rome, and the punishment, more sever than the law of talion,[87] which will strike the lordly cities of the world. It is worth our while to document a few passages which characterize this anti-Roman hatred: "However many riches Rome has received from tributary Asia, three times as many will Asia receive from Rome, and it will deduct from Rome penance for the violence that has been done; and however many men of Asia become servants in the residences of the Italians, twenty times as many miserable Italians will work for their wages in Asia, and every one will be the debtor

---

86 The Book of Revelation of John, the last book in the New Testament, which includes a series of prophetic visions or *apokálypsis* (Ancient Greek: ἀποκάλυψις) surrounding the rise the Anti-Christ and the Second Coming of the Christ.

87 The Law of Talion, more commonly known as "an eye for an eye," derives from the Latin *lex talionis*, the law by which punishment must be equal to injury.

to dozens" (III, 350).[88] "O Italy, to you shall come no foreign Mars [to succor you], but the wretched blood of your own people, not easily destroyed, shall devastate you who are renowned and brazen. And you, lying amidst the still hot ashes, unforeseeing in your soul, will give yourself over to death. You shall be mother of men without goodness, you shall be the nurturer of brutes" (III, 460-470).[89] And here follows an entire film of disasters and catastrophes, described with sadistic complacency. The references to Judaism become ever more distinct toward the end of the third book and the beginning of the fourth. Prophecy becomes history in IV, 115:[90] "Also to Jerusalem will come a wicked tempest of war from Italy which will raze the great temple of God." But in catastrophes of every kind the Romans "must recognize the wrath of the celestial God, for they have destroyed the innocent people of God." Rome, also the ancients, were perhaps perfectly aware that it was Babylon's yearned-for collapse which was described with Grand-Guignolesque[91] hues similar to those of the Johannine Apocalypse, because it, together with Italy, had murdered many of the faithful saints and the genuine people (that is, Israel) amongst the Jews. Lactantius, for example, writes (*Div. Inst.*, VII, 15, 18): *Sibyllae tamen aperte interitum esse Romam locuntur et quidem iudicio dei quod nomen eius habuerit inuisum et inimica iustitiae*

---

88 Evola is evidently working from a different manuscript than that commonly available in English. I will therefore indicate the corresponding passages in Milton S. Terry's blank-verse English translation. The present quotation is to be found at III 425.

89 III 580-590.

90 IV 162.

91 The Grand Guignol, *le Théâtre du Grand-Guignol*, was a Parisian theater which opened in 1897 and closed in 1962. It was based on a peculiar kind of artistic realism, and featured gory horror plays.

alumnum ueritatis populum trudidarit.[92] In IV, 167 *et seq.* the text continues, "Alas, O wholly impure city of the Latin soil, O Maenad that adores vipers, you will be sedated as a widow upon your hills, and the river Tiber will weep for you, her consort, that you possess a homicidal heart and an impure soul. Know you not of what things God is capable, and what he is preparing for you? But you say: I alone am, and no one will destroy me. And now instead the everlasting God will destroy you and all your own, and there will be no trace of you in that land, even as it was before the great God invented your glories. You remain alone, O wicked one; immersed in the flaring fire, you will dwell in the wicked Tartarian region of your Hades." Against the condemned Romulean city and the Italian land stands the "divine race of blessed heavenly Jews" (248).[93] Book III (703-5)[94] repeats: "But the men of the great God live all of them around the temple, delighting in those things that will be given them by the creator, the judge, the only sovereign... and all the cities will proclaim: how he loves these men, the Immortal God!" The passages 779 *et seq.*[95] reproduce almost to the letter the noted prophecies of Isaiah, and the messianic and imperialistic Jewish dream takes shape, which has as its center the Temple: the "prophets of the Great God" will take up the sword after the cycle of catastrophes and of destruction, and they will be

---

92 Latin: "Nonetheless the Sibyls say openly that Rome shall be destroyed, and indeed by the judgement of God, because it held his name in hatred, and as the enemy of justice massacred the sons of the true people" (translation mine). The citation is from the work of Lucius Caecilius Firmianus Lactantius (c. 250-c. 325), an early Christian writer of North African origin. He was very highly regarded by the humanists of the Renaissance period, who considered him a "Christian Cicero" for the grace of his style. The present quotation comes from his *Divinae Institutiones* (*Divine Institutions*), Book VII, Chapter 15.

93 The longer quotation comes from V 225-242. The "divine race of heavenly Jews" is from V 337.

94 Beginning from III 877.

95 Beginning from III 925.

the kings and the executioners of all peoples. These new prophets, all descendants of Israel, are destined to be "the leaders of life for the entirety of humankind" (580).[96]

It is a singular contrast to the fact that, while on one hand, as has been mentioned, the authors of these writings attempt a pagan alibi—meaning they wish to give to their prophetic expressions the authority proceeding from the antique Roman Sibylline tradition—nonetheless in the fourth book (1-10) they completely betray their true positions. In this passage the *Sibylline Books* contain indeed a lively polemic against the rival pagan Sibyls, and she, into whose mouth one had placed the expression of hatred's hopes and of the chosen people's vendetta, suddenly claims to be prophetess not of "the liar Phoebus," not of the Apollinian god "that foolish men called a god and wrongly a prophet, but of the great God"—of the God who does not tolerate graven images; the which manifestly means Jehovah, the god of Mosaism.[97]

With which—as one might say in Hegelian language—the negation comes to negate the negation,[98] so as to bring to light the essential fact of this entire "tradition." The "liar Phoebus" that the God of Israel would supplant is in realty the false Apollo: for, even if the Sibylline religion makes reference to Apollo, it does not mean the pure divinity of light, the symbol of the solar cult of Hyperborean (Nordic-Aryan) origin,

---

96   Probably taken from III 724.

97   Jehovah is one of the names of the Jewish God, and the reference is the second commandment, "Thou shalt not make unto thee any graven image," Exodus 20:4. Mosaism: the religion and doctrines of Moses.

98   Hegel's doctrine of negation of the negation, which later became a central aspect also for Marx's dialectic materialism, was a key part of Hegel's dialectical understanding of history. What *is* (that which Fichte later called the thesis) is then negated (antithesis); but this negation is then also negated (sublation or synthesis). The "negation of the negation" represents in part a return to the original thesis, but in a new and changed form. The key movement for historical progress of any kind is therefore this third step, sublation, the negation of the negation.

but it means rather the Dionysized Apollo, who is associated with the feminine element;[99] and this element above all uses his revelations as an organ, exhuming the principle of the ancient Demetric-Pelasgian gynecocracy. That which remains is therefore the continuity of an anti-Roman influence, which clarifies itself ever more, and which in the period between the first and the third century comes incontestably to depend on, or at least to make common cause with, the Semitic-Jewish element, in relation to which it assumes the extremest forms and, so to speak, finally reveals the *terminus ad quem*,[100] the final aim of this entire fount of inspiration: "O wholly impure city of the Latin soil, Maenad that loves vipers, immersed in the flaring fire, you will dwell in the wicked Tartarian region of your Hades."

---

99 Apollo was thought to be foremost amongst the deities worshiped by the Hyperboreans, the race of men who lived in the far northern land of Hyperborea, where the sun never set. The Hyperboreans were physically powerful, exceptionally tall and long-lived, and were thought to be the most blessed of peoples.

100 Latin: "limit to which," the final destination or aim of a thing.

10. ORIENTATIONS ON MASONRY

No one who would gain awareness of the influences to which the modern epoch owes its forms can neglect the study of Masonry. Up until yesterday, this study had a particularly topical character for many, and it was common even to draw practical and political consequences from it. Once the role that Masonry has played as an historical power has been ascertained, it is impossible in fact to refrain from taking a stand on it, in a manner conforming to the principles which one defends. As is known, fascism from the first took sides against Masonry (and here no one will want to broach what presumably happened with racism and antisemitism in fascism—namely, that this taking of sides occurred almost coersively, owing to external influences).[101] Equally well known is the anti-Masonic campaign undertaken by official Catholic circles, especially by the Jesuits; and up until yesterday one could find expressions in various writings, for example those of Father Gemelli,[102]

---

101 Although many remarks from Mussolini and other fascists make it clear that fascism was often conceived as the proper society for "this our Aryan and Mediterranean race" (Mussolini in a speech from 1921), fascism did not take racial concerns as its core in the same way that Nazi Germany did. As ties between Mussolini and Hitler tightened during the War, race became a growing concern in fascist Italy on account of Nazi pressure, and some believed that this reflected less something inherent to fascism, than the mere influence of the Axis alliance. Evola's point here is that the fascist opposition to Masonry cannot be considered alien to fascism in the same way that a certain kind of racism might be.

102 Agostini Gemelli (1878-1959), an Italian Franciscan friar and physician.

as for instance "Jewish-Masonic coteries," used to indict the forces that in the shadows continued the already secular battle against the Church and traditional values.

But in general there are no clear and well-founded ideas regarding this entire subject. The judgements made on Masonry oscillate between the judgement of those who see in Masonry an occult power, with its secret masters and wide-ranging plans on the one hand, and on the other a number of rather superficial estimations of the most recent circumstances by those who see in Masonry nothing but a gang of individuals sustaining each other for material and absolutely profane benefits, without any transcendent purpose, adopting titles and symbolic ceremonies as a mere ostentation. It will be useful therefore to come to the point in all this for the orientation of those readers of the Right who are interested in this problem.

Let us mention before all of the effective origins of Masonry. Not only its enemies, but also many eminent Masons have, in this regard, highly vague and approximate notions, believing in general that Masonry has always been what it is today. In particular, they think that the positive origins of Masonry date from 1717, the year in which the Grand Lodge of London was founded.[103] In reality matters stand quite differently. Masonry antedates that year, which was not the date of its birth but rather of a profound crisis and of a species of secularization and inversion of polarities which the precedent tradition underwent.

That which was thereafter organized and diffused in an ever vaster manner throughout Europe was in reality so-called *speculative Masonry*, which in the modern Masonic circles is distinguished from

---

103 The Grand Lodge of London and Westminster (which refers, not to a building, but to a governing body) was founded in 1717 when a number of extant Lodges united into one. John Montagu, Duke of Montagu and a British peer, became involved in the lodge, thus providing a bridge between Masonry and high society. The very fact that the Grand Lodge of London was formed by the unification of prior lodges calls into question the idea that Masonry was born in 1717.

operative Masonry. It is not easy to speak briefly on the essence of this last, because it would necessarily take us into a realm which most people would find unusual. According to the most superficial and profane interpretation, operative Masonry was formed by corporations of actual masons, to whom various elements were later added. It was operative, therefore, because these elements performed a real material activity, as the builders of edifices, perhaps also cathedrals. Ancient Masonry surely had intimate relations with certain kinds of corporative traditions, dating from the Medieval Period and perhaps from yet before. But the fact is that these external traditions possessed also an internal tradition, based on the symbolic transposition of principles and of procedures of the art of building onto the spiritual plane of concepts. Material construction became a simple allegory for a creative and secret internal work; the exterior temple was symbol for the internal one; the rough stone to be squared was the common human individuality, which must be rectified that it might qualify for the *opus transformationis*,[104] that is for an overcoming of human caducity and for the acquisition of knowledge and superior liberty. The degrees of this realization corresponded to those which originated the true hierarchy of "operative," not "speculative," Masonry.

In scattered organizations, where art and "operativeness" had this special significance, which therefore had nothing to do with the political, social, and ideological plane, a process of degenerescence must have emerged between the end of the seventeenth century and the commencement of the eighteenth century, which process permitted the action of obscure forces and the infiltration of elements that gradually came to control those organizations, instilling in them another spirit and carrying their action onto the ideological and revolutionary plane through the distortion of a number of fundamental ideas. Though we risk reductionism, we must once more limit ourselves here to sketching

---

104 Latin: "work of transformation."

this last point. In the ancient organizations the central ideal was a higher liberty based on an effective superiority, in the following terms: all dogma and authority was considered a simple expedient, legitimated in view of individualism and of the intellectual limitation of the many. In order that certain truths of transcendent order might be recognized and protected from every attack or critique, it was necessary to present them in the form of dogmas and to sustain them by a categorical authority—formality, however, which is completely useless for whomever is enlightened, because such a one would be capable of recognizing these truths directly, without any coercion, sufficiently to extend himself beyond dogma and beyond any particular extrinsic traditional obstruction. Moreover, at the level of true knowledge, one arrives at something universal, anterior and superior to all the particular and variously conditioned dogmatic forms. And one of the principle distortions to which we have alluded, was taking that which is proper to this superior, uncommon, super-personal level of consciousness and conscience, and relating it to simple human reason—thus making of this human reason the supreme judge, and transforming the impulse to carry oneself altogether higher than dogma and any exterior authority into a critical and destructive attitude with respect to traditional values. This last attitude was dramatically proposed to an "emancipated" humanity in need of liberation from every "obscurantism" and every "tyrant." This shift appears already in the mutating significance of the term "enlightenment." In its origins this term referred to the "Illuminati,"[105] a secret group who strove to accomplish the spir-

---

105 Plural of the Latin *illuminatus*, "enlightened." The term "Illuminati" refers to any number of secret Enlightenment societies. These societies, directly contrary to the original meaning and purpose of Masonry, dedicated themselves to opposing "superstition" in society—which to their minds included every form of religious or spiritualistic thought—and to the establishing of a new order of liberal, secular states. The first group to bear this name were the Bavarian Illuminati, founded (most suggestively) in 1776. Though the earliest societies were rigorously suppressed, it is thought that this action simply drove them underground, and to this day the name is implicated in a variety of theories surrounding the establishment of a New World Order.

itual and super-rational enlightenment of which we have spoken; but this soon came to apply itself to the whole orientation of anti-traditional and rationalistic criticism, negator of every principle of authority. The term "enlightenment" in its current and historical sense corresponds precisely to this orientation, referring as it does to the ideological movement which prepared the French Revolution and, more generally, the revolution of the Third Estate.

After the construction of the Grand Lodge of London "speculative" Masonry went on to act ever more in this direction; it abandoned the spiritual sphere, concentrating itself on the political, social, and ideological, and, as a tactic, employed cloaked, subtle, and indirect action. This internal and degenerative transformation appears moreover in the clearest way in the contradiction existing between the internal and rigorously hierarchical structure of Masonry with all of its grades and pretentious dignities (though they be atimes put together in an inorganic and synchretistic way, especially in the Scottish Rite[106]) and the external egalitarian, democratic, anti-authoritarian and humanitarian ideology which it professes. The contrast appears also in certain antique Masonic constitutions which included in their statutes the duty to fidelity not only toward the sovereigns of the country but also toward the Catholic Church itself, compared with that orientation which translates into a number of rituals of the so-called Grades of Templar in Scottish Masonry, in which the neophyte, to consecrate his solemn commitment to combat the "double tyranny" (that is the principle of authority both in the political sphere and in the religious) must take up a dagger and strike, in symbolic act, the emblems of this dual authority, the crown and the tiara.

---

106 There are different grades or degrees in different orders of Masonry. The Scottish Rite (or the Ancient and Accepted Scottish Rite of Freemasonry) for example has 33.

All of this has for some time now been much more than mere theory, for it has been proven (by the dossiers of the Holy Office,[107] moreover) that in a secret convention of Masons, of Illuminati and pseudo-Rosicrucians, held near Frankfurt on the vigil of the French Revolution (A. Dumas, himself a Mason, describes the same event in novelized form in his *Joseph Balsamo*[108]), the project was announced to overthrow first the house of France, in the commencement of a blaze which subsequently would ignite all of Europe, and then to strike against the Church. Masonry in this sense has also acted, more or less behind the scenes, in all the revolutionary movements that continue the French Revolution in Europe (after an absolutely essential role they played in the constitution of the United States and its corresponding democracy), especially in the revolutions of 1848-1849.[109] Their aim has been the overthrow of all that which subsisted of traditional Europe, of the regimes of the First and Second Estates—those Estates, that is, which stood on an authoritarian, spiritual, dynastic and aristocratic basis—and the feeding of the revolution of the Third Estate with liberalism, democracy, laicism, anti-Catholicism, constitutionalism, and almost even a tending internationalism. From this arises the Church's

---

107 The Holy Office, or the Sacred Congregation for the Doctrine of the Faith, is one of the nine congregations of the Roman Curia. It takes as its duty the promotion and the defense of Catholic dogma throughout the world. This gives it a certain juridical power as well within the framework of the Church.

108 Alexander Dumas (1802-1870), famous French author of numerous works, but best known for his *The Count of Monte Cristo* and *The Three Muskateers*, among others. *Joseph Balsamo* is the story of the historical Giuseppe Balsamo, better known as Cagliostro, a magician whose name has been associated since his death with charlatanism. Dumas' book follows Cagliostro's escapades in Masonry and his direct involvement in the French Revolution.

109 Reference to the Revolutions of 1848, a series of democratic revolutions that sprang up around Europe, aiming at the liberalization of numerous European countries. Particularly effected was the Northern part of Europe, including Austria, Denmark, the Netherlands, and France.

stance and its condemnation of Masonry: condemnation—it is well to underline this—related to that orientation of the Church that many Catholics of today do not hesitate to call "anachronistic" or "medievalistic." The Church in those days appeared as a "reactionary" power allied to the *ancien régime*, and it considered liberalism in the same terms in which the liberals of today consider for example communism.

In reality, wherever one speaks of "immortal principles," of "liberty," of "democracy," of egalitarianism based on humanitarianism and internationalism, and so forth and so on, these are but the many ramifications of that anti-traditional religion of the Third Estate, for which Masonry was the principle harbinger. The role that Masonry played even in the Italian Risorgimento[110] is well known (especially in its manifestations as Carboneria) in those aspects of the Risorgimento which were not patriotic so much as ideological-revolutionary. Less known, but no less real, was the role it played in the First World War in presenting that conflict as a democratic crusade against the central Empires, which, apart from Russia (which was to be equally devastated through a game of concordant action and reaction) constituted the part of Europe most immune to the revolution of the Third Estate. It had the same role also in Italy, in

---

110 Italian: "resurgence." Also known in English as the Italian Unification, the Risorgimento was the almost sixty-year period during which the extremely varied and fragmented pieces of the Italian peninsula were welded together through political and military maneuvering into the unified nation we know today. The Carboneria, mentioned by Evola here, was a revolutionary group which took the place previously occupied by the Masons, who were forbidden from meeting starting in 1815. It is likely if not certain that the repressed Masons were absorbed into Carboneria, and it is possible that key Masons directed the ideology and actions of this subsequent group. Like the Masons, the Carboneria met in secret. Many of its members occupied visible roles in the unification movement. For the social and political changes in Italy which generally followed the Risorgimento, the novel *The Leopard* by Giuseppe Tomasi di Lampedusa is highly to be recommended.

the crisis of the Triplice[111] and in the same interventionism (here, too, despite all patriotic varnish, which was used as a means to an end). Even before the war ended, an international convention of Masons in Paris revealed its true, unconfessed aims ("to force a new great step forward of the ideas of the French Revolution"), which were the very same aims of the League of Nations, whose project it already then began to sketch. In the United States Masonry and Judaism often found themselves entwined intimately and tactically, and it is to their influence that we must certainly attribute the ideological aspect of "crusade" and the radicalism of the American intervention in Europe, also in the Second World War. Here too is to be found, more generally, much of that which defines the United States' pretensions toward being a paladin nation-leader of democracy, of "progress" and of "civilization."

Certain circles survived in Masonry in which the tradition of ancient "operative" Masonry was partially conserved, especially in Germany, in England, and in the Nordic countries. A typical case is that of Joseph de Maistre, the greatest Catholic exponent of the principle of pure authority from the heights and of divine right. Maistre was also a Mason—he belonged to the lodge "*La parfaite sincérité*" of Chambery of the Rectified Scottish Rite, with the name of *Eques a floribus*.[112] Frederick the Great was also a Mason (so much so that one connects his name, arbitrarily, but not for this less significantly, to

---

111 The Triplice, or Triple Alliance (1882-1914), is the name of the military alliance between Germany, Austria-Hungary, and Italy, which was formed in secret in 1882 to guarantee a unified military front between these powers in case of any attack against them on the part of another great power. It was broken with the Treaty of London, with which Italy was induced to join the Triple Entente in World War I.

112 *La parfaite sincérité* is French: "perfect sincerity." This Lodge was founded in the French town of Chambery in 1739 by the Marquis de Bellegarde François Noyel. The mystical name *Eques a floribus* (Latin: "Servant of the flowers") was evidently bestowed on Maistre at his initiation.

one of the principle Masonic buildings),[113] as were numerous illustrious Englishmen of high birth; in certain circumstances the Church accused even a number of personalities very near to Metternich of Masonry—Metternich, the *bête noire* of the liberals and the democrats of that time.[114] But in the unfolding of the great historical forces and the revolutionary current, all of this weighed nothing whatever, and nothing issued from it which might modify Masonry's essential meaning today. There is no known case of dignitaries, recognized by this surviving operative Masonry, who have disavowed and condemned the ideology and the action of speculative Masonry—which in reality is the only form of Masonry to exercise a perceptible influence in the period which we here are considering.

In view of such action, it was natural for fascism to take up a position against Masonry, and to proceed to the suppression of the lodges. It is a fact that in an early day Masonry (none other than the Scottish Rite) tried to repeat with newly-born fascism the game of "means to an end" that it has so often been able to play with "patriotic" movements. It gave aid to fascism in the insurrectional period while keeping itself invisible, because it counted on certain revolutionary, secular and republican tendencies, which Mussolini's State knew how to immediately overcome. The incompatibility between fascism and Masonry was declared on the basis of the moderate thesis proposed by those who noted Masonry's internationalism: a sovereign national State can-

---

113 Frederick II of Prussia (1712-1786), known for his spreading of Enlightenment ideals in his country. He was responsible, for instance, for abolishing torture and reducing press censorship and religious discrimination. He was a friend of Voltaire. I have been unable to find the source of this reference to "one of the principle Masonic buildings."

114 Klemens von Metternich (1773-1859), German diplomat and statesman remembered by his detractors and his proponents alike for his strength as a diplomat and for his staunchly conservative mindset. Evola dedicates a number of reflections to him further on: see Chapter 27.

not permit its members to be tied by an oath of obedience to a secret or semi-secret international and super-national organization. The radical thesis of the battle against Masonry—as against the occult powers which, in strict connection with secularized Judaism and international finance, control the world—this radical thesis was defended in fascism only by several groups of scholars, above all the group of writers headed by Giuseppe Preziosi.[115] The assassination attempt against Mussolini which General Capello,[116] a Mason, instigated, together with not a few other lesser known facts, demonstrate how Masonry sought to strike at fascism, which had unexpectedly become the principle obstacle to its entire action in Italy, where it had maintained such a strong position on account of its Risorgimental precedents.

After this retrospective glimpse at the genesis, the nature and the direction of the action of modern Masonry, we can touch upon what Masonry might signify in the game of forces today in motion. In general, it is safe to say that the hour of Masonry is passed. It has naturally enjoyed a revival in the new democratic Italy, but its political influence is limited to minor parties—to the republican, liberal, radical, and social-democratic parties: thus one cannot say that it has or could have any determining role. In France its positions are solid to this day, and it seems that one must attribute to its hidden action the obstruction of the recent national and military movement of the right. Likewise un-

---

115 Preziosi (1881-?) was an Italian Catholic intellectual. As a young man he traveled in the United States, where he became aware of the international influence of the Jews. He founded the journal La vita Italiana (Italian Life) in 1915, which he used as a platform to talk about the Jewish problem and its connections to Masonry.

116 Luigi Capello (1859-1941), an Italian general who was very highly esteemed for his military work in World War I. He was an initial supporter of fascism, but later grew extremely hostile toward it. He had attained the thirty-third and highest grade of the Scottish Rite, and, according to official investigations, it was through the efforts of an "important Mason" that he was incited to involve himself in the 1925 attempt on Mussolini's life.

changed are the positions of American Masonry. But there are certain considerations of a general nature which make one think that Masonry has no future—considerations regarding the comprehensive meaning of history. As we have observed on many occasions, and as even Marxist historiography has foreseen—by positing as progressive that which is in fact regression and decline—from civilizations, systems, politics and societies controlled by the First Estate and based on pure spiritual authority, we have passed on, by a fairly precise, general, and uniform rhythm, to aristocratic, feudal and monarchical civilizations and regimes (the Second Estate). With the crisis of this epoch, it is the Third Estate that has come to power in the cycle of democracies, in the form of bourgeois society and that capitalism which is its economic counterpart. But the tendency we have already outlined is toward another descent of level, toward the revolution of the Fourth Estate under the sign of Marxism or of communism and, as more attenuated forms of transition, everything in which the collectivist and "social" element predominates.

In this whole game of forces, the role of Masonry, as we have said, has been to prepare the revolution of the Third Estate, to contribute actively to the crisis and to the destruction of the subsisting systems of civilization of the First and Second Estates, and to develop all the consequences of the ideology of "immortal principles" in national and international offices. But in the accomplishment of this work, far from leading, as its utopia proposes, toward a definitive final stage, Masonry has simply and fatally prepared the ground for the subsequent wave, for the world of the Fourth Estate. This is the well recognized dialectic of Marxist historiography, in which the bourgeois and liberal revolution open the breach for the socialist revolution. This counts also in part for Judaism in its aspect of international power strictly connected to capitalism—that is to say, the civilization of the Third Estate: one cannot any longer count it among the determining powers at the close of the cycle. We therefore see that Masonry, after having acquitted its task, has found itself ever more undermined and supplanted in the most recent times; the forces it has liberated have passed or are passing to other hands in the battle for the conquest of the world. Apart from the Marxified and communist areas, where Masonry and Judaism have been banned, forces have organized even in the "West" which have in large measure liberated themselves practically from Masonic obedience (this, in case one believes there is an out-and-out super-ordinate Masonic plan), and for which the original Enlightenment and democratic ideology is merely an adornment and an accessory. Thus the true danger here and now is not to be found any longer where the anti-Masonic (and in part anti-Jewish) polemic had located it during the period of the crisis of traditional Europe.

There is no reason to speak here of certain sporadic attempts to redirect Masonry toward its "operative," that is, spiritual, tradition. Leaving aside certain groups of scholars, and the appeals that some, taking inspiration from the ideas of René Guénon, have promoted in this direction, it would seem that in the great lodges these appeals have had as little echo as they have had in the high Catholic hierarchies, where men of the right would like to see Catholicism enter the field resolutely and without compromise against all the forces of modern subversion. Certain Catholic tendencies toward "putting oneself in step," certain gangs of political Catholicism aligned with Masons, or at least with ideologies whose Masonic and anti-traditional origin is extremely evident, should be enumerated amongst the signs, and certainly not the edifying signs, of the times.

11. THE TWILIGHT OF THE ORIENT

It is no longer doubted by anyone that the prestige and the hegemony of the white race are now in full crisis. In the first place, the Orient is awakening and moving to the offensive. The recent revolutions, which above all take the yellow race as their epicenter, cannot logically be considered as other than the precursors of a vaster and more general motion, of an unleashing destined to render our future yet more problematic. It is interesting to investigate both the origin of all this, as well as its deeper meaning.

In the first place we must recognize that the white races are but harvesting the fruits of what they have sown. If their hegemony is presently reducing itself to a myth, if forces are taking shape in the spaces they have already colonized, forces which now turn against them, one sees in all this nothing more than the effect of a species of historical Nemesis.[117]

The white races called this upon themselves

Let us return a moment to the origins. The fact that for centuries a certain group of peoples was able to subject the entire remainder of

---

117 Nemesis was the Greek goddess who brought retribution against men for their hubris, or their overweening pride and their exceptional good fortune. She has been connected with the ideas of equilibrium and law. She was the daughter of Night, and was thought to bring a just leveling to the overly-blessed. She was thus seen as a balance against the excesses of Fate and Fortune.

the world to its own will is unique in universal history, especially when one keeps in mind all the cases in which such a hegemony of the whites had nothing like the counterpart of a true, which is to say spiritual, superiority. A spirit of adventure might well have acted at the beginning of the conquest, toward the epoch of the Renaissance—a boldness, a decided will, a hardness of character, together with gifts of organization; but especially with regard to the Orient the idea of "superiority of civilization" was a mere presumption of the white races, as was the conviction that Christianity made the Occident the bearer of the true faith, authorizing it to a haughty detachment from the rest of humanity, which it considered "pagan" and barbaric.

But these same heroic-religious factors were rapidly to fail. In the period of the *conquistadores*,[118] they were supplanted by economic exploitation on the part of various commercial companies, who came with armed forces to impose the exchange of merchandise and "free trade" even on those who did not minimally feel the need of such things. The myth of superiority, which in the end justified every sort of abuse and oppression, rested on the progressivist superstition—that is on the idea that science and technological civilization constitute the last word on the history of the world, and assure the Europeans of the global right to a general "civilizing" work. As the era of nationalism, of capitalism and of democracy developed, this system was to be struck to its very foundations, and the First World War with its ideology constituted the decisive turning point. One can here touch with one's own hand the inner contradictions of this civilization of which many of our contemporaries are still so proud.

---

118 Spanish: "conquerors." The conquistadors were the military colonizers that Spain sent to South America in the 16th century. They were responsible for practically eradicating several extensive civilizations of that region, as the Aztec in Mexico and the Inca in Puru. Their conquest was linked decisively with the lust for gold.

First of all, to disseminate the gospel of "the rights of man," to proclaim the dogma of the fundamental equality of every being with a human appearance, signifies the virtual destruction of the presuppositions for every hegemony which cannot be reduced to oppression pure and simple. If men—at least by right—are equal, it is "unjust" that one people dominates another, whatever that other might be, and it is for half-wits to think that the white color of the epidermis signifies something more than any other color.

Versailles has sown, the Orient has harvested[119]

Next comes the contribution of the so-called "principle of sovereignty" or of the "self-determination of peoples." The Western democracies took this principle in hand at Versailles to overthrow everything in Europe which yet took inspiration from an aristocratic and imperial idea; but this same principle is a demon which has evaded its summoners. One cannot see how it might be limited in its validity to Western peoples alone, or how every colonial people should not likewise invoke it. For which reason Westerners, in a species of masochism, were reduced in the end to preaching anti-colonialism. Attempting to save something of the past—and attempting also to save face—they adopted the role of

---

119 Reference to the infamous Treaty of Versailles which, by many estimations, simultaneously closed World War I and paved the way for World War II, by bringing unduly and, some would say, vindictively harsh reparations against Germany. The references to "sovereignty" and "self-determination of peoples" are to certain principles which the Treaty was thought to embody. "Self-determination" in particular was one of the ideas sponsored most avidly by President Woodrow Wilson in the post-war period. In a famous speech of 1918 he stated that "national aspirations must be respected; people may now be dominated and governed only by their own consent"—which of course is but a restatement of the democratic principle itself, to the utter exclusion of both the aristocratic and imperial principles.

the lackey who has mere "mandates" over other peoples, who is at their service to "educate them" and "civilize them," that is to lead them to the state of consciousness and technological efficiency that in the end will give them the means to show him the door.

Added to this, as its apex, is the internal contradiction which Leninism indicted in what it called "moribund capitalism."[120] This is the capitalism which, from its own financial blockage, is forced to "industrialize" every remaining area of the world, thus creating everywhere the new phenomenon of a local proletariat ready to aggregate with the international front of communism. One of the fortes of communism, as is known, is precisely in drawing equivalence between non-European peoples and that oppressed proletariat exploited by the bourgeois and by imperialism. And the imperial bourgeois are supposedly represented by those white peoples who are already the lords of the world.

So much for the causes. In few other cases can one see so clearly the effect of an immanent justice, of an historical Nemesis. The West has elected for a materialistic and plebeian civilization which then bears forth its consequences, as if in ricochet.

Except that we must now emphasize the other point—the significance which "awakening" has for entire continents, and above all for Asia. Such significance is clear: it means setting out down the same descending, spiritually inverted road which we Westerners have taken. The Orient in particular rises as an antagonist and a danger for the West only when it assimilates the most perverting Western ideas, defaults in its traditions, directs outwardly the entire spiritual tension which previously—according to what is right and fitting to every civilization centered in super-mundane and metaphysical values—it had gathered above all inwardly and directed toward the heights. In this

---

120 Lenin's term for imperialism, which he believed was the final expression of capitalism prior to the revolution.

way the waking of the Orient is precisely equivalent to the *twilight of the Orient*, in the same sense in which Spengler could already speak of the "twilight of the West."

No one can grasp the scope and the peril of the unleashing which can be expected when the Orient, already ascetic and spiritual, hurls itself entirely in this direction. No one can grasp this, that is, save that man who has a sense of the whole potential, of the whole expansive, explosive, overwhelming force, which spiritual intensity makes possible, when it detaches itself from its natural non-terrene object, and expands outwardly, as a material, politico-social, and also military force.

Atavistic contest between America and Asia

Already we have seen anticipations of all this. Indeed, we would like to know where everyone has suddenly gone who used to speak of the Orientals as listless, passive, contemplative. When the Orientals are released from their traditions, one sees how they have the capacity to give lessons even to the Americans, those "activists" *par excellence*, so soon as they have been familiarized with technology. And in combat, one witnesses how these forces form precisely an impetus, a fanaticism, a total contempt for death, which gives rise to unedifying comparisons with the soldiers of the Western democracies.

Let us not forget the inestimable factor represented by a traditional vision of life, such as that predominant in the Orient, which does not consider our birth on this planet as the beginning, nor our death as the end, but understands this entire existence rather as a mere episode. Certain it is that in such a view every tragedy becomes relative, and a disposition emerges toward a leap or absolute sacrifice, which is careless of life or death.

All of this should be considered as part of that Oriental "potential" which has been freed—that is, which the West has freed—and which the red subversion is now mobilizing and organizing, often bringing about in a small number of years (as in the case of China) that landslide-movement from the Empires to Marxism, which in Europe required the course of centuries.

This might not form the horizon even of the immediate tomorrow. But what counts is ever the direction. Political and economic solutions here, in our opinion, are naught but trifles. The unique radical formulation must if anything rest on those cyclical laws which regulate the unfolding of civilizations. Pursuant to these, the last forms of every civilization lose their original spiritual character, they materialize, they thicken and in the end they dissolve, disorderly and "atavistically," until a new animating and organizing principle bursts forth.

The West now finds itself visibly toward the end of a cycle of this kind, but precisely for this it finds itself also nearer, perhaps, to a new beginning: nearer to those populations which only now, in adopting the modern civilization and "liberating themselves," are setting out down the road which, beyond the mirages of the technological-social civilization and its derivatives, will conduct them fatally toward the same crises which have been active amongst us already for some time. If it may be given to us to overcome these crises, a position of primacy with respect to them could newly be guaranteed to us, and in terms much different from those with which already one wishes to legitimate the supremacy and every violence of the whites.

Problematic though it be, this, in our opinion, is the only perspective which remains open, if one has the courage to think these problems through to their depths.

12. DIONYSUS AND THE "LEFT-HAND PATH"

The conceptions of Dionysus and Apollo, as they are sketched in the exposition of one of the first and most evocative works of Friedrich Nietzsche—*The Birth of Tragedy*[121]—have but scarce correspondence with the meaning that these entities owned in antiquity, especially in their esoteric understanding. This notwithstanding, we will take precisely the Nietzschean treatment as our point of departure, with the aim of defining fundamental existential orientations.

We commence from the presentation of a myth.[122]

Immersed in the luminosity and the fabulous innocence of Eden, man was a blessed immortal. In him the Tree of Life flowered, and he himself was this luminous life. But suddenly there arises a new, unheard-of vocation: the will for a *dominion* of life, a will to overcome it, a will for the power of being and non-being, of Yes and No. The "Tree

---

121 Friedrich Nietzsche (1844-1900), beyond being one of the most influential German philosophers of all time, was also very influential in Evola's intellectual development. Nietzsche's first book, *The Birth of Tragedy* (1872), garnered little attention at its publication, but later came to be seen as a seminal study of Ancient Greek culture. It was an investigation into the origins of Greek tragedy, and proposed a dual origin of tragedy in what he famously called the Apollonian (the world of order and balance, measure and appearance) and the Dionysian (the mad and the disorderly, the universal unity in which all particular individuality is suppressed or destroyed). Greek tragedy was seen in this work as the unification of these two principles into a single form of art.

122 The first part of this myth derives from the account of the Hebrew Bible. See Genesis 2 and 3.

of Good and Evil" can be related to this. In the name of this vocation
man detaches himself from the Tree of Life, which entails the collapse
of an entire world in a flash of a value which discloses his reign: the
reign of him who is, according to a hermetic saying, superior to the
very gods, insofar as together with the immortal nature, by which the
gods are constrained, he has in his power also the mortal nature—the
infinite together also the finite, affirmation but also negation (which
condition was signified by the expression "Lord of the Two Natures").

But man was not sufficient to this act; a terror seized him, by which
he was overwhelmed and broken. As a lamp beneath too intense a
splendor—as is said in a Kabbalistic text[123]—as a circuit struck by too
high a potential, the essences were damaged. To this we should relate
the meaning of the "fall," and even of "sin" itself. Then, the spiritual
powers that should have been his servants were unleashed by this terror, and immediately precipitated and froze in the form of objective,
autonomous, fatal existences. This power, *suffered* and rendered external and fleeing to itself, took the species of an objective autonomous
existence, and liberty—whose dizzy apex would have instaurated
the glory of a super-divine life—transformed itself instead into the
indomitable contingency of phenomena, amongst which man strays
like a perturbed and wretched shadow of himself. It could be said that
this was the curse flung by the "murdered God" against him who was
unable to assume his heritage.

With Apollo, understood ever in Nietzschean terms, that which
derives from this failure unfolds itself. One must relate to Apollo, in his
elementary function, the will that discharges itself, which does not any
longer live itself as will, but rather as "eye" and as "form"—as vision,
representation, conscience. He is precisely the artificer of the objective

---

123 The Kabbalah refers to a tradition of mysticism and esotericism originating in
     Judaism. It is complex and multifaceted, but it centers on the investigation of
     secret teachings originally of the Old Testament, concentrating on the interpre-
     tation of those texts and on the numerical significance of the Hebrew language.

world, the transcendental foundation of the "category of space." Space, understood as the means of "being outside," as that for which things are not lived in function of will but rather under the species of images and of visuality—space so understood is the primordial objectivization of fear, of the disintegration and of the discharge of the will: transcendentally the vision of a thing is the fear and the suffering regarding that thing. And the "manifold," the indefinite divisibility precisely of the spacial form, reconfirms this meaning, reflecting precisely the failure of tension, the disintegration of the unity of the absolute act.[124]

But as the eye has no consciousness of itself if not in function of that which it sees, so being, rendered objective and exterior to itself by the "Apollinian" function of space, is essentially dependent, bound: it is a "being which rests on," which draws its own awareness from the other. This need of resting on generates the "categories of limits": the tangibility and solidity of material things are its incorporation; they are almost the very *syncope*[125] of the fear which arrests the insufficient being on the limit of the "Dionysian" world. For which one might call it the "fact" of this fear, while space is the "act." *Law* is a particular case of this limit. While he who is in himself does not fear the infinite, chaos, that which the Greeks called the *apeiron*,[126] because he rather sees reflected in it his own profoundest nature of "a being substantiated of liberty," he who instead defaults transcendentally has a horror

---

124 [Evola's note] In this context one might recall Henri Bergson's theory, which explains space precisely as "the undoing of a gesture," in a process which is the inverse of that wherein multiple elements are, at a blow, gathered and fused together in a qualitative simplicity. [For more on Bergson, see note 315 to Chapter 29 below. -*Trans.*]

125 From the Ancient Greek συγκοπή, "a cutting up." Syncope comes to mean by extension, for example, the loss of sounds within the pronunciation of a word due to the suppression of unstressed vowels, and in medical terms it means fainting—the temporary loss of consciousness.

126 Ancient Greek ἄπειρον: "infinity, eternity," literally "without end or limit," a term connected in Greek philosophy and mythology with the primordial Chaos.

of the infinite, flees from it and seeks in law, in the constancy of causal sequences, in the predictable and in the ordered, a surrogate for that certainty and that possession from which he has fallen. Positive science and every morality could, in a certain sense, be included in such a movement.

The third creature of "Apollo" is *finality*. For a god, the ending does not have any sense, given that he outside of himself has nothing—no good, nor any true, any rational, pleasant, or just—from which to draw norms or to be moved; but good, true, rational, pleasant and just are identified with that which he wants, simply insofar as he wants it. In philosophical terms, one could say that the "sufficient reasons" of his affirmation is the affirmation itself.

Beings outside of themselves, on the other hand, have need of a correlation in order to act, of a motive for action or, better say, semblance of a motive for action. In fact, in decisive cases, outside of banally empirical contexts, man does not want a thing because he finds it, for example, just or rational, but he finds its just or rational simply because he wants it (psychoanalysis has made, in this connection, a few valid contributions). But he is afraid to descend into the profundities where want or impulse nakedly affirm themselves. And here it is that "Apollonian" prudence preserves one from the vertigo of a thing that might happen without cause or scope, that is, for itself alone, and by the same movement with which it frees the will in visibility, it now makes all deep affirmations appear in the function of ends, of practical utility, of ideal and moral motives which justify them, and on which they rest. It makes these affirmations appear through the categories of "causality" and the so-called "sufficient reason."

So the whole life of the great mass of men has the sense of a flight from the center, of a will to stupefy themselves and to ignore the fire that burns in them, which they do not know how to tolerate. Severed from being, they speak, they stir, they seek, they love and they mate in reciprocal desire for confirmation. They multiply their illusions and so erect a great pyramid of idols: the constitution of society, of morality, of ideality, of metaphysical ends, of the reign of the gods or of a tranquilizing providence—all of this supplies to existence a central reason, a fundamental meaning. All the "luminous spots to cure eyes damaged by gruesome night"—to use the words of Nietzsche.[127]

Now, the "other"—the object, the cause, the reason, etc.—as it does not exist in itself, being only a symbolic apparition of the deficit of the will to itself, in reality only confirms the very deficiency of the will in the very act in which this will asks the other for confirmation.[128] Thus man wanders, similar to one pursuing his own shadow, eternally parched and eternally disillusioned, creating and devouring forms that "are and are not" (Plotinus).[129] Thus the "solidity" of things, the Apollonian limit, is ambiguous; it fades as it is grasped, and postpones desire and need recurrently to a subsequent point. Whence comes also, beyond that of space, *the category of time* as well, and the law of becoming of forms that rise and dissolve—indefinitely—because for a single moment of rest, for a single instant in which he does not act, does

---

127 *Birth of Tragedy*, Section 9. Translation Walter Kaufmann's.

128 [Evola's note] To this one might associate the deeper sense of the Patristic doctrine according to which the body, the material vehicle, was created at the moment of the "fall" so as to impede the further fall of the souls (cf. for example Origen: *De princip.*, I, 7, 5). Apollo is such a prudent god. Moreover one should think of a paralysis owing to fright: it is like a withdrawal, and throwing oneself behind the *I*, by way of which that which was dominated and concluded organically in a living and pulsing body becomes something inert, rigid, alien. The objective world is our "great body" paralyzed—frozen and fixed by the conditions of limit, through fear.

129 Plotinus (204/5-270) was a Greek Neoplatonic philosopher whose metaphysical writings became the inspiration for subsequent mystical movements. His transcendent "One," which encompasses all experience and being and thus lies beyond all experience, both "is and is not." (See *Enneads*, Book VI, esp. 2 and 3.) This same concept has echoes throughout Greek philosophy: see Heraclitus, Fragment 49a: "We step and do not step into the same rivers; we are and are not." Also Plato, *Republic*, 479a-d.

not speak, does not desire, man would feel the collapse of everything. So his security amongst things, forms, and idols is spectral, as much as that of a somnambulist who walks along the edge of an abyss.[130]

Nevertheless this world might not form the final demand. As it indeed has no roots in the other, as it is only the *I* which is responsible, and as this *I* keeps within itself the causes, it has as a matter of principle the possibility of working its resolution. Thus the tradition which has been attested regarding the "Great Work," the creation of a "second Tree of Life." This is the expression used by Cesare della Riviera in his book *The Magic World and the Heroes* (2nd ed. Milan, 1605),[131] wherein this task is associated with "magic" and in general with the hermetic tradition and the magical. But in this context it is interesting to consider that which is proper to the so-called "Left-Hand Path."[132] This path requires the courage to tear away the veils and the masks with which "Apollo" hides the originating reality, to transcend form in order to put oneself in contact with the elementalism of a world in which good and evil, divine and human, rational and irrational, just and unjust do not any longer have any sense at all. At the same time, it requires knowing how to carry to its apex everything wherein the originating terror is exasperated, everything which our naturalistic and instinctive being does *not* want; knowing how to break the limit and dig ever more deeply, feeding the sensation of a dizzying abyss, and *consisting*, maintaining

---

130 [Evola's note.] Cf. C. Michelstaedter: *Persuasion and Rhetoric*, Part II and *passim*.

131 I have been unable to find any information on Cesare della Riviera. His book *Il Mondo Magico degli Heroi* was republished in 1982 in modernized Italian by Evola himself, who included his own commentary. It has not been translated into English.

132 The term "Left-Hand Path" derives from the Sanskrit *Vāmācāra*, and described a heterodox approach to spirituality. Despite this, it historically had its own rules and forms. In modern times it has come to be associated with black magic. For more on this, see the remainder of the present chapter, as well as Chapter 18 below.

oneself within passing away, wherein others would be broken. From this arises the possibility of establishing a connection also with historical Dionysianism—not "mystical" and "Orphic" Dionysianism, but rather Thracian Dionysianism,[133] which had certain frenetic, orgiastic, and destructive features. And if Dionysus reveals himself in moments of crisis and collapse of the law, even "guilt" might enter this existential field; in guilt the Apollonian veil is rent and man, come face to face with the primordial force, plays the game of his perdition or of his making himself superior to life and to death. It is interesting that the German term for crime contains the meaning of a break (*ver-brechen*).[134] An act can be called guilty insofar as it is an act which one fears, which one does not feel capable of assuming absolutely, so that one fails at it—an act which we unconsciously judge to be something too strong for us. But an active, positive guilt has something transcendent—so Novalis wrote.[135] When man wants to become God, he sins, almost as if this were the condition for such becoming. In the Mithraic mysteries[136] the

---

133 Orphism was a religious practice centering around the myth of Orpheus and his descent to, and return from, the underworld. These practices were connected to the so-called "Dionysian Mysteries," a set of rites and cults which initiated their members through the use of intoxicants and music. Thracian Dionysus was the version of the god to come from the Thracian deity Sabazios (Sabazius was an alternate name for Bacchus amongst the Romans). Sabazios was a greatly powerful sky god associated with horses.

134 *Ver-* is a German suffix deriving from Proto-Germanic "far"; the German *brechen* shares the same etymology as our English "break."

135 Georg Philipp Friedrich Freiherr von Hardenberg (1772-1801), known universally by his *nom de plum* Novalis, was a German poet and author best known for his poetry and his mystical and philosophical aphorisms. He influenced such artists as Hermann Hesse, Richard Wagner, and Jorge Luis Borges. The reference here is possibly to *Spiritual Songs*, I.

136 The mysteries of the cult of the god Mithras, originally the Persian god Mithra, deity of covenants and justice. Mithraism became a notable force in the Roman Empire, and is discussed at some length in Chapter 17 of the present work.

capacity to murder and to impassively watch a murder (if need be a simulated murder) constituted an initiating trial. One might refer to this same context certain aspects of sacrificial rites, when the victim was identified with the divinity itself, and yet the sacrificer had to kill it, so that, superior to curses and catastrophe, the absolute was liberated in him—and so was liberated also in the community which magically converged in him. Such is transcendence in the tragic nature of sacrifice and guilt.

But the act can also be carried out on oneself in certain varieties of the "initiatory death." That is: to do violence against the life in oneself, in the evocation of something elementary. Thus the path which in certain forms of tantric yoga opens the "*kundalinî*" is called the path in which "the flame of death flares."[137] The tragic act of the sacrificer here is interiorized and becomes the practice with which the very organic life in its roots is deprived of every support, is suspended and dragged beyond itself along the "Royal Road" of the so-called *sushumnâ*, "devourer of time."[138]

It is known that historically Dionysianism has been associated with forms of frenetic, destructive, or orgiastic unleashing, as in the classic type of the bacchants (Dionysus=Bacchus),[139] votaries and priests alike, and of the Maenads and the Korybantes. But here it is difficult to separate what is inspired in these experiences on the one

---

137 The *kundalini* is the energy point at the base of the spine which is to be "awakened" in the course of spiritual preparation in a variety Oriental traditions.

138 The *sushamna* is one of the *nadis*, energy channels which run through the human body. The *sushamna* runs along the spinal cord.

139 The bacchants were worshipers of Dionysus. The Maenads were the female revelers who, possessed by Dionysus, entered into a state of ecstatic frenzy, in which they were said to kill animals and humans and to shred them. They dressed in animal skins and carried with them the thyrsus, the symbol of Dionysus—a rod covered in ivy with a pine cone upon its end. The Korybantes were the dancing worshipers of Cybele. They dressed in armor and wore crests upon their heads, and their ecstatic dance was said to have an initiatory aspect.

hand from phenomena of possession on the other, especially when one speaks of institutionalized forms tied to a tradition. In any case it must always be remembered that here one finds oneself on the "Left-Hand Path" which skirts abysses; and to proceed on that path, as is said in a number of texts, resembles walking on the blade of a sword. The presupposition, both in the field of the a-providential vision of life, as well as these behaviors themselves, is awareness of the mystery of transformation from venom to medicine, which constitutes the highest form of alchemy.

13. THE MYTH OF THE FUTURE REGALITY

In a previous work we have referred to a number of predictions that philosophers, such as Vico[140] and Spengler, have formulated on the course of history. These thinkers have recognized that the most critical point of the terminus of any historical cycle, might be precisely the same point at which the principle of authority, and of "monarchy" in the literal sense of "dominion of one alone," recovers its vigor. While we indicated the suspicious side of this view—precisely because such a power would not be anointed by any higher legitimacy—we noted that those philosophers have in their way once more taken up a motif of universal character, which is present in the traditions and the myths of many peoples.[141]

Let us now bring this to our attention—in the name of simple curiosity, if you please—by selecting out a few points from amongst this extremely vast material. One might speak of this as an "origin myth." At the same time it takes the form of a historical prediction. The basic idea in both cases is the same: as if in an abrupt volte-face, a new principle manifests itself at the maximum point of disorder—a principle

---

140 Giambattista Vico (1668-1744) was an Italian philosopher and historian, best known for his 1725 work *The New Science* which is considered one of the first works of philosophy of history. It attempted a systematic understanding of historical cycles in the form of *corsi e ricorsi*, or "occurrences and recurrences," and the movement between civilization and barbarism.

141 Evola is probably referring here to the ninth chapter of *Revolt Against the Modern World*, "Life and Death of Civilization."

which sometimes has supernatural and sacral features, but at other times also heroic and regal ones. An example of this is the well-known Hindu theory of the *avatâra*,[142] "descents" or periodic manifestations of a power from the heights, when the law in a society has been violated, when the castes no longer exist, and impiety, disorder, and injustice prevail. Thus in some future period the so-called Kalki-avatâra[143] is awaited, who, together with the kings of the "solar dynasty" and the "lunar dynasty," will do battle with the forces of chaos.

This bears comparison with the ancient Persian myth of the advent of Shaoshyant.[144] In the eternal battle between the luminous god Ahuramadza and the anti-god Ahriman, Shaoshyant will appear as a sovereign sent by the Ahuramadza to instaurate a new, triumphant reign of all those faithful to the principle of order, of light, and of truth. Now, it is interesting to note that the Jews drew their idea of the Messiah precisely from this most ancient Iranian concept. Only in late prophetism did the Messiah acquire those merely mystic and religious features which anticipated the Christian theory of the coming of a super-terrestrial kingdom. In the ancient Jewish conception the Messiah was rather he who, emanating from the "God of armies," would secure the "chosen people" power over this world and dominion over all its enemies.

It is a little known fact that the origin myth had a peculiar strength in the imperial Roman period. The ascent to the throne of each new Caesar

---

142 The avatars are deities incarnated on earth. The word is most often associated with Vishnu, representative of the forces of conservation or preservation; hence the reference here to violated laws and to injustice.

143 Kalki is the tenth avatar of Vishnu, whose arrival will end the Kali Yuga, the present age of the world, which is considered a Dark Age for its lack of spirituality.

144 Shaoshyant is the divine figure of the Zoroastrian tradition who will bring the final victory over evil in the world. Ahuramadza, whose name means "mighty lord of wisdom," is the Zoroastrian God, and Ahriman is the spiritual principle of malign negation: though he had the possibility of doing good, he willfully chose to do evil. According to a certain offshoot of Zoroastrianism, Ahuramadza and Ahriman were brothers in constant battle with each other, and would remain so until the coming of Shaoshyant.

was nominated *adventus*.[145] If Virgil, already in his well known Eclogue,[146] heralded the end of the iron age at the coming of Augustus and the dawn of a new golden age, so afterward the mood of a kind of messianic waiting encircled each new emperor, who was saluted with the liturgical formula, "Come, you whom we have awaited!" In a very interesting work (*Christus und die Caesaren*) Staufer[147] brings to light precisely these aspects of the Roman mysticism of the *Regnum*,[148] which to a certain extent involuntarily prepared the ground for the Christian idea.

But perhaps the Medieval period presents the most evocative formulations on our present theme. The Romano-Germanic and Ghibelline *restauratio imperii*[149] was associated with a group of legends

---

145 The same Latin term which later transformed into the Christian Advent, the period of waiting for the birth of Christ.

146 Publius Vergilius Maro (70-19 BCE), commonly known as Virgil, Roman poet, orator, and statesman. He is best known for being the author of the epic *Aeneid*. His *Eclogues* were pastoral poems (for which they are sometimes also known as the *Bucolics*) about the simple rural life of shepherds.

147 Ethelbert Staufer (1902-1979), a German Protestant theologian. He dedicated many of his studies to analyses of those features of Roman civilization which paved the way for Christianity, or which were later absorbed into it. The book cited here was his first (1952), and it has been translated into English as *Christ and the Caesars*.

148 Latin: "kingdom." The *Regnum Romanum* refers to the first period of Roman history after its semi-mythical founding, during which the Roman state was a monarchy. It lasted about a quarter millennium, from around 750 BCE to around 500 BCE.

149 Latin: "restoration of the empire." The Ghibellines were originally Italian supporters of Frederick Barbarossa, who subsequently sought to expand the Holy Roman Empire into the lands directly or indirectly controlled by the Pope—hence their attempt to "restore the empire," to bring the Holy Roman Empire back into Rome, which had been the point of its origin in the times of the Ancient Romans. The Ghibellines were opposed by the Guelfs, the supporters of the Pope, and the conflict between them became a central piece of Medieval politics, lasting some three hundred years, from the twelfth to the fifteenth century.

and myths, which were enhanced by a higher, transcendental, universal significance. From this derives first of all the legends of the Grail. As we have demonstrated in our book on this subject, the core of these legends has little to do with Wagner's romantic mystico-Christian digressions. Here we are dealing essentially with the anticipation of him by whose virtue a fallen kingdom would rise again in new splendor.

The imperial myth in the Medieval Ghibelline period had many other variants. The Dantesque theme of the new flourishing of the Tree of Empire comes from the same source.[150] Yet even more interesting is the motif of the "last battle." This is associated with the idea of the *interregnum*,[151] of a latent regality. A regal or imperial figure—identified in the saga with some historical personage or other—in truth would never die. He would withdraw into an inaccessible abode (for example, Frederick Barbarossa in Kyffhäuser)[152] and he would await his hour to reawaken and remanifest himself, to wage, alongside all those who remained faithful to him, a decisive battle against the forces of disorder, of injustice, and of the darkness.

---

150 Dante Alighieri (1265-1321), author of *The Divine Comedy*, is widely regarded as the greatest Italian poet, and is famous for bringing the vernacular Italian of his time into poetry, which later led to the Tuscan Italian of that period transforming into Italian as we know it today. The present reference is not to Dante's *Comedy*, but rather to his work *De Monarchia*, his political treatise on secular versus religious power in political authority.

151 Latin: "between reigns," referring to any period between two regimes (as between the death of one king and the coronation of the next) in which there is no official ruler. Here, Evola evidently means the term somewhat more broadly, to include also our own time as a time between the legitimate rule of the First or Second Estates.

152 Frederick Barbarossa (1122-1190), whose nickname was given to him during his campaign in Italy (*Barbarossa* means "red beard.") He was known as an excellent emperor and general, and made lasting contributions to jurisprudence. The Kyffhäuser is a mountain in Germany, in which Frederick was said to have a cave. Legend has it that he and his knights would sleep there until the time comes for their awakening, whereupon they shall rise and restore the Empire.

It is interesting to note that in a variant of this saga, the hour of his return coincided with the bursting forth of the peoples of Gog and Magog,[153] whose coming Alexander the Great had barred off with a wall of iron. These demonic peoples might well symbolize the world of the godless materialized masses in revolt, and it is interesting to note that they would burst forth at that point where no one but the wind any longer sounds the trumpets that have been placed at the summit of the wall. That is: so soon as one realizes that there is no one any longer behind the apparent defenses of a world in crisis, no one who can grant these defenses solidity and true legitimacy, in this same moment the unleashing of the lower forces will come. As usurpation and consequent disorder reach their extreme limit, the crisis arrives and with it the decisive moment: the last battle, whose outcome will determine the possibility, or the lack thereof, for initiating a new positive cycle, a new manifestation of the *Regnum.*

Enclosed in all these variations of the "origin myth," there is thus perhaps an invariable meaning—a meaning to validate, in the truths of a nigh perennial tradition, the faith of all those today who are not yet broken.

---

153 Gog and Magog figure in the Bible (see Ezekiel 38:2 and Revelation 20:8) as enemies of God. In the original reference, Gog is named a prince in the land of Magog, but in later references they both appear as lands, individuals, or peoples. The legend of Alexander comes from the Jewish historian Josephus, who identified Gog and Magog with the Scythians. Alexander was said to have barred the Scythians with an iron gate.

14. QUO VADIS, ECCLESIA?[154]

Some years ago, before the war, Julien Benda[155] wrote a book which had noteworthy resonances as an indictment of a characteristic phenomenon of the latest times, which he designated with the words *trahison des clercs*. Taking the term *clerc* in its ancient sense,[156] Benda related it essentially to the type of the intellectual and thinker of ethical orientation, whose function in other times was the defense and the testimony of values opposed to the materialism of the masses, opposed to biased passions, opposed to the interests of mere human existence. Benda observed that the *clercs* did not delude themselves that they were able to realize the ideal values that they defended (and here a certain dualistic and pessimistic orientation manifested itself, which stopped them from recognizing that in the civilizations of the past those values stood

---

154 Latin: "Where are you going, o Church?" The "quo vadis" comes from a legend surrounding St. Peter. It is said that Peter, to save his life, had decided to flee Rome during the persecution of the Christians. As he was departing the city, he suddenly saw Christ entering. He fell upon his knees, saying to him, "*Quo vadis, Domine?* (Where are you going, Lord?)" And Christ replied that he was going to be crucified once again. Peter took this for a sign, and returned to the city, where he became a martyr.

155 Benda (1867-1956) was a French writer, most famous for the book which Evola cites here, *La Trahison des Clercs* (1927), translated into English as *The Betrayal of the Intellectuals*, which argued that the intellectuals had become a species of adulators of raw power, and have thus forsaken their traditional duty.

156 The French word *clerc*, just as our English "cleric," "clergy," and also "clerk," derives from the Latin *clerus*, member of the priestly class.

effectively at the center of traditional organic institutions); yet still they at least hindered all that which was material, inferior, and merely human from making itself into a religion, or usurping and attributing to itself a higher meaning.

Now, the latest times have offered us the spectacle of the desertion and the betrayal of the *clercs*. These—as Benda observed—have abandoned their posts and have gone to put their intellectualism, their thought, and their very authority at the service of material reality, together with those processes and forces which are affirming themselves in the modern world. By such an act the *clercs* thereby gave these processes and forces a justification, a right, a value. The which has done nothing but bring an unprecedented acceleration and strengthening to those forces and to those processes.

Since the time that Benda wrote his book the phenomenon he indicted has only broadened. We think it well to note the fact that this phenomenon seems now to invest the representatives of the very religion which has come to predominate in the West—that is, Catholicism. Indeed one is no longer dealing only with so-called "committed" intellectuals, with "progressivists and "historicists," one is not dealing with the ideologies at the service of party interests and of the harbingers of the "new humanism," but also of the *clercs* in the proper sense of the term. A part of the clergy, up to the highest ranks, seems to incline toward the "betrayal" which Benda has indicted.

In fact, Catholicism has gone so far in adopting such an orientation, that they who truly defend traditional values, which is to say the values of the Right, must ask themselves up to what point they can yet count on Catholicism here—up to what point a new choice of vocations and of traditions is potentially leading the Church in the same direction as the forces and the subversive ideologies which predominate in the modern world.

Since the population of Italy is predominantly Catholic, and since Catholicism is even now rooted in wide strata of this population, it constitutes also a political force. Thus during the electoral campaigns one has often attempted to win over a part of the masses by harking back ostentatiously to Catholicism and to "moral Catholic values," even when this is reducible to mere words or even atimes to mendacious hypocrisy. But today we are arriving at a point in which even this tactical and opportunistic justification seems to fail, and we must ask ourselves whither the Church is going and whither it wants to go, so that we may courageously orient ourselves in consequence.

That Catholicism for some time has set aside the values of true transcendence, of high ascesis and of contemplation (so much so that all the truly contemplative Orders live a wretched life and risk extinction), or has made them tertiary; that it has preoccupied itself, over and above all, with a parishioner's moralism, a bourgeois moralism, concentrating itself ever more on the plane of community—all this is well known. But we can glimpse in this regression the outline of a successive phase: that of the politicization and of the growing "progressivism" of Catholicism.

It must be said without mincing words that a not indifferent part of the disastrous outcome of the latest political elections in Italy,[157] with the advancement of Marxism and communism, hinges on precisely this new course of the Church. Its tacit consecration of the Christian Democrats was not in any way revoked in the platform of the famous center-left, which was put up by that party. On the contrary: Pope

---

157 Reference to the 1963 elections, which saw a decided decline in the influence of the comparatively conservative Christian Democrats (who took their bearings by the Church), and a corresponding rise in the fortunes of the communists and the socialists. The Christian Democrats took the majority of seats in Parliament (260), while the communists took 166. If one adds together the seats of all the liberal, socialist, and communist parties after the election, one finds that they took 325 of the 630 seats.

Roncalli[158] did not lose the chance to profess his "progressivism," his anxiety for "social progress" conceived precisely in the material and immanent terms that previously were proper to secular ideologies. He treated the solemn condemnation of Marxism on part of his predecessor practically as if it had never been uttered; instead he advanced the dangerous thesis that it is necessary to disassociate ideology from its possible practical effects, and that if these effects are good (according to the metric alluded to), one can compromise in ideology. Here the reference to Marxism, if not to communism itself, is sufficiently visible. The fundamental ethical criterion, according to which what truly counts are not facts and utility but rather intentions and spiritual foundation, is thus effortlessly tossed aside.

We have spoken, with respect to the contemporary Church, of a new choice of its traditions which today presents an extreme peril. Indeed in the history of Christianity there appear forms of a "spirituality" which—one cannot fail to recognize it—could favor precisely the present subversive "social" theories. From the sociological point of view original Christianity was effectively socialism *avant la lettre*;[159] with respect to the classical world and civilization it represents an egalitarian revolutionary ferment. It leveraged itself upon the mood and the needs of the masses, of the plebs, of the disinherited and of the traditionless members of the Empire; its "good news" was that of the inversion of all established values.

This background of Christianity and its origins was more or less limited and rectified with the formation of Catholicism—thanks, in grand part, to a "Roman" influence. This overcoming was manifested

---

158 Pope John XXIII (1881-1963) held the papacy from 1958-1963. He was a much beloved Pope, and was responsible for the famous (or infamous, depending on one's point of view) Vatican II, which led to a great many changes in the Church, as for instance the substitution of vernacular for Latin during masses.

159 French: "before the letter," meaning that a certain phenomenon occurred before it was named or conceptualized.

also in the hierarchical structure of the Church; historically it had its apogee in the Medieval Period, but its orientation did not fail in the period of the Counter-reformation—nor, finally, in that which was called the "alliance of the throne with the alter,"[160] Catholicism's consecration of legitimate authority from the heights, according to the rigorous doctrine of Joseph de Maistre and Donoso Cortés,[161] and with the Church's explicit condemnation of liberalism, democracy, and socialism—and lately, in our century, in the period of modernism.

But now this entire valid superstructure of Catholicism seems to crumble and to bring the emergence precisely of the promiscuous, anti-hierarchical, "social" and anti-aristocratic substrate of primitive Christianity. The return to such a substrate is, moreover, the best means for "marching with the times," for keeping oneself up-to-date with "progress" and with "modern civilizations"—while the position that a truly traditional organization ought to take today should be absolutely the contrary: namely, a triplicated, inflexible intransigence, which puts in the foreground the true, pure spiritual values, against this entire world "in progress."

We have heard Catholics like Maritain and Mounier affirm that the true Christian spirit today lives in "social" movements and socialistic laborers; even De Gasperi,[162] in an ancient speech which was almost forgotten until yesterday, had reaffirmed such an idea, quite

---

160 Reference to the ideas of Joseph de Maistre. See note 36 to Chapter 3 above, and the whole of Chapter 31 below.

161 Juan Donoso Cortés (1809-1853) was a Spanish conservative diplomat and political theorist, who dedicated much of his thought to the analysis of the relation of religion and political power and the concept of sovereignty. His ideas influenced Carl Schmitt and Metternich among others. For more on Cortés, see Chapter 28 below.

162 Alcide Amedeo Francesco De Gasperi (1881-1954) was one of the founding fathers of both the the Christian Democratic party (which was unequivocally the most important political party in the young years of the Italian Republic) and also the European Union. He served many years as Prime Minister.

beyond the absolute concordance between the Christian spirit and the democratic spirit. With an authentically progressivist vernacular, high exponents of the Church have spoken of "Medievalistic vestiges" from which Catholicism must liberate itself (naturally, one links those values which are truly transcendent, spiritual, and sacral, to such presumed "vestiges"). If the Church yesterday exercised itself in more or less artificially building the symbol of "King Christ," today it has put up the symbol of "Christ the laborer" (with reference to the period during which Jesus supposedly worked as a carpenter for his putative father—almost as of this had any sensible connection with his salutary mission), in supine adhesion to the dominant myth (the "laborer" is sacrosanct—woe to whomever touches him!). The theories of the Jesuit Teilhard de Chardin,[163] who has harmonized Catholicism with scientism, evolutionism, and the myth of progress, although his books (as of yet) have no imprimatur,[164] have a large following amongst the Catholics (another significant symptom: for the diffusion of the thought of this highly "modern" Jesuit, an international committee has been constituted, under the patronage of Maria Josè, the wife of Umberto II).[165] We have seen Pope Roncalli cordially receive the daughter of Khrushchev[166] in audience with her worthy husband,

---

163 Pierre Teilhard de Chardin (1881-1955) was a French Jesuit priest and intellectual. He studied geology and paleontology (he was involved in the discovery of Peking man, an early human skeleton) and dedicated much of his academic work toward the synthesis of his scientific and religious beliefs.

164 That is, it has not been officially approved by the Holy See. All of Chardin's scientific writings have been refused the imprimatur to this day.

165 Umberti II (1904-1983), the last King of Italy, who reigned for all of thirty-four springtide days, for which he was dubbed the May King. After the fall of the monarchy, he passed the remainder of his life in exile in Portugal. His wife, Marie José of Belgium (1906-2001), was a devout and influential Catholic.

166 Nikita Sergeyevich Khrushchev (1894-1971) was First Secretary of the Soviet Union from 1953-1964. His daughter Rada, and her husband Alexei Adjubei, editor of an official Soviet newspaper, were received by the Pope in 1963.

evidently forgetting the world of which they are the exponents (even as one whines and "prays" for the destiny of the "Church of Silence" in the countries under the communist regime). If to all this, as worthy consummation, we add the encyclical *Pacem in terris*[167] and the not unconfessed center-leftist tendency of the major Catholic Italian party, is there any reason to be amazed that many Catholics have felt liberated from their scruples and, "making alliances," have facilitated the advance of the left?

The apotheosis which was made of John XXIII upon his death is significant; it is deplorable that the press of national and philofascist orientation has so conformistically associated itself to this. Naturally, we would not have asked anyone to speak harshly of the dead; but certain precise reservations ought to have been formulated, to break the uniformity of the chorus of eulogies—which chorus was not, naturally, without its influence in the conclave's decision to elect Cardinal Montini.[168] The good intentions, the goodness and humanitarianism of the Pope, might have been recognized, without this impeding an indictment of the almost infantile ingenuity of a mind drunken with democratic and progressivist ideas (the deceased Pope in his time was, moreover, a good friend of Ernest Buonaiuti,[169] a defrocked priest of modernist and socialized ideas, and naturally an antifascist). Thus the dominant motive for his last encyclical was an optimism which brought

---

167 *Pacem in terris* (Peace on Earth) was Pope John's famous 1963 encyclical, which treated of the question of nuclear non-proliferation in the midst of the Cold War. Quite beyond its presumed subject, however, it has had an enormous influence throughout the Catholic world for its progressive stance on human rights.

168 Pope Paul VI, who had been very close to Pope John. He continued the reforms of Vatican II while attempting to alleviate the doubts that had arisen in its wake on the part of certain traditionalist elements in the Church.

169 Buonaiuti (1881-1946) was an Italian historian who was divested of his university chair for his opposition to the fascists, and excommunicated from the Church for his modernist stance. His friendship with Pope John was much commented at the time.

the Pope to improbable and exceedingly dangerous judgements on the positive character of a number of "signs of the times." The same thing was also the motive for a number of initiatives, rectification of whose deleterious effects "will require decades," according to one cardinal.

The very interesting proceedings of a recent Council were leaked to the public. In this Council, a plan of openly conservative character was presented regarding the Sacred Scriptures and the Tradition; according to the procedure, a hundred votes were lacking for this plan's rejection. The Pope, on his own initiative, rejected it regardless, and forced the elaboration of a new plan. At the beginning of the Council he had declared himself "against all these prophets of misfortune who say that everything goes from bad to worse...as if we were nearing the end of the world."

We have received a little book from a group of French Catholics who express their most serious concerns, should the line advocated by Papa Roncalli in that Council be maintained (the title of the little book is actually "*S.O.S. Council*"). This group has been able to procure one of the new plans regarding the subject of the Council, and it has translated this from Latin with commentary, to demonstrate the strident contradictions between many of its expounded ideas on the one hand and the Gospels on the other. The Gospels, for instance, are explicit with regard to the last times: they speak of a period of false prophets, of the seduction of the masses, even of the coming of the Antichrist and the definitive separation between two parts of humanity. This is exactly the contrary of the progressivist conception of present-day humanity, which would direct itself continuously toward a better world. Moreover, apart from the strongly-hued mythologico-apocalyptic pictures of the Gospels, quite a different interpretation of the "signs" of the times in the present epoch is common to an entire series of eagle-eyed writers: for them, we live in a "dark age," despite all its splendors. One can start from the Catholic existentialist Gabriel Marcel (*L'homme contre l'humain*) up to René Guénon (*Le règne de la quantité et les signes des temps).*[170] It seems therefore that that greatest light which, theoretically, should be infused into a pontificate by the Holy Spirit, has in the present case served little or nothing.

The idea that well-being and material and social progress facilitate true moral and spiritual progress—as is affirmed in that Council's plan, and as Pope Roncalli himself has asserted—finds no basis at all in the Gospels, and the effective spiritual level of "more progressed" peoples (for example, the United States or Western Germany) confirms one's doubts. The "sign of the times" in the ascent of the working class (beyond that of woman)—a sign deemed to be a positive one—is another pure concession to the socialist, if not even the proletarian, mentality. These French Catholics in their critique opportunely recall that, according to the Catholic conception, work is only a species of obscure punishment, a consequence of the "fall," and that in the traditional Catholic moral theology, only work corresponding to a true vocation and to the pure necessities of one's state is approved—quiet different than every mania to leave this state at all costs and to "ascend." The traditional Catholic conception is precisely contrary to the current ones.

In the encyclic *Pacem in terris*, we see the exceedingly grave consequences of what one must call (in an almost psychoanalytic sense) a "peace complex"; and precisely the place this complex was accorded by the Pope Roncalli ("the Pope of Peace"), by his meeting human weakness halfway, was one of the causes of the great popularity which he enjoyed. But here one must put things to their proper place. His point of departure is, naturally, the specter of atomic war and of humanity's complete self-destruction. It is obvious that if this specter could be exorcised in a positive way, this would be comforting (but neither should the possibility of a non-atomic war be excluded, in the same way that even in the direst straits of the last World War,

---

170 Marcel's book has been translated into English with the title *Man Against Mass Society*. Guénon's book has been translated into English with the title *The Reign of Quantity and the Signs of the Times*.

not one of the belligerent nations resorted to chemical warfare). When supreme values are at stake, however, precisely the representatives of spiritual authority should formulate a *non possumus*[171] even in extreme cases. In fact, so far as peace goes, one must even ask oneself what ends peace should serve: whether it should be the end of rendering things easier to millions of collectivized beings who toil in the terrestrial Marxist-Lenninist paradise or, on the other hand, to millions of others who think only of nourishing themselves, of drinking, of proliferating, of accumulating electrical appliances and of brutalizing themselves in various ways in the climate of "Western" prosperity.[172]

In this encyclical we are given to recall the words of Christ: "I leave you my peace, I give you my peace"—without however placing the same emphasis to the remainder of the phrase—indeed, rather by silencing it: "But I do not give it as the world gives it, etc."[173] The true idea, here, is that of a peace synonymous with calm and of interior steadfastness, of maintaining oneself even in the midst of catastrophe.

It is on this that we would have preferred to hear further words, *in alto loco*,[174] rather than of the "peace complex" which, in an entirely profane spirit (the peace that "the world" can give), might bring one to indulge in compromises, arrangements, transactions and illusory

---

171 Latin: "we cannot." The term traces its origins to certain Christian martyrs who declared this "we cannot" in the face of those authorities who would have prohibited their beliefs or practices; and in consequence of their refusal to bend to secular authority, they lost their lives. This phrase came to play a certain diplomatic role in the Church, becoming the policy of several popes in the face of temporal powers which would limit the role or power of the Church.

172 Evola uses the English word "prosperity" here.

173 John 14:27. In corroboration of Evola's point here, it might be noted that in the passage immediately following this citation in Pope John's encyclical (section 171), the Pope speaks explicitly of his hope in the "proper material welfare" of the peoples of the Earth.

174 Latin: "in a high place," used to describe the words or doctrines which come from authorities or rulers.

relaxation. Almost as if the distance which separates the positions of a spiritually-founded politico-social doctrine which recognizes the true values of the person, from the positions, for example, of the atheist and anti-religious ideologies of the "Orient" and of the acolytes of the "Orient"—almost as if this distance were no greater than that which in other cases and in other times brought the Church to decide, even at the cost of persecutions, on its *non possumus*. Thus let it not be forgotten that it is likewise said of the Christ, that he came to earth to bring not peace but rather war ("the sword") and division, even between those who have the same blood, with reference to precise spiritual fronts (Matthew 10: 34-35; Luke 12: 48, 52). And the gesture of the Christ who drives out the merchants from the temple (we ought to add: "and from around the temple") with a whip, would seem more topical than ever today, with respect to the parties which proclaim themselves Catholic but which walk arm in arm with the Masons and with radicals, "opening themselves to the left" and prospering in the climate of unheard-of corruption of the democratic parliamentary regime of politicizing profiteers.

Apart from certain of his suspect precedents, it is not yet clear what orientation Cardinal Montini, as Pope, will choose: whether or not he will follow the footprints of his much acclaimed predecessor.[175] *Quo vadis, ecclesia?* The first possibility is precisely to compromise as much as one can with the "modern world," by the failure (typical in Pope Roncalli) to recognize the negative side of those predominant and

---

175 With the benefit of hindsight, we can say that Pope Paul VI, despite certain attempts he made to walk the line between various hostile camps within the Church, very much followed the modernizing tendencies of Pope John. He brought a great many (if often subtle) changes to the symbols of the Church. One can take the measure of his papacy by the proliferation of unheard of demands which were made during and after his pontificate—such as demands for the marriage for priests, reintegration of divorced Catholics, and the acceptance of homosexuality.

determinant currents which do not permit us to indulge in any kind of optimism—neglecting the lessons so many times imparted by history, that whoever deceives himself that he is able to direct the forces of subversion by bending or endorsing their course, has always ended up being crushed by them. The second possibility is an energetic reaction, an intransigent stance in the sign of spiritual, sacral and transcendental values, which could not do other than lead to a radical revision of the relations with that majority party which in Italy abuses the qualification "Catholic," and which is doing everything to irresponsibly prepare the way for communism. The possibility of a new concentration of truly anti-communist forces could perhaps follow.

Unfortunately there are not many reasons to be optimistic, not only regarding a possible positive decision in the face of this alternative—that is of a courageous change of course on the part of the Church—but also regarding the will to recognize and to confront the problem decisively, obeying no mere influence of the times. Things being as they are, we must believe that the forces of the Right ought to maintain a precise distance from the Church, as uncomfortable as this might be. Just as we cannot approve the by now useless tactical appeal to Catholic values in the electoral campaign, given the plane to which they have descended and the facility with which the opposing forces have leveraged upon "progressivist," democratic and "social" Catholicism—so we would not know how to approve of certain small groups of "traditionalists" who persist in faltering valorizations, which are verily voided of all sense when those invested with authority in Church do not take the initiative with them in the upper hierarchy.

Whoever knows our work, perforce knows the position which, from the point of view of doctrine and of philosophy of history, we generally take in the face of Catholicism. We have even had occasion to write that "whoever is traditional by being Catholic, is not traditional but halfway." Nonetheless in our fairly recent book *Men Among the Ruins* we have stated, "If today Catholicism, feeling that the decisive times are nigh, had the force to detach itself truly from the contingent plane and to follow a course of high ascesis—if it, precisely on such a basis, almost in a recovery of the spirit of the best Medieval Crusade, made its faith into the soul of an armed bloc of forces, compact and irresistible, directed against the currents of chaos, of yielding, of subversion and of the political materialism of the modern world—certainly, in such a case there could be no doubts (on our part) as to what side to choose. But matters unfortunately do not stand in this way." If therefore no substantial change takes place, if the convoluted development, which we have here indicated in some of its aspects, continues apace, it will be necessary to regulate ourselves in consequence, renouncing one of the factors that otherwise might have played a not negligible role (given the traditions subsisting in various strata of the Italian people), and determining to follow an independent course of action (we refer to the "national" parties or those of the Right)—a course of action which is certainly more difficult, but which is at least clear and without compromise.

15. "LOVE FROM AFAR"

In the sphere of interior relations, and of that which has been called by the neologism of ethology,[176] one can distinguish two fundamental forms, countersigned respectively by the formulae "love of the near" and "love of the far" (the Nietzschean *Liebe der Ferne*).[177] In the first case one is attracted by that which is near, in the other that which is far. The first is relevant to "democracy" in the widest and above all most existential sense of the word; the second relates to a higher type of human being, and is attainable predominantly in the world of Tradition.

In the first case, in order that a person, a master, should be followed, he must be felt to be "one of us." Thus someone has coined a

---

176 From the Greek ἦθος, meaning customs, manners, and also disposition and character. Ethology is the study of human character and its formation and evolution.

177 I have been unable to find this exact phrase in Nietzsche. Most probably, this is a reference to *Thus Spoke Zarathustra*, Part II, Section 15, "On Immaculate Perception." The reference may also be to Section 15 of *The Gay Science*, "Aus der Ferne," ("from a distance") in which Nietzsche speaks of one's perception of a mountain from below and from above, and says that "some greatness...wants to be beheld from a distance and by all means from below, not from above" (translation, W. Kaufmann). The point of Nietzsche's passage here, however, seems to be precisely the contrary of what Evola intends. Nietzsche's concept of the "heights" and of "distance" in many cases does not correspond perfectly to Evola's. See also *Beyond Good and Evil*, Sections 57 and 211. Evola might also be thinking of the "*pathos* of distance" here—see section 257 of *Beyond Good and Evil*—but again, this refers more to the inner state of one who is distant, than the outer perception of the distances.

happy formula, "oursism." There is an evident relation between this "oursism" with "popularity," with "moving toward the people" or "amongst the people"—and indeed, on the other hand, with the intolerance for every qualitative difference. Everyone knows certain recent aspects of this orientation; here one can include even the insipid circulating and "traveling" of the Pontiffs themselves, where it would be instead more natural to nourish a near-inaccessibility, through which certain sovereigns appear to the people like the "solitary heights." We should underline the pathos of the situation here, because there can be a physical nearness which does not exclude, but even maintains, the interior distance.

One knows the part this "oursism" has played also in the totalitarian regimes of yesterday and today. Really pathetic scenes have been portrayed and disseminated, of dictators who gratify themselves by appearing amongst "the people." If the basis of power is more or less demagogic this is, moreover, almost a necessity. The "Great Comrade" (Stalin) never ceased to be a comrade. All this corresponds to a specific collective atmosphere. Already more than a century and a half ago, Donoso Cortés, philosopher and Spanish statesman, wrote with bitterness that there are no longer sovereigns who truly know how to present themselves as such; for if they did so, it might be that no one would follow them. Thus a kind of prostitution seems to impose itself, emphasized by Weininger,[178] in the world of politics. We risk nothing by affirming that if today there were masters in authentic aristocratic sense, they would be constrained to conceal their nature and to pre-

---

178 Otto Weininger, Jewish Austrian philosopher, was born in 1880 and died at his own hand in 1903. The reasons for his suicide remain obscure. Evidently he had had the thought of killing himself for years prior, and one of the most plausible motivations which are adduced to explain his act, was a certain self-loathing on account of his Jewish heritage. He wrote several books in his short life, and is most famous for his *Sex and Character*, which was notorious for its intrepid but harsh judgement of Jews and women.

sent themselves in the attire of democratic mass agitators, in order to exercise any influence at all. The army is the unique sector which in part remains immune to such contamination, even if it is not always easy to find in it that severe and impersonal style which characterized for example Prussianism.

An essentially plebeian type of human corresponds to "oursism." We might refer to the opposite type with the formula of "love of the far." Not "human" nearness but rather distance arouses a sentiment in such a one, which basically elevates him and, simultaneously, urges him to follow and to obey, in very different terms than are characteristic of the other kind of human being. In elder times one could speak of the magic or the fascination of "Olympian superiority." In this, quite different chords of the soul vibrated. Speaking for a moment from a different sphere, we surely cannot perceive any progress in the passage from the man-god of the classic world (symbol or ideal though it was) to the god-man of Christianity—the god who makes himself man and founds a religion which is at bottom human, with a love which is supposed to associate all men and to draw them near to one another. Not erroneously did Nietzsche detect in this the contrary of that which he designated with the word *vornehmen*, translatable by "distinct" or "aristocratic."[179]

The nocturnal starry night above exalted Kant for its ineffable distance,[180] and this sentiment is felt by many non-vulgar beings in a totally natural way. Here we find ourselves at its limit. However we can extend a reflection also to planes which are infinitely more condi-

---

179 The more common English translation of this essential concept in Nietzsche is "noble." See *Beyond Good and Evil,* Book IX.

180 From the famous statement of Kant in *Critique of Practical Reason*: "Two things fill the mind with ever new and increasing admiration and awe, the more often and steadily we reflect upon them: the starry heavens above me and the moral law within me" (5:161.33–6, translated by Guyer).

tioned. To "anagogic" distance (that is, the distance which elevates),[181] one can oppose that which not rarely hides beneath the garments of a certain humility. It was Seneca who said that there is no more detestable pride than that of the humble.[182] This saying derives from an acute analysis of the fundament of the ostentatious humility of persons who, at the end of the day, are proud of themselves, being intimately intolerant of whomever is superior to them. In such men, feeling themselves together is natural, and brings them to that end which we have here indicated.

As in many other cases, the considerations here explicated, which naturally go against the grain, are meant to establish discriminating criteria of measure.

Regarding this mania for the popularity of the great, we cannot resist the temptation of recounting a personal episode. Years ago we tendered one of our books to a certain sovereign, following the normal rules of etiquette—that is to say, not directly but through an intermediary. Now, we tell the plain truth if we affirm that we felt almost a shock[183] when we received a letter of thanks that began with the words "Dear [!] Evola"—though I had never in person met this personage, nor had ever even spoken to him. This "democraticality" seems to make for good tone today. Yet it must disgust anyone who yet has a sensibility for ancient values.

In an exceedingly banal sphere, we might remember, as index of the same matter, a usance which is extremely common to the United

---

181 From Ancient Greek ἀναγωγή, meaning "leading upward."

182 Probable reference to Seneca the Younger (c. 4 BCE-65 CE), Roman stoic philosopher. I have been unable to find the source.

183 It is perhaps not superfluous to note that Evola uses the English word "shock" here. This word has been absorbed into Italian directly from English and now forms a part of the Italian lexicon; Evola himself uses it several times in the present work. Nonetheless, there might be something particularly suggestive of his present use of an English term.

States, the most plebeian Country of all the world. Especially in the newest generation, one cannot engage in the smallest of talk with anyone there without him inviting you to call him by his first name, Al, Joe, etc. Contrariwise, we are led to remember those children who spoke in terms of respect with their own parents, and we recall also a certain person, very close to us, who continues to use the respectful *thou* form with girls (respectable ones) even after he has been to bed with them; even while films reflecting customs from overseas present us with the stereotype of "he" who after a simple, insipid kiss, immediately begins calling the woman "you."[184]

---

184 Italian, as most languages, has two "you" forms, the formal (used with persons of importance, strangers, etc.) and the informal (used with friends). English had such a form, but it fell into disuse in the last few centuries. Evola's point is that the formal "you" was used much more commonly in the past than it is now; or that the level of formality between persons who do not know each other has considerably decreased.

16. THE FETISH FOR MAGIC

This constant talk surrounding "magic" constitutes a phenomenon of our days worthy of notice. Magic has become almost fashionable, and references to it are observable not only in literature, but also in other spheres, cinema not excluded. Books on magic multiply. We leave aside that part of all this which attracts the masses, the lowest strata of the population, which is credulous and inclined toward superstition, and which furnishes the clientele of "wizards," seers and like salespeople. We would like to consider rather almost a "cultural" phenomenon, as one would say today, which merits a certain attention on our part.

For a general interpretation, one can refer in part to the very causes which have generated neo-spiritualism in its myriad theosophic, orientalistic, "occultist" varieties. Here one is dealing with an impulse of man toward escapism in the strange and the unusual, almost of an attitude which is incapable, for its lack of principles, of distinguishing that which is positive in this "spiritualism" from that which is negative. The mask of such "spiritualism" is seemingly luminous, but its true face in many cases is not so at all. (We have undertaken a close examination of all this in a book entitled precisely *The Masks and the Visage of Contemporary Spiritualism.*) From the start, two fundamental causes have favored the "spiritualist" phenomenon: on the one hand, the suffocating materialistic and scientistic conception of the world; on the other hand, the fact that the dominant religion has demonstrated itself ever less capable of giving something more, something transcendent, beyond simple dogma, liturgy, devotion, and confessional practice. Thus one searches for such things elsewhere.

But there is something peculiar in the case of interest in "magic," because it has a more active appearance; it makes one think of super-sensible forces which can potentially be used to obtain concrete results. While the features of a threadbare mystical "spiritualism" are feminine, those of "magic" are indubitably masculine. This does not exclude the possibility that various illusions might arise in this connection.

If in the title of the present notes we have spoken of the "fetish" for magic, we do not wish with this to suggest that magic is a pure superstition. We might immediately observe that so-called modern "metapsychic" research has in fact verified, under stringent scientific controls, the objective reality of a series of paranormal phenomena. This alone would suffice to ground "magic," if only the corresponding conditions were different—which is to say, if only such phenomena were not sporadic and thus often bound to reduced states of con-sciousness, like those of the mediums, but were susceptible to being methodologically reproduced in perfect mental lucidity. But precisely in view of this essential psychic displacement there is the danger that with magic one must really speak practically of a fetish.

The non-specialized reader might be interested in a summary indication of the presuppositions which are necessary if magic is to have any reality. These presuppositions have an essentially existential character. We are not dealing with "arcane mysteries," nor with special occult operations that can be performed by just anyone. We are speak-ing rather of seeing in whom and in what measure it is possible to revive an interior state, and also relations between man and world, which belong in large part to the past, to civilizations and to an envi-ronment radically diverse from that of the man of today.

For the man of today, a barrier stands between the *I* and reality or nature. Reality, nature is something which exists in itself, in a spacial exteriority (just as they are considered, essentially, by positive science). This was not the case, or was not in equal measure the case, in the world wherein magic formed an organic part. The barrier in that world was permeable, and this fact was accompanied by a perception of reality which was not merely "physical." A double possibility derived from every potential removal or attenuation of that barrier. On the one hand, it was possible that invisible forces of reality might invade man from without, injuring his personality (whence what Frazer called "the perils of the soul",[185] in which one finds the *raison d'être* of many rites of protection in ancient civilizations and also amongst primitive populations). On the other hand, a movement in the opposite direction was possible: namely that man, having removed the barrier, might penetrate into nature and act on it precisely in terms of "magic." Analogous conditions were necessary also for his action on other beings.

This is the objective condition by which magic becomes something more serious than mere superstition or suggestion. If, in referring to current times, we have spoken of magic as a "fetish," we have done so because in a civilized society of the modern kind the existential structure of man and environment are by now essentially diverse from those just now indicated. Thus, apart from those populations which are still "primitive" and exotic, magical possibilities today can be observed, if at all, in our countrysides, amongst persons whose imagination yet has a particular potency, a vehemence, which has not been paralyzed by the hypertrophied intellectualism that characterizes modern civilized man. This last is especially true of that type of modern man who lives in large complex urban centers wherein, moreover, as someone has justly observed, a further species of "petrification" of the exterior aspect of natural reality can be perceived, rendering him yet more impenetrable.

---

185 Sir James George Frazer (1854-1941), a Scottish anthropologist, most famous for his book *The Golden Bough*, a comparative study in religion and mythology. The "perils of the soul" (Evola here uses Frazer's original English phrase) comes from the title of Chapter XVIII of that work.

Leaving aside exceptional cases of persons who should be considered as the holdovers of that precedent human type, in most cases it would be necessary to reactivate the non-dual state of which we have spoken. It is this which magical rituals in less remote times have sought to bring about, producing forms of exaltation and of ecstasy capable of "opening," of reestablishing contacts. Today some risk such adventures, even attempting blitzes into that territory, possibly including the use of drugs, but rarely proceeding with precise ideas and precise connections to a tradition. The clarion path of interior discipline and of mental concentration (in a way partially similar to that of yoga), which requires particular forms of preparation, is struck upon much less commonly, and it attracts fewer: for it is near to a true, uncomfortable ascesis, and moreover leads rarely to the principle aims of magic.

This is why, speaking realistically, magic today can serve almost exclusively as a distraction, or else as an ingredient (associated frequently with sex) for that man who goes on the hunt for experiences which are as "intense" as they are turbid. These experiences act almost always as a surrogate to compensate for the absence of a profound and strongly rooted sense of existence. All of which, moreover, rarely carries one beyond the merely subjective field, while there is a real danger of ending up in spiritually regressive forms, or else of opening oneself, sometimes unintentionally, to the "nether" forces, reintroducing therefore the "perils of the soul" of other times, almost without even being aware of it.

17. NOTES ON THE MYSTERY OF MITHRAS

E. Renan[186] wrote: "If Christianity had been arrested by some mortal illness, the world would have been Mithraicized"—that is, it would have adopted the religion of Mithras. In general, it is recognized that Mithraism was Christanity's most redoubtable antagonist. After penetrating Rome around the midpoint of the first century before Christ, it enjoyed its apogee toward the third century, diffusing itself as far as the most distant provinces of the Empire, attracting above all the legionaries and colonizing veterans, who found it congenial for its combative and virile orientation. Emperors, such as Hadrian, Commodus and Aurelius, made themselves initiates into its Mysteries.[187] Mithraism was officially recognized toward the end of the second century as a religion of the Empire, and Mithras was conceived as its protector and champion. His cult was fused, moreover, with that of the Sun, Helios, god of divine potency, sovereign and invincible. The date of one of

---

186 Ernest Renan (1823-1892) was a French historian and linguist, best remembered for his *The Life of Jesus* (1863), which attempted to humanize Jesus and to render him more Aryan as an historical figure. Perhaps the most revolutionary aspect of this book, however, was simply its attempt to look at the life of Christ from the point of view of history rather than theology.

187 Hadrian (76-138) is famous for his eponymous wall in Britain. Commodus (161-192) was physically powerful, though he was known to be a somewhat simple and ignorant man, and he is often remembered as the emperor who partook as a gladiator in the gladiatorial contests, to the great scandal of the Romans. Marcus Aurelius (121-180) was a Stoic, and wrote his *Meditations* in that spirit.

his most important festivals, on which his rebirth was celebrated (*dies natalis Solis invîcti Mithra*),[188] was fixed at 25 December (the winter solstice). In their supplanting work, the Christians appropriated this date for their Christmas. The story has it that Constantine himself vacillated between Christianity and Mithraism, and Emperor Julian was certainly an initiate to its mysteries[189]—the same Julian who, as can be read in a subsequent essay of the present volume, looked to Mithraism in particular, together with Neoplatonic metaphysics and to the mystery cults, in his ardent and noble attempt to restore the Roman cults against the flood of Christian beliefs.

Regarding the thesis that the ancient world might have been Mithracized rather than Christianized, we should nevertheless make a few reservations. If it were to advantageously compete with Christanity, Mithraism would have had to descend to Christianity's level. Had it maintained its integrity it could only with difficulty have won over those promiscuous popular masses, amongst which the religion of Jesus essentially gained its footing with its doctrine of salvation and its universal sentimental basis. As an emanation from the ancient Iranian Mazdaism,[190] Mithraism adopted the central theme of a battle between the powers of light and those of darkness and of evil. It too had its religious and exoteric forms, but its core was constituted by its

---

188 Latin: "the day of the birth of the unconquered Sun Mithras."

189 Constantine the Great (27-337) was the Roman Emperor famous for being the first to convert to Christianity. It is said he converted when he saw a cross descending from the sun, bearing the words *In Hoc Signo Vinces*, "In this sign shall you conquer." Many of the subsequent successes of Christianity are attributed to Constantine. Emperor Julian (331/332-363) is often known as the Apostate for his attempt in the opposite direction. For more on Julian, see Chapter 26 below.

190 Another term for Zoroastrianism, one of the world's oldest religions, which comes from the teachings of the prophet Zoroaster. Due to its conception of the world as being divided between two contrary forces of good and evil and its monotheism, it is often taken as a forerunner of Christianity, though it would be a mistake to attempt too close a parallel between the two religions.

Mysteries—that is, by initiation in the proper sense. This constituted its limitation, even if it made it into a more complete traditional form. Subsequently, we witness however an ever more decisive historical separation between religion and initiation.

We will consider the Mysteries of Mithraism in the present notes by seeking to indicate their nature according to the testimonies which have reached us—that is, those testimonies which are consistent on one hand with the reports of the ancient writers, and on the other with the figurative monuments discovered in the physical centers of that cult and of those Mysteries. Beyond the testimonies gathered by Franz Cumont[191] in his classic works, we might consider "The Mithraic Ritual of the Great Magical Papyrus of Paris," entitled *Apathanatismos*;[192] its text, translated and annotated, can be found in the first volume of our work *Introduction to Magic*.

Before all, for our present purposes, we must consider the myth of Mithras in its interior sense, as it can be seen through the various episodes as they are portrayed in a quantity of sculptures and bas-reliefs, some of magnificent workmanship. Indeed we should remember that myths of this kind acted as dramatizations of the very experiences that the initiate must traverse, almost identifying himself with god by repeating his deeds.

In the myth, Mithras is born from a stone (*theos ek pétras petrogenos Mithra*), he is generated from a stone (*petra genetrix*), as a manifestation of the originating Uranian light. This birth occurs beside a "river": it is a miraculous birth witnessed only by several "guardians" hidden atop some hills. We can refer these last to the "Invisible Masters," not unrelated to those beings of the origins

---

191 Cumont (1868-1947) was a Belgian archaeologist and historian who is well known for his investigations into Mithraism.

192 Ancient Greek ἀπαθανατισμός: "immortalization."

who, according to Hesiod,[193] would never die, but as the "Wakeful Watchers" would continue to live through successive ages.

The "waters" on one side, the "stone" on the other might allude to the duality constituted by the flux of becoming and the principle that rules it. Various interpretations of the "stone" are possible; as is known, it figures in myriad traditions. There is temptation, moreover, to establish an analogy between this genesis of Mithras and a theme of the Arthurian cycle, which features a sword that must be extracted from a stone floating on the waters.[194] And indeed, as he rises from the stone, Mithras holds in one hand a sword, in the other a torch, the first a symbol of strength, the other of light, of an illuminating power.

In the "stone" one can also see a symbol of an indestructibility and an interior steadfastness, qualities required of the initiate as the fundament of his rebirth.

In fact, from ancient reports, especially those transmitted to us by Nonnus the Grammarian,[195] it appears that in the mysteries of Mithra the neophytes had to brave a number of trials, passing intrepidly across fire and water, enduring cold, hunger and thirst. According to another report, the neophyte, to put his impassibility to the trial, was

---

193 The Greek poet, highly esteemed by the ancients, who probably lived between 750-650 BCE, author of *Works and Days* and the *Theogony*. The reference here is to the former work; see lines 121-125. The reference to Uranus in the earlier part of the passage is rather to the Greek god Ouranos, god of the sky, son of Aether, god of heavenly light.

194 Reference to the legends surrounding King Arthur. According to the most widespread version of this, the young Arthur, by his royal blood, is the only one capable of extracting the magical sword Excalibur from a stone.

195 Reference to Nonnus of Panopolis, a poet born in Hellenized Egypt in the fourth or fifth century. He wrote an epic poem (no exaggeration; the poem is 48 books long) about the story of Dionysus entitled *Dionysiaca*. This poem has proven to be an exceptional fount of Dionysian myths, and its main value is taken to lie in this fact—hence perhaps the curious fact that Evola refers to Nonnus, unconventionally, as "Nonnus the Grammarian."

made to take part in the simulated killing of a man. And the story goes that Emperor Commodus, who wished to become an initiate, aroused the indignation of his milieu by taking that simulated killing seriously, thereby causing the death of a man. It may be that all this—that a qualification of the kind—could have relation to the symbol of the "generating stone," that is, to one of the conditions of the initiatory rebirth.

However, the qualities just mentioned appear to be required for the successive developments of the myth of Mithras, as Mithras must withstand a furious wind which immediately assails him and which flagellates his naked body; but he goes directly toward a tree, he makes a garment of its leaves and he feeds of its fruits. Given the initiatory meaning of the tree, here one might think of the tree whereupon Adam wished to put his hand to become "similar to one of us" (to a god), but from which he is barred by the Jehovah of the Old Testament.

This meaning might be confirmed in a subsequent episode of the myth, which seems to relate a confrontation between Mithras and the Sun, the flaming Aion. This episode concludes however with an alliance between the one and the other, such as to make Mithras the bearer of the sovereign force of that divinity. One treats of the *hvarenô*[196] of the ancient (Iranian) Mazda tradition, of "Glory" conceived of as a supernatural fire which is proper before all to the celestial divinities but which descends also to illuminate the sovereigns, to consecrate them and to vouch for them through victory. The sovereign upon whom this "Glory" descended was built up beyond men and was considered by his subjects as an immortal. And it is for this reason that, in the assimilation of Mithras with Sol,[197] ever newly victorious over the darkness, the same Mithras was esteemed as the protector and champion of the Roman Empire.

---

196 "Glory" which is often connected with a crown of light, or an aureola.

197 Sol (Latin: "sun") was the Roman sun god, Sol Invictus ("the unconquered sun"), connected also with Mithras.

But this dignity of Mithras has also another relation with the central episode of the myth—with the killing of the bull. Mithras spies the bull; so soon as the bull comes out of his "cavern," Mithras leaps upon him, he rides him, gripping onto his horns. The quadruped takes to galloping, transporting Mithras on a furious race. Mithras does not cease his grip, he lets himself be transported without letting himself be bucked off until the animal, exhausted, reenters his cavern from whence he issued. Then Mithras kills him with his sword.

We see here the confrontation with the elemental "nether" force of life and of its transformation by the work of him who has recruited it upon its surfacing (consider the ride) and has also conquered it. In fact, the blood which gushes from the wound of the bull transforms itself into "ears of wheat"; falling on the earth, these produce "vegetation." One has only to impede foul beasts from rushing to drink of that blood (these are to be seen in the depictions of the myth)—the which has likewise an esoteric significance: when the hero or the initiate is not "pure," that which in him remains of inferior nature will be strengthened thanks to the liberated energy, and not only will the transformation not take place, but the result could be fatal (this is a danger which, using a different symbolism, has often been also indicated in the texts of alchemical hermeticism[198]). According to a variant of the myth, the blood of the bull transforms into *wine*: possible allusion to the effect constituted by a kind of magical inebriation.

This episode of the myth fulfills such an important role that it gives place to a specific rite of initiation of the mysteries of Mithras, which consist of a baptism of blood. The Mithraea, or the places where such Mysteries were celebrated, were so built as to include a higher and a

---

198 Hermeticism is an esoteric tradition which takes its name from Hermes Trismegistus ("thrice-great Hermes"), the god who is said to have penned the *Hermetic Corpus*. This enigmatic text subsequently became the basis for the hermetic tradition, which had a deal of influence in the West, particularly beginning from the Renaissance.

lower part (they were almost always subterranean, which had its own significance). The neophyte who had overcome the preliminary trials was taken to the lower rooms; naked, he received the blood of a bull which was killed ritually by the hierophant in the upper part of the sacellum;[199] this blood was poured on him. Particular experiences brought about by this whole event were tied to this baptism of blood, which took the place of the Christian baptism.

In general, the experiences of the Mithraic initiate can be referred in part to the above-mentioned ritual, *Apathanatismos*, even if other elements are to be found intermixed with the Mithraic ones—other elements proper to gnosticism and to magical traditions. Dieterich,[200] who was the first to publish a translation of this evocative text in 1903, called it a "liturgy." This designation is inexact, because one is not dealing with a ceremony with hymns and such, but rather of a ritual with instructions, magical formulae and invocations together with signs of the corresponding experiences. The ritual seems to presuppose a preliminary initiation, inasmuch as the subject in the first invocation declares that he has been purified by the "sacred ceremonies" and that he has been uplifted by "the strong force of forces" and by the "incorruptible Right," sufficiently to be able to aspire to "immortal birth," to subtract himself from the law of necessity which reigns in the lower world, and to contemplate the gods and Aion,[201] "lord of the crowns of fire." There is talk of doors which open, of the "seven" visions, first in their feminine aspect, then in the masculine aspect as the "Lords of the Celestial Pole." The theurgical action car-

---

199 The hierophant was the overseer of sacred mysteries. The sacellum is a small chapel-like part of the Mithraea.

200 Albrecht Dieterich (1866-1908) was a German philologist and scholar of religions. He dedicated many of his studies to the religion of the Greco-Roman world.

201 Hellenistic deity connected to eternity and the afterlife, later taken to be the protector of Roman rule unto perpetuity.

ries visibly beyond the Seven, until, amongst flashes and lightning, a figure appears which is Sol-Mithras himself; and the initiate must know how to fasten this god to himself and then, with a command, to prohibit the god from departing from him, so as to transform himself into this god (to assume the god's nature) to such an extent as to "die integrated in palingenisis and, in the integration, to reach fulfillment."

The ritual includes many other details upon which we cannot linger here. The reader is referred to the text which, as noted, has been reproduced, translated from Greek with commentary, in the first volume of our work *Introduction to Magic*.

Here we will only add that Mithraism too knew of the retrograde voyage across the seven planetary spheres, no longer in the descent in which the soul is taken bit by bit into the "spheres of the necessary," subjected to gradual conditioning up to the state of a mortal man, but rather in a re-ascension which goes beyond such spheres, in a "denuding," up to attainment of the Principle of the Unconditioned.

The "seven" is found also in the number of grades of Mithraic initiation in its institutionalized form, so to speak. The grades bore these names: Raven (*Corax*), Occult (*Cryphies*), Soldier (*Miles*), Lion (*Leo*), Persian (*Perses*), Messenger of the Sun (*Heliodromos*), Father (*Pater*).

Toward an interpretation of these grades, one might think of a preliminary "mortification" of the inferior nature (with the which, moreover, a correspondence is stabilized to the alchemical-hermetic symbolism of the Raven, frequently used to allude to the *nigredo*[202] phase, to the "Black Work"). After which the initiate takes on an occult existence (second grade); in the third grade he becomes a soldier of the ranks of the Mithraic initiates who, conforming to the warrior spirit of that tradition, were conceived of as a militia. The subsequent

---

202 The phase of alchemical work which is associated esoterically with the death (even the murder) and the decomposition of the false self.

grade represents a strengthening of this quality, while the "Persian" grade plausibly established a connection with the original lineage of Mithraism, with that of the Iranian religion of the Light. Regarding the *miles*, Tertullian[203] relates that during the act of conferring this grade, a sword and a crown were granted to the neophyte. The neophyte took the sword but rejected the crown, saying, "My crown is Mithras."

As "Messenger of the Sun" (the sixth grade) the initiate reflected the same quality attributed to Mithras in the myth, after his confrontation with Helios. Finally the *Pater* corresponded to the dignity of initiator (initiatory paternity) and of lord of a Mithraic community (*pater sacrorum, pater patrum*).[204]

From the which it appears that, had Mithraism ever prevailed over Christianity while maintaining its central core, the consequences would have included also the maintenance of a regular initiatory tradition, constituted by such a core, in the subsequent history of the West; while for its exterior, religious side, the quality of *Soter*[205] (the Savior, He who gives health), which is sometimes attributed to Mithras, would have held sway. More, there was the aspect which made of the "unconquered god"—*Invictus Mithra*—the solar patron of the Roman empire: for which one saw in him the dispenser of the Mazda *hvarenô* which conferred victory, in a confluence with the ancient Roman tradition of (*Fortuna Regina*, the Latin translation of *tùke basiléos*).[206] This was

---

203 Christian apologist (155-240) of the early period, Tertullian was the author of many religious works.

204 Latin: "father of sacred things, father of fathers"

205 From the Greek Σωτήρ, "deliverer," which was the epithet of various principle Greek gods, including Zeus, Poseidon, Dionysus, Apollo, and Athena.

206 Latin and Greek, respectively: "Queen Fortune." The goddess Fortuna was connected with fate; she was often depicted as being blind or blindfolded, in representation of the unpredictable vicissitudes of life.

expressed also in the object of a cult, that same *Victoria*[207] whose statue was erected in the Roman senate.

One sees from this nevertheless that Mithraism constituted a cultural, sacral and initiatory complex which for its very nature could not avoid being excised during that retrograde process which has carried the West away, distancing it ever more from the horizons of glory and of luminous potency, until, at last, with the exception of an initiation which was no any longer an integral and central part of a system but only a subterranean vein with sporadic reemergence despite Christianity, every real contact with the super-sensible was interrupted.

---

207 The Roman goddess of victory, equivalent of the Greek Nike. The statue to which Evola makes reference was installed in the Senate in 29 by Augustus to celebrate the victory at the Battle of Actium, and the Senators upon arrival there were accustomed to burning a sprig of wheat before it. It was removed in 357 by Constantine in order to placate his new god; then it was subsequently restored by Julian and removed a final time by Emperor Gratian.

18. ON THE "LEFT-HAND PATH"

To form an idea of the nature of Divinity and of its relations with the world one can follow two paths: the *deductive* path and the *inductive* path.

Whoever chooses the first way, commences from a conception *a priori* of Divinity deduced from a Revelation or from a dogma, and seeks to perceive how it might accord with the factuality of mundane reality. The problem presents various difficulties when Divinity is conceived, as it is in Christianity, with "moral" attributes, which stand under the species of a Creator, God of light, of love, and of providence. Indeed there are aspects of the world and of life that are undeniably dark and problematic, which therefore cannot definitively be brought into accord with that theological conception. *Theodicy* is the part of theistic theology which attempts to get to the bottom of such antitheses. The best known example of Christian theodicy is that of Leibniz,[208] who wanted to demonstrate through speculative arguments that ours is "the best of all possible worlds." Such a formula, however, is ambiguous, because the "possible" can also be interpreted as "everything which can be done," that is, more or less, as "it couldn't have been done better."

---

208 Gottfried Wilhelm Leibniz (1646-1716) was a German philosopher and polymath, and he is (unfortunately) best remembered for the sentence which Evola cites here, which was later ridiculed by Voltaire in *Candide*. Leibniz, who was neither a fool nor a madman, obviously did not mean to assert with his phrase that this world is the best world *conceivable*; he meant rather that it was the best which could be attained, given the constraints of possibility.

This would oblige however a redimensioning of the "moral" conception of Divinity. In antiquity, such was undertaken in the most drastic way by Marcion,[209] who took the other path, the "inductive" path. It is affirmed—Marcion says—that God is wise, good, and omnipotent. But these attributes are irreconcilable with one another because, considering the world as it is, one must deduce either that God is wise and good but not omnipotent (we return to the "what it was *possible* to create"), or else he is good and omnipotent but not wise, or else he is wise and omnipotent but not good. The Marquis de Sade,[210] the "divine marquis," went yet further in this direction. As Mario Praz[211] has well brought to light, Sade was not an atheist; he believed in the existence of God, but in a wicked God. For him, this was demonstrated by the prevalence of evil and of destruction in the world. Sade drew practical consequences from this idea as the basis of an upside-down ethics: if evil is the predominant force in the universe and the expression of the divine nature, evil, vice, and corruption, for their conformity to the universal law, will be forever happy and prosperous (consider the title of his novel: *Justine ou les prosperités du vice*[212]), while good and virtue will be forever unhappy and unlucky, not to say damned.

---

209 Marcion of Sinope (85-160) was a Christian theologian who dedicated himself at a very early date toward attempting a reconciliation of many of the thorniest issues of Christian theology, which have indeed remained common themes of the theologians since.

210 Marquis de Sade (1740-1814) was a French aristocrat and erotic novelist, who has made his permanent imprint on our language with the terms *sadism* and *sadist*. He was famous for his immorality and blasphemy. The epithet "divine marquis" which came to be associated so closely with Sade's name was evidently applied in a spirit of thoroughgoing French irony.

211 Praz (1896-1982) was an Italian art critic.

212 Evola here confuses two similar titles of De Sade's novels: *L'Histoire de Juliette ou les Prospérités du vice* (*The History of Juliette, or the Rewards of Vice*) and *Justine, ou Les Malheurs de la Vertu* (*Justine, or the Ills of Virtue*). In any case, his point stands; indeed, the second title only strengthens it.

These difficulties, this *aporia*[213] and these antinomies, derive from keeping to a fairly limited point of view; also from considering rigid moral categories (as good and evil) rather than ontological categories. The Orient above all offers vaster and freer horizons.

One can make reference before anything to the doctrine of a Supreme Principle which encompasses, reunites, and transcends all opposites (this idea, moreover, has been adumbrated sporadically in the Occident by several mystics and by a number of metaphysics; cf. the *coincidentia oppositorum*, up to William Blake's "marriage of heaven and hell".[214] Secondly, and above all, one might recall the Orthodox Hindu doctrine of the triple aspect of Divinity. This doctrine is apparently obtained by applying the method here called "inductive," that is inferring the correct concept of the Divinity from concrete experience. Factually, one observes creative processes, subsistent forms, as well as destructive processes in the world. Correspondingly three faces are attributed to divinity: that of God who creates, that of God who conserves, and that of God who destroys, the corresponding religious hypostases being Brahmâ, Vishnu and Shiva. These gods have furnished the points of reference for a differentiated cult, but also for various paths of action—paths which are distinct but, in the last analysis, equivalent.

---

213 Ancient Greek ἀπορία: "without passage." An aporia is a philosophical enigma due to an apparent contradiction in premises.

214 *Coincidentia oppositorum*, Latin: "coincidence of opposites." The term comes most likely from the work of the German theologian Nicholas of Cusa (1401-1464), but was taken up by many thinkers after. The concept refers to the unification of apparent contradictions in a higher level of reality. William Blake (1757-1827) was an English poet, printmaker, and visionary, known for the often mysterious spiritualistic tendencies of his work. *The Marriage of Heaven and Hell*, a collection of his poems and his illustrations and etchings, is one of his most famous and enigmatic works; as its name suggests, it sought a cosmic transcendence of apparent opposites.

It is in this view that the concepts of the Right-Hand Path and the Left-Hand Path are properly defined. The first path relates to the first aspects of the Principle (Brahmâ and Vishnu) and, on the plane of comportment, of ethics and of cult, it is characterized by affirmation of what exists, by the sacralisation of what exists, by conformity to law (*Dharma*) and to the positive precepts of a given traditional order of earthly life. Meanwhile the Left-Hand Path—Vârnâcara—stands essentially under the sign of Shiva (or of his Sakti[215]—for example Durgâ and Kâlî), that is, of the destructive aspect of divinity; it entails not only detachment and the release from every existent order and norm, but an "anomia" (=*adharma*, having no *nomos*=a law). So Shiva was capable of being both the god of ascetics who withdrew from the bonds of the world, as well as of the outlaw himself.

In this respect however as many misinterpretations can arise (and effectively have arisen) as deviations. It is in this sphere that the concept of "destruction" is associated with that of "transcendence": however, not destruction for destruction's sake, but destruction for transcendence (the etymology of the word "transcend" is surpassing by rising). Also, it is obviously not so much a question of material destruction as, above all, of destructive *experiences*, because here one is dealing with the paths to spiritual realization. The reference here made to "transcendence" is reductionistic; the orientation toward the heights is the constant and inescapable presupposition. It distinguishes the world of which we are speaking unequivocally from the sinister world, mentioned above, of Sade and the like, despite the obscure ecstasies that this last might provoke.

It is natural that whoever follows the Left-Hand Path makes apologia for it; so one reads in a certain text that this path is to the Right-Hand Path as wine in milk, and that they who have a qualification or

---

215 Or *shakti*, meaning "power." According to Hinduism these are the primordial cosmic forces.

a vocation for *Vîra* (=a virile or heroic orientation) are attracted to it. But a positive title for this claimed preeminence might really exist, which emphasizes precisely the dimension of "transcendence": because that which has a character of transcendence is necessarily destructive (destructive of the finite), and such a character was attributed, beyond Shiva, to the Supreme Principle itself. This appears in an orthodox text which has almost the same popularity in India as the Bible enjoys in the West: namely, the *Bhagavad-gîtâ*.[216] In the eleventh chapter of this text, a destructive and crushing force is indicated as a "supreme form" of the divinity, and the warrior Arjuna is exhorted to become its human incarnation by conquering every agony and every weakness of soul. This orientation can absolutely be related to the Left-Hand Path: combat, death, destruction receive a metaphysical anointment if their foundation is in the impulse toward transcendence, in the adumbration of an essential divine attribute.

But customarily the Left-Hand Path is not referred to the "Path of the Warrior" (despite the evident convergences) but rather to particular experiences in which also figures, as in Occidental Dionysism, the orgiastic element, which is to say the specifically sexual element.

In such experiences one seeks something destructive in view of its "deconditionalized" qualities. Thus it would be a grave error to think that, for example, when sex and woman are used on that path, one aims at "pleasure" as it is commonly understood: the "voluptuousness" counts rather as a shattering of the door in the opposite direction. In the Right-Hand Path sexual unions are ritualized, are made in the image of the *ieros gamos*,[217] of the intercourse of a divine couple or

---

216 The Hindu Sanskrit scripture, and part of the epic Mahabharata, whose warrior protagonist (the same Prince Arjuna mentioned in sequel here) is connected simultaneously to both the human and the divine.

217 Ancient Greek ἱερὸς γάμος: "sacred marriage," the union between god and goddess which are reproduced by humans in certain rituals, particularly in the Hindu and Buddhist traditions.

a mythological archetype. Meanwhile in the Left-Hand Path sexual unions must "kill," by realizing the ancient formula love=death. It can be observed that Western alchemical hermetism has enumerated the use of women amongst those means that it, in its cyphered polivalent jargon, has called "corrosive waters" or the "philosopher's venom."

An eminent Hindu scholar, Das Gupta,[218] has indicated connections between the Left-Hand Path and certain "obscure religious cults." We have stated above that very widespread misunderstandings of a moralizing character exist with respect to the essence of this Path; we must note also a number of its degraded and degenerate forms. In fact, we stand on rather treacherous ground here, especially if we proceed to true and proper "evocations." There are practices the ultimate meaning of which could be summarized thus: *to activate (or evoke) that which stands beneath form, in order to carry oneself above form.* By "form" here is meant all that which is variously conditioned and ordered with a certain fixity in the human being or in a given structure. Every order is defined as a form which yokes and ties the formless and elementary—the "demonic," if you please, in the ancient and non-Christian moral sense of the term. The formless or elementary is now liberated; by emerging, it cannot help but act destructively on form. If we stop here, we find ourselves in the field of obscure rites of witchcraft. Forms of possession (potentially not perceived as such) might result. If rather the destruction of form carries beyond and above form, all of this might acquire a kind of positive character. One could even speak of a "white manipulation of the black magic" (which extends so far as to include even the so-called "black masses"),[219] and this might form an aspect

---

218 Probably a reference to the Bengali Surendranath Dasgupta (1887-1952). Dasgupta lived many years in the West, renowned for his investigations into the philosophers of the East.

219 Black or Satanic masses are rituals proposed by certain traditions of black magic and witchcraft. They are the liturgical and spiritual inversion of the traditional Catholic mass.

of the Left-Hand Path. Whence the references made by Das Gupta. Everyone perceives the risks that are encountered in such practices. It is important to observe, on the other hand, that in India the Left-Hand Path is not taken by isolated individuals who are attracted by one or the other of its aspects; there, several traditions correspond to it, with several spiritual masters (guru) and it often even entails initiations. Initiation, in the aspect which ought to be considered in this context, is taken to arouse in the single individual a power which, if it does not immunize him completely to every danger (in such a case he would no longer be a man), it at least helps him to keep his feet—naturally, if he knows how to look clearly into himself, if he knows his own possibilities, and if the ultimate aim is kept constantly present.

19. THE SENSE AND ATMOSPHERE OF ZEN

One knows of the interest that so-called Zen Buddhism has aroused, even outside of specialist spheres, from the time that D.T. Suzuki[220] introduced it in his books *Introduction to Zen Buddhism* and *Essays in Zen Buddhism,* which were subsequently translated also into French. This interest derives from a kind of paradoxical meeting point. For the West in crisis, Zen represents indeed something "existentialistic" and surrealistic. Even the conception of Zen as a spiritual realization free from all faiths and all obligations, together with the mirage of an instantaneous and in a certain sense gratis "breaking of level"—one which is capable, moreover, of resolving every agony of existence—this conception could not have done other than exercise a particular fascination on the many. But to a great extent all of this regards only the appearances: the "philosophy of crisis" in the West, which is the consequence of an entire materialistic and nihilistic development, and Zen, which ever takes as its antecedent the spirituality of the Buddhist tradition, present very distinct spiritual dimensions, for which every authentic encounter with Zen presupposes in a Westerner either an exceptional predisposition, or else the capacity for that *metanoia,* that inner revolution, which has less to do with intellectual "attitudes," than with what has been conceived in every time and place as something much deeper.

---

220 Daisetsu Teitaro Suzuki (1870-1966), Japanese scholar of Buddhism. His famous *Introduction* issued in 1934, and was followed by a great many other works on Zen.

Zen has value as a secret doctrine which was transmitted, outside of the scriptures, by Buddha himself to his disciple Mahâkâçyapa. It was introduced in China around the 6th century by Bodhidharma[221] and then carried on through a succession of Masters and "patriarchs" both in China and Japan, where it yet lives and has its representatives and its Zendo ("Meditation Rooms").

As far as its spirit goes, Zen can be considered as a recovery of original Buddhism itself. Buddhism was born as an energetic reaction against the theologizing speculation and empty ritualism into which the ancient Hindu priestly caste, which already possessed a sacred and living wisdom, had finally fallen. Buddha made of all this *tabula rasa*; he posed rather the practical problem of overcoming what in popular expositions is presented as "the pain of existence" but which in internal teaching appears to be, more generally, the state of caducity, of agitation, of "thirst" and oblivion of common beings. Having himself traversed the path to awakening, to immortality, without anyone's aid, he indicated the way to whomever felt his vocation to lie in it. Buddha, as is known, is not a name, but an attribute, a title; it signifies "the Awakened One," "he who has attained awakening" or "illumination."[222] The Buddha remained silent as to the content of his experience, so as to prevent his pupils from giving themselves over once again to speculation and philosophizing, rather than to acting. So he did not speak, as his predecessors, of Brahman (of the Absolute), nor of Atmâ (the transcendental *I*) but used only the negative term nirvâna, even at risk of furnishing pretexts to those who, in their incomprehension, would see in nirvâna the "nothing," an ineffable and evanescent transcendence almost at the limit of the unconscious, a blind non-being.

---

221 Mahâkâçyapa was one of the most important of Buddha's disciples, and is considered as a major figure in the traditions both of Zen and of Buddhism as such. Bodhidharma was a Buddhist monk who immigrated to China in the fifth or sixth century, bringing Zen with him.

222 The name given to him at birth was Siddhârtha Gautama.

Now, in the subsequent development of Buddhism precisely the situation against which Buddha had reacted was repeated, *mutatis mutandis*; Buddhism became a religion with its dogmas, with its rituals, with a scholasticism of its own, with a mythology of its own. It divided into two schools,[223] the one—the Mahâyâna—richer in metaphysics, gratifying itself with an abstruse symbolism, the other—the Hînayâna—more severe and naked in its teachings, but too preoccupied with the simple moral discipline carried out along more or less monastic lines. The essential and originating core, that is the esoteric doctrine of illumination, was almost lost.

And it was here that Zen intervened, to make of everything once again *tabula rasa*, to declare the uselessness of all these by-products, to proclaim the doctrine of Satori. Satori is a fundamental interior occurrence, an abrupt break of existential level, corresponding in essence to that which we have called "awakening." Its formulation however was new, original, and arrived almost as a kind of capsizing. The state of nirvâna—the presumed nothing, extinction, the already distant final term of an effort of liberation, which according to some could require even more than one existence—is now indicated as the *normal state* of man. Every man has the nature of Buddha. Every man is already "freed," superior to birth and to death. One must only become aware of it, realize it, *"see it in one's own nature,"* the fundamental formula of Zen. A wide-opening outside of time—this is Satori. On one hand, Satori is something improvised and radically different from all the states to which men are accustomed, like a catastrophic trauma of ordinary conscience; at the same time it is that which brings one again

---

223 Reference to two Buddhist sects with many particular differences. The Mahâyâna ("Great Vehicle") sect of Buddhism considers the Buddha a kind of deity and holds that everyone can become Buddha, while the Hînayâna ("Lesser Vehicle") considers the Buddha a human being who attained enlightenment or illumination. Hînayâna is considered by many to be closer to the original teachings of Buddha.

precisely to what should, in a higher sense, be considered normal and natural; thus it is contrary to an ecstasy or a trance. It is a rediscovery and a taking possession of one's own nature: illumination, or light, which draws out of ignorance and out of the subconscious the profound reality of that which one has always been and never can cease being, no matter one's condition.

The consequence of the Satori would be a completely new vision of the world and of life. For whomever has experienced it, everything remains the same—things, the other beings, one's own self, "the sky, the rivers, and the vast earth"—and yet everything is fundamentally different: as if a new dimension had been added to reality and the meaning and the value of it had been transformed completely. According to what the masters of Zen say, the essential trait of the new experience is the overcoming of every dualism: dualism between inner and outer, between *I* and *not-I*, between finite and infinite, between being and non-being, between appearance and reality, between "empty" and "full," between substance and accident—and the other such indiscernables of every value posited dualistically by the finite consciousness and obfuscated in the individual, up to certain paradoxical limits. These are a single thing, the liberated and non-liberated, the enlightened and the non-enlightened, this world and the other world, fault and virtue. Zen effectively takes up the paradoxical equation of Mahâyâna Buddhism: nirvâna=samsara,[224] and also that of Taoism:[225] "infinitely distant is the return." All of this as if to say: the liberation is not to be sought in the beyond; this very world is the beyond, is liberation; nothing has need of being liberated. This is the point of view of *Satori*, of perfect enlightenment, of "transcendent wisdom" (*prajnâpâramita*).

---

224 Nirvana—as Evola outlines above—is an inner state of freedom and quietude brought about by spiritual awakening. Samsara is the cycle of birth and rebirth in which most beings are trapped. These are, of course, the commonplace and outer meanings given to these words.

225 Taoism is a philosophical tradition of Chinese origin.

In essence, we are speaking of a displacement of the center of the self. In any situation and in any occurrence of ordinary life, even in the most banal, the place of common sense, dualizing and intellectualistic in itself, is assumed by a being that does not know any longer the contraposition of a non-I, which transcends and recovers the terms of every antithesis, so as to enjoy a perfect liberty and incoercibility: even as that of the wind, which blows wherever it wants, and also of the naked being which, precisely because it has "slipped the grasp" (another technical expression), because it has abandoned everything ("poverty"), becomes everything and possesses everything.

Zen—at least the predominant current of Zen—insists on the discontinuous, improvised, unpredictable character of the opening of Satori. With reference to this, Suzuki went beyond the pale in polemicizing against the techniques in use in the Hindu schools, in the Sâmkhya and in Yoga,[226] but contemplated also in certain of the originating texts of Buddhism. The simile is that of water that at a given moment transmutes to ice. Also given is the image of an alarm which at a given point, from some particular jolt, begins to ring. There is no effort, discipline, or technique which in and of itself conducts to Satori. It is said, rather, that sometimes it intervenes unexpectedly, when we have exhausted all the resources of our being, above all of our intellect and our logical capacity of comprehension. Other times violent sensations, even a physical pain, can bring it about. But the cause can be also the simple perception of an object, any given fact of ordinary existence, given a certain disposition latent in the soul.

Here, certain misunderstandings can arise. As Suzuki himself recognizes, "The satori is not a thing to be gained through the

---

226 Samkhya is an ancient Indian philosophy, which in some of its forms denied theism, and aimed instead at the elimination of ignorance as the road toward freedom. Yoga is a related practice which focuses on meditation, concentration, and control of mind and body, toward the end of attaining that same freedom.

understanding."[227] He, however, speaks of the necessity of passing first through a "true baptism of fire." For the rest, the necessity of a preliminary preparation, which can even take the period of many years, is indicated by the very institution of the so-called "Meditation Rooms" wherein they who wish to reach the Satori subject themselves to a regime of life analogous, in part, to that of certain Catholic Orders. The essential thing would seem to consist in a process of maturation, identical to that of nearing to a state of extreme existential instability, within which the smallest shock suffices to produce a change of state, the breaking of level, the opening which leads to the "dazzling vision of one's true nature." The Masters know the moment in which the mind of the disciple is mature and the opening is on the point of producing itself; at that point they give, if possible, the decisive push. Sometimes it can be a simple gesture, an exclamation, something apparently irrelevant, even illogical, absurd. This suffices to produce the collapse of the entire false individuality, and, with Satori, the "normal state" takes over, one assumes one's "original visage," "that which one had before creation." One is no longer a "hunter of echoes" and "follower of shadows." We are brought to think, in certain cases, of the analogous existentialist motif of "failure" or "shipwreck" (*das Scheitern—*

---

227 This quote taken from *Introduction to Zen Buddhism* (as found in *Zen Buddhism: The Selected Writings of D.T. Suzuki*, 1996, Chapter 4, IV). I am uncertain about Evola's original citation, but the subsequent reference to "baptism of fire" in this same paragraph is probably taken from section I of the same work. Here is the Italian, for anyone who wishes to pursue the matter further: "*in genere non sono state date indicazioni sul lavoro interiore che precede il* satori." ("In general no indications have been given as to the interior work which precedes Satori.")

Kierkegaard, Jaspers[228]). Indeed, as has been noted, often the opening comes precisely when one has exhausted all the resources of one's own being and, so to speak, has one's back up to the wall. One can see this in relation to several practical methods of teaching Zen. The most commonly used instruments on the intellectual plane are the *kôan* and the *mondo*;[229] the disciple is put before certain sayings or responses of a paradoxical, absurd, sometimes grotesque or "surrealistic" nature. He must utterly wear out his mind, if necessary for whole years, unto the extreme limit of every normal faculty of comprehension. If, then, he dares take yet one more step forward, he might produce the catastrophe, the upheaval, the *metanoia*. He has attained Satori.

At the same time, the norm of Zen is that of an absolute autonomy. Nothing of gods, nothing of cults, nothing of idols. Emptied of everything, even of God. "If on your way you encounter the Buddha, kill him," says one Master.[230] It is necessary to abandon everything, to rest on nothing, to go forward, with one's essence alone, unto the point of crisis. To say anything further on Satori, to make a comparison between it and the various forms of mystic and initiatory experience of the Orient

---

228 *Das Scheitern* is German: "failing, defeat, foundering." The concept was used by the German psychiatrist and philosopher Karl Jaspers (1883-1969) to describe the precondition for the conscious awareness of mental limits, in order that these might be transcended. Similar ideas appear in Søren Aabye Kierkegaard (1813-1855), Danish philosopher and theologian and forerunner of existentialism, who wrote at length of the emotional and psychological preconditions for faith (see for instance *Fear and Trembling*). These preconditions are in many ways similar to what Evola describes here.

229 The *kôan* are succinct paradoxical statements particularly in the Japanese Zen tradition employed by Zen Masters to prepare novices mentally for awakening. The *mondo* are recorded dialogues between pupils and masters which are then used as guides for instruction.

230 This *kôan* is attributed to Linji Yixuan, a Chinese Buddhist Master and founder of a school, who was known to shout at his students and even to strike them in order to bring about their awakening.

and of the Occident, is very difficult. Apropos the Zen monasteries, it is worth noting that one passes only the period of preparation therein. Whoever has attained Satori leaves the convent and the "Meditation Room," returns to the world, choosing the way that most behooves him. One might think that the Satori is a kind of transcendence which then carries any particular form of life to immanence, as to a natural state.

The new dimension which is added onto reality following Satori issues in a certain comportment, for which the maxim of Lao-tzu[231] is relevant: "To be whole in fragments." In relation to this, one has observed the influence that Zen has exercised on the life of the Far East. Moreover, Zen has been called "the philosophy of the Samurai,"[232] and it can be affirmed that "the life of the Zen is identical to the way of the bow" or "of the sword." By which is meant that every activity of life can be permeated by Zen and so elevated to a higher meaning, to a "whole" and to an "active impersonality." There arises a sense of the irrelevancy of the individual, sense which does not paralyze but assures a calm and a detachment, permitting an absolute and "pure" engagement in life—in certain cases up to extreme and typical forms of heroism and sacrifice, which for the greater part of the Occidentals are almost inconceivable (consider the case of the Kamikazé in the last World War[233]).

---

231 An ancient Chinese philosopher (the name literally means "Old Master") of the 6th century, who is reputed to be the author of the *Tao Te Chung*.

232 The Japanese Samurai were a warrior caste of Japan which emerged around 700 and declined in the 1800's. They took on many forms over the centuries of their existence, in some cases being a formal part of the Japanese military and even government, and in other cases playing a more mercenary-like role. In many of their manifestations they were renowned for their discipline and training, and they kept themselves to a strict code of honor.

233 The Kamikazé (Japanese: "divine wind") were Japanese aviators during the war who would take their own lives by attempting to fly their airplanes into enemy vessels. Many of the Kamikazé fighters were steeped in military codes of honor along the lines of the Samurai, in which Zen Buddhism was a prevalent current of thought.

What Jung[234] says is a joke—namely that, more than any other current of the West, psychoanalysis is that which can understand Zen. According to him, the Satori would result in same wholeness, devoid of complexes and scissions, at which psychoanalytic treatment presumes to arrive when it removes the obstructions of the intellect and its pretensions to supremacy, and reunites the conscious part of the soul with the unconscious and with "Life." Jung is unaware that in Zen, both its method and also its presuppositions stand opposite his own: the "unconscious" does not exist as an entity in itself, to which the conscious must open itself, but we are speaking rather of a *super-conscious* vision (enlightenment, the *bodhi* or "awakening") which carries in its act the luminous "originating nature," and with this *destroys* the unconscious. Nonetheless one can keep to a feeling of "totality" and liberty of being which manifests itself in every act of existence. It is important however to specify the level to which one refers.

In point of fact, tendencies have arisen, especially in its exportation amongst us, to "domesticate" or moralize Zen, veiling in it, even within the sphere of simple conduct of life, the possible radicalist and "antinomistic" consequences (=of antithesis to the ruling norms) and insisting instead on the obligatory ingredients of the "spiritualists," on love and on service to one's neighbor, be they ever so purified in an impersonal or a-sentimental form. In general, no doubts can arise as to the "practicability" of Zen, in relation to the fact that the "doctrine of awakening" has an essentially initiatory character. Thus it cannot ever pertain to anything but a minority, as opposed to late Buddhism, which took the form of a religion open to everyone, or else of a code of simple morality. Zen ought to have constrained itself to esotericism in its reestablishment of the spirit of originating Buddhism.

---

234 Carl Jung (1875-1961) was a Swiss psychiatrist, and one of the most influential writers of psychiatry.

In part, it has succeeded in this: it suffices to consider the legend of its origins. However we see that Suzuki himself was inclined to present things in a different way, and that he has valorized those aspects of Mahâyâna which "democratize" Buddhism (after all, the denomination "Mahâyâna" has been interpreted as the "Great Vehicle" also in the sense that it would be adapted by wide circles, not by the few). If one is to follow it, certain perplexities on the nature and the scope of Satori itself would arise; it would be necessary to ask oneself if such an experience regards simply the psychological, moral or mental domain, or if it invests also the ontological domain, as is the case for every authentic initiation. However this last question car arise only for a very small number.

20. PERSPECTIVES ON THE BEYOND

As early as 1927 Oxford University Press published a Tibetan text, the *Bardo Tödol*, in an English translation edited by W.Y. Evans-Wentz and by the Lama Kazi Dawa Samdup. This text, to which was given the title *The Tibetan Book of the Dead*, immediately attracted the attention not only of historians of religion, but also of a considerably wider public.

This text was related by many to the Egyptian "Book of the Dead";[235] but, as we will immediately note, comparisons could also be made with ancient Occidental wisdom teachings.

Such texts offer somewhat perturbing perspectives to whomever is not a materialist, but who is yet familiar only with the Christian conceptions of the afterlife. The Christian conception has indeed a static and stereotypical character. Before all it postulates as a dogma an immortality attributed to any and every soul; thus it does not distinguish between a possible simple and precarious survival on the one hand and a true immortality on the other. In the second place, Christianity considers the beyond as an almost automatic process, meaning that the passage into the states called paradise, inferno and purgatory is determined only by the kind of life the individual leads on this earth, as judged in terms of religious morality. On the other hand, the beyond is presented in the texts just now cited in terms which are considerably

---

235 A collection of ancient Egyptian texts dedicated to helping the journey of the dead in the afterlife. They thus contain a number of religious and magical rites and incantations.

more dynamic and dramatic, with myriad alternatives and destinies which are not entirely predetermined.

Regarding certain of the fundamental themes already known also to pre-Christian Occidental antiquity, one can refer to what Plutarch relates in his tract *De facie in orbe lunae*.[236] He says here that there are two kinds of deaths. The first is the death which comes on earth and in the reign of Demeter; it is that in which the body decomposes and returns, as a cadaver, to Mother Earth, of which Demeter is the goddess. The spiritual-soul complex however survives such death, where "soul" is understood as the whole of the psychic, affective, instinctive faculties, with memories, impulses etc., while "spirit," on the other hand, is understood as the supernatural principle of the personality—principle which however so rarely emerges in ordinary life, that one might say the common man knows well enough about his "soul," but remains almost totally ignorant about his "spirit" in the eminent sense.

Now—continues Plutarch—this same complex dismembers in a phase subsequent to the death of the physical body, and this is the "second death," which does not occur on earth, but, symbolically, on the Moon, and in the sign of the goddess Proserpina. Then in its turn the soul detaches from the higher principle of being, and is reabsorbed into the vital cosmic substance, understood properly as that which is the inexhausted root of repullulating evanescent existences in the "circle of generation."

An exact correspondence can be noted here with the ancient traditional Hindu teaching, which speaks of the "two paths": two paths, because at this point an essential alternative presents itself, to which one may relate the sense both of the blessing, "May you escape

236 Plutarch (46-120) was a Greek writer best known for his *Parallel Lives*, a series of biographies of great men, paired off with each other to emphasize similarities or contrasts between them. His dialogue *De facie quae in orbe lunae apparet* (Latin: "On the Face which Appears in the Orb of the Moon") treats of cosmological matters, including spiritual and eschatological questions.

from the second death," as well as the curse, "May you die from the second death." The notion of the "second death" was known also in Ancient Egypt, from which an echo passed into the Old Testament. For the rest, the Jewish term corresponding to the Christian "hell," the "gehenna of fire,"[237] also designated the place where the refuse of a city was destroyed; it includes therefore the fundamental idea of a destruction (not of a place of punishment) and alludes moreover to the possible negative outcome of the events of the afterlife—to that case in which, after an intermediate ephemeral existence, after a more or less lengthy survival in the after life, nothing would remain of the personal conscious being upon the dissolution and the re-absorption of the "soul": this death would be an effective extinguishing. This—says Plutarch—is what becomes of those who were completely attached to the Earth, who identified all their being with materiality, with the life of the sensations, of the instincts and of the passions, without ever "awakening," without ever throwing their glance toward the heights. The classic conception of Hades, place wherein nothing survives but "shadows," can be brought back to an analogous order of ideas.

But for others the "second death" might signify the liberation or the possibility of liberation. Precisely the detachment of the soul (after the death of the physical body) becomes the condition for "going beyond," for an effective immortalizing transfiguration, for a "rebirth on high" in an integration of the "spirit." And Plutarch calls them "victors" to whom it is given to participate in this destiny; "the crown of the initiated and of the triumphant" belongs to them.

These perspectives on the beyond grow more complex if one compares the principle of the present chapter to the Oriental texts cited, and above all to the "Tibetan Book of the Dead," because they present yet more differentiated possibilities, which require for their determi-

---

237 Gehenna was also the place in the Hebrew Bible where the kings of Judah consigned their children to the flames (see Jeremiah 7:31 and 19:2-6).

nation given attitudes or given actions (or reactions) of the soul. They supersede everything which in a certain measure is automatic in the processes spoken of by Plutarch. If the Egyptian "Book of the Dead" keeps itself to an almost magical plane with the formulae and the incantations it furnished to the dead, almost as a viaticum,[238] so that they might abscond from the "second death," and subsist and reaffirm themselves in the afterlife, in the Tibetan teachings emphasis is rather given to the capacity to dissolve a phantasmagoria of apparitions and of visions which are only projections of the content of the deepest unconscious strata of one's being, and which are tied also to one or another cosmic potency. This capacity determines a variety of destinies. The highest possibility, that of a truly immortalizing liberation, corresponds to the moment in which the soul reveals itself after death as "pure Light" in its transcendence; everything depends on its being able to identify itself actively and intrepidly with that light. In the scheme related by Plutarch this would be equivalent to an integration of the "spirit" in its true origin, in the moment in which it is released from the "soul" complex or, better say, in which this complex abandons it, ceases to offer it a support, but ceases also to be its final constraint.

It is symptomatic that such a view (merely unusual to most), beyond eliciting a lively interest today in the field of spiritual studies, has found some who believe it susceptible also to practical experimental applications. This is demonstrated by a book which has been issued already in four editions by the University Press of New York, a book entitled *The Psychadelic Experience* and subtitled "A Manual Based on the Tibetan Book of the Dead." The authors—T. Leary, R. Metzner and R. Albert—believe that the interpretation of the Tibetan text as a compendium of teachings exclusively regarding states and actions of the afterlife, is one-sided and little "profound." They believe this text

---

238 The viaticum (Latin: "provisions for a journey") is the Catholic administration of the final communion to the dying.

might have value also for the living, toward the attainment of the same ends. It should be recalled how from antiquity on the correspondence between the provocative states of death and those which are traversed through initiation and "initiatory death" has been recognized. From this issues an *ad hoc* interpretation of the Tibetan text, in a framework of "psychadelic" evocations—that is of projections of one's deepest being, which can be rendered possible above all with the aid of drugs. The problematic and adventurous character of such assumptions is clear. Moreover, it has also been the cause of a mishap for the first of the three authors of the book just cited, Professor Leary, who has been ousted from his teaching by the academic authorities for having encouraged his students in the use of LSD and other drugs, toward the ends hereabove mentioned.[239]

---

239 Timothy Leary (1920-1996) is most often remembered in connection to his controlled psychedelic experimentation. Leary was officially dismissed from Harvard for having missed a number of scheduled class lectures, but Leary himself denied these accusations, and it has been speculated that his encouragement of drug use amongst his students was the real motive for his dismissal.

21. THE TWIN FACE OF EPICUREANISM

The fortune enjoyed by the doctrine and the schools of Epicurus[240] in Rome is usually interpreted as a proof of the lack of elevation in Roman thought. Epicureanism is indeed conceived as synonymous with materialism, with atheism and with the glorification of pleasure. And this is just what was needed (so it is said) for decadent Rome, for idle patricians or for soldiers who, shorn of their arms, knew not how to interest themselves in anything higher. The distinctly anti-metaphysical and anti-speculative tendency of Ancient Rome is confirmed through Epicurus and his fervent Roman apostle, Lucretius. This opinion, taken up again in the very texts which make up the basis of the common education of the young, is in part one-sided, and in part false. A few brief considerations apropos this question will not be devoid of interest.

Let us commence by putting the meaning of the doctrine of Epicurus itself into the right light. This doctrine is composed of a physics and an ethics, the one in strict dependency with the other. "Physics" for Epicurus was meant as an introduction and propaedeutic

---

240 Epicurus (341-270 BCE) was one of the major Greek philosophers, remembered for his hedonistic philosophy. As Evola points out in this chapter, such a philosophy is open to many misinterpretations. Epicurus was a prolific writer but the vast majority of his work has been lost. His philosophy comes down to us in fragments and second-hand reports, and in its fullest expression in *De rerum natura* (*On the Nature of things*), the philosophical poem of his late-come Roman disciple Lucretius (99-55 BCE).

for ethics. That might seem strange, if one considers that the physics of Epicurus is neatly detached from previous metaphysical and religious interpretations of nature, while in its orientation it has diverse traits in common with modern physics. It wishes to explain both physical phenomena and also psychic phenomena through pure natural causes. It excludes every supernatural agent, and the soul itself is thus considered even as one considers a thing, with nothing mystical and romantic. The gods and providence are banished from the drama of things. The survival of the soul is disputed. One may therefore ask: how can such a conception have ethical value?

Epicurus responds: by virtue of that interior liberation, that brightening of vision which Epicureanism produces through its realism. Epicurus expresses without reticence his intention to destroy all anguish for death and for the beyond through his physics, to eliminate all the insane pathos of yearning, of hoping and of imploring which already in Greece corresponded to a period of decadence and to an alteration of the originating heroic, Olympian spirituality, and which unfortunately also in Rome would have the significance of an alteration of the ancient ethics and the ancient ritualism. The physics of Epicurus aims therefore at bringing man back to himself, at detaching him from disorderly imaginations, at training him to realism and at creating in him a calm interior. After which, a discipline of life might arise, the details of which cannot be examined here, but which in any case has little to do with the search for "pleasure" as it is today commonly meant—above all when one applies the epithet "Epicurean" to someone.

In this respect it would suffice already to note the similarity which the ethics of Epicurus has with the Stoic ethics[241] on many points, even

---

241 Stoicism was a Hellenistic philosophy which later had an important influence in Roman civilization. Its founder was an Athenian, Zeno (344-262 BCE), and it later counted a number of very important exponents, such as Seneca, Epictetus, and Marcus Aurelius. (See above note 182 to Chapter 15, note 65 to Chapter 8, and note 187 to Chapter 17, respectively.)

in its very terminology—for, as one knows, the Stoic ethics is one of the most severe. As with the Stoics, likewise in Epicurus one of the aims of interior disciple is "autarchy," that is self-sufficiency, the dominion of one's own soul, the withdrawal of oneself from the contingency of impressions, from the impulses, from irrational movements. Here Epicurus, as against the Stoics, speaks of "pleasure." He does not believe, as the Stoics do, in an arid "virtue" or in a cold rigidity before the human passions. He holds that an intimate happiness, an unalterable enjoyment, almost a calm joy-giving light, inheres in a soul which has arrived at possession of itself, state which nothing can perturb and before which every vulgar inclination for a fleeting happiness or voluptuousness reveals itself to be despicable. This is "positive" pleasure, which Epicurus poses as an end, distinguishing it from "negative" pleasure, that is, from pleasure which is to be realized by withdrawing oneself from every cause for agitation or suffering in body and soul. Epicurus considers this second pleasure only as a means, and only insofar as it does not obstruct the manifestation of the first. And he adds to this that whoever realizes the "pleasure" which Epicurus intends shall never fail in it, not even in front of the most atrocious torments, not even finding himself in the "Brazen Bull"—that is in the prison of bronze formed as a bull, within which the condemned man was made to die by slow fire. From which one sees how little authentic Epicureanism has to do with the vulgar concept one has made of it. True, Epicurus denies the gods as entities which intervene arbitrarily in the events of the world, or which are invoked in the small doings of the human soul, or, also, which serve only as bugbears for weak spirits—but he admits them in an ethical role, and, verily, precisely according to the ancient Hellenic Olympian conception: as detached, perfect, passionless essences, which to the Sage count as supreme ideals.

If Epicureanism incorporates such meanings in its better and essential aspects, its adoption by the Romans obviously presents itself in a much different light than that which is usually cast on it. In truth, owing to the fact that the many have a preconceived and partial idea about the "spiritual," they presume to measure everything by this idea, they are unable to see anything beyond it. Now, it should be kept in mind that if the Roman was originally anti-speculative and anti-mystical, he was not so on account of his inferiority, but rather at bottom on account of his superiority. That is, he possessed a congenital style of life which shunned pure mysticisms and sentimental effusions; he had a super-rational intuition of the sacred, strictly connected to norms of action, to rites and precise symbols, to a *mos* and a *fas*[242] and to a peculiar realism. He knew no evasions. He did not fear death. He possessed an immanent meaning in living. He ignored the frights of the afterlife. He conceived only of his masters and his divinized heroes as survivors of the eternal slumber of Hades. The subsequent speculative, pseudo-religious or aestheticizing forms which took hold in Rome through exotic or pre-Roman elements have, compared to all this, the significance of degeneration. It was for an instinctive reaction of the ancient Roman soul that Epicureanism was accepted. Epicureanism contained the seeds of a simplification and a liberation from the superfluous: physics as a clear and realistic vision of the world, ethics as an immanent discipline of life, thanks to which the good of an unalterable and omnipresent happiness emerges from measure, from autarchy, from tranquility of soul, almost as the anointment of a wholeness which, according to a saying of Epicurus himself, "renders one similar to the Olympians."

The fact that these seeds in part bore fruit and redirected the ancient Roman soul, in part degenerated on account of soil already adulterated—this fact is secondary. Here we want only to bring to light, as the true cause of the success of Epicureanism in Rome, a

---

242 *Mos*, Latin: "habit, custom, manner" (as in our English "mores"), considered exclusively in a human sense. *Fas*, also Latin: "divine law or will; that which is lawful or permitted."

certain correspondence of motifs, all related to something which was superior as much to every vulgar hedonism or materialism, as to every formless, agitated, and meandering mysticism.

22. FACES AND MUSH

One of the episodes which most characterize the spirit of Bolshevism[243] was the so-called Vavilov affair.[244] Professor Vavilov is a Russian biologist who wound up in Siberia, together with some colleagues—not for properly political reasons, but for the simple fact that he is an exponent of "genetic" theory. Geneticism is that current of biology which admits a preformation in man—that is, dispositions and characteristics which are congenitally man's (based on so-called "genes"), and which do not derive from external things.

This theory has been declared "counter-revolutionary." Marxism indeed would like everything in man to be the result of his environment, and, in particular, of economic-social forces and conditions. It is on the basis of such a view that communism seriously believes itself capable of giving life to a new human being, to collective proletarian

---

243 The Bolsheviks (from the Russian *bol'shinstvo*, "majority") were the original victorious communist faction which eventually rose to power in the wake of the Russian Revolution and transformed at last into the Communist Party of the Soviet Union.

244 In the original text, Evola erroneously provides the name "Vasilloff." Nikolai Vavilov (1887-1943) was an eminent Russian botanist and geneticist who dedicated his life to the study of plant improvement, and amassed the world's largest seed collection in the process. He made the error of critiquing the work of a fellow scientist, Trofim Lysenko, promoter of a non-Mendelian conception of genetics; the case was brought before Stalin, and Vavilov was sent to Siberia, where he starved to death in the space of three years.

man, who is freed "from the individualistic accidents of the bourgeois era." Such an assumption would be frustrated however if one had to admit that man has an interior form, that there exist *persons*[245] with a nature proper to them, with their own quality and, if you please, their own destiny, rather than being the atoms of a mass ready to undergo an external mechanical action and to produce, in consequence, any type of collective desired. A timely campaign, conducted by a biologist of Marxist orientation, Lysenko, therefore brought to light the dangerous germ of heresy which is contained in the theory of geneticism—even if it be simply anthropological—and professor Vavilov was forced down the road to Siberia, the place where one "reeducates" spirits in Russia today.

"Behaviorism," together with the views of Dewey, are among the theories most expressive of the North-American mentality.[246] "Behaviorism" has it that anyone may become whatever he wants, given only a congruous pedagogical and technical process. If a given person is what he is, if he has given gifts—if he is, let us say, a thinker, or an artist, or a statesman—this does not depend on his particular nature, and does not speak to any real difference. Anyone else can become as *he* is, only if such a one wants it and knows how to "train himself to it." This is, evidently, the truth of the self-made man,[247] who from the plane of practical success and of social climbing, proceeds to

---

245 Evola stresses this word, certainly so as to remind his readers of its etymology: it comes from the Latin *persona*, meaning "mask" or "face," thus leading us back to the alternative suggested by the title of this essay: either human beings with distinct faces, or the faceless formless mush-like mass.

246 Behaviorism is the psychological theory most often associated with B.F. Skinner (1904-1990), which holds that all human action, inner and outer, is reducible to simple mechanical response to environmental stimuli. It thus proposes that human behavior is inherently controllable and manipulable. John Dewey (1859-1952) was an American intellectual who is associated with pragmatism, liberalism, and education reform in the United States and abroad.

247 Evola uses the English "self-made man."

extend himself into every domain, thereby corroborating the egalitarian dogma of democracy. Indeed, if such a theory is true, one can no longer speak of real differences between human beings, of diversity of nature and of dignity. Anyone can presume to possess virtually everything that another is; the terms superior and inferior lose their significance; every sentiment of distance and of respect becomes unjustified; all roads open to everyone, and we really are in the regime of "liberty."

Thus we find ourselves before a fundamental viewpoint in which Bolshevism and Americanism meet in a significant way. Just as the Bolshevik-Marxist theory, the American expresses intolerance toward everything which has a character in man, an internal form, a quality which is its own and inimitable. A mechanistic conception is likewise counterposed to an organic conception: for whatever one can build up, commencing almost from nothing, cannot ever have anything other than a "constructed" character.

There is surely the appearance of activism and individualism in the American viewpoint which might lead one astray here. But practically speaking one sees the meaning of these things in the Americans themselves. They are the living confutation of the Cartesian axiom, "I think, therefore I am," because "they do not think, *and yet* they are."[248] Infantile, "natural" even as a vegetable is natural, the American psyche is perhaps yet more formless than the Slavic; it is open to every form of standardization, from that of the culture of *Reader's Digest*[249] to the varieties connected with conformism, to manipulated public

---

248 This devastating wordplay is on the most famous *Cogito ergo sum* (Latin: "I think therefore I am") of the extremely influential early modern French philosopher René Descartes (1596-1650). Descartes presumed in this little sentence to outline the first indisputable truth which he would subsequently use to build his entire philosophy.

249 The *Reader's Digest,* founded in 1920, is a "general-interest family magazine" which remains among the most popular and best-selling in the United States.

opinion, to advertising, to the *idée fixe* of democratic progress. It is on the basis of this background that the theory above mentioned must be understood. The counterpart of "I can be that which anyone is" and of pedagogy in its egalitarian function, is a qualitative regression: man becomes internally formless.

This formless man, however, is that which both communism and also Americanism want—leaving aside the differences of these two, which do not touch on the essential. The two views of which we have spoken have both a symbolic value as well as an aggressive efficacy. They are the trenchant contradiction of the traditional ideal of the personality, and they strike at those foundations which the man of today could still use as defense and reaction against the chaos of his civilization.

In fact, in an epoch wherein not only the idols have collapsed, but also many ideas and many values have been prejudged by rhetoric and by an internal insincerity, only a single way remains open: to seek within oneself that order and that law, which outside oneself have been rendered problematic. But this means also: to be able to rediscover in oneself a form and a truth, and to impose it on oneself, to realize it. "Know oneself *to be oneself*"—this was already the watchword of classical civilization.[250] "That our thoughts and our actions are our own, and that the actions of everyone belong to him"—so wrote Plotinus, and from the Roman-Germanic world up to Nietzsche the ideal of

---

250 "Know thyself," γνῶθι σεαυτόν, was one of the maxims inscribed in the forecourt of the Apollonian Temple of Delphi. "Become yourself," imperative later taken up by Nietzsche (see *Gay Science*, section 270, and also the subtitle of *Ecce Homo*), traces its origins to the Greek poet Pindar (c. 522-c. 443), who wrote in his Second Pythian Ode, line 72: "Become what you are, having learned what that is" (γένοι' οἷος ἐσσὶ μαθών). It is probable that Evola's "*conoscer se stessi per essere se stessi*" is taken directly from Pindar's Ode. For the reference that Evola subsequently makes to Plotinus, see Plotinus' *Third Ennead*, section 4.

an internal form, of fidelity to that which one is, was maintained, in opposition to every disorderly tendency.

Does all of this fall perhaps only within the domain of individual ethics? We would not say so. If we search for the prime causes of the present disorder, departing from those raging in the economic-social field so far as to preclude almost any possibility of healthy equilibrium, we find these causes in a mass betrayal of the traditional ideal. One does not know and one does not want to know any longer what one is; therefore neither the place which suits one in the whole, the fixed framework within which one might, without letting oneself be distracted, develop one's being and one's possibilities and realize one's own perfection, such as to truly confer a sense and an interiority to one's own life and to actuate at the same time one's corresponding part in a hierarchically ordered world. Is it not perhaps even along this road that the "economic era" has been determined on the one hand by the paroxysm of the most unrestrained capitalism, and on the other hand by a livid hatred for class? Is it not perhaps thus that we have arrived at a world composed predominately of maniacs and sociopaths, where not "being," but arriving at this or that position, is important?

But if matters stand in this way today—and little though one might wish to reflect on it, one cannot fail to recognize it—is it not then perhaps deception and self-deception to place one's hope in the power of some system or other, before one initiates a detoxification and a rectification of one's own internal sphere of attitudes, of interests, and sense of life?

Certainly, this by now cannot be demanded from the many, nor all at once. Orienting the best, however, is always possible. It is possible to demonstrate that at that point wherein one no longer has a proper way, wherein one cedes rather to the fascination of external forms of growth, of affirmation and of production—at that point one opens oneself to the forces which make the Marxist and democratic doctrines true, even on the biological plane. One thus validates the

Marxist work of atoms, of mass and of mush rather than of men and of faces. Everyone must decide this on his own: whether to arrest himself, to rediscover the basis for a right force in his proper mode of being and in his *proper* equilibrium, or else—even while believing he is doing quite the contrary—to give a new lure to a collectivizing process which flares up nowadays every which place. But this decision is also requisite, if one's ideas and efforts in these political struggles might acquire a real basis, a form and a prestige—so that the structures might finally be determined which ought to exist between men and masters of men.

23. DOES THE WEST HAVE ITS OWN IDEA?

The problem connected with the question, "Does the West have its own idea?" is verily fundamental for our entire civilization. It would be presumptuous to seek to scrutinize it in depth in a brief essay. Here we will fix only a number of essential points of reference, and we will do this through the examination of a writing which bears precisely this title (*Hat der Westen eine Idee?*), by the author Walter Heinrich.[251]

Heinrich is one of the principle living traditionalist writers, to whom we owe various works of sociology, history of religions and critique of the times. His ideas draw on those of the school of the Austrian philosopher Othmar Spann,[252] known advocate of an organic and anti-individualistic conception, which he has formulated in myriad fields. What Heinrich says in his brief but dense work touches the essence of the argument, and goes beyond the commonplaces and the easy formulae of the better part of those who write on it.

Heinrich frames the question in the following terms: that world, not yet well united, which is counterposed to the "Orient" on the plane of political forces, cannot hope for success if it does not know how to make itself in the image of its own true and specific idea, if it does not

---

251 Walter Heinrich (1902-1984) was a German sociologist and the writer of many books, none of which has been translated into English. Given Evola's high praise of him here, this is particularly regrettable. He was the pupil of Othmar Spann (see next note).

252 Spann (1878-1950) was an Austrian economist and sociologist known for his conservative ideas.

know how to seriously adopt that idea—and not merely discourse on it—and to follow it faithfully in the effort of realizing it.

The Western world, whatever possible superiority it might secure, especially in the technologico-industrial sphere, will not be able to hold its ground in the face of the Orient without such an idea. To be sure, a principle of defensive super-statist economico-military organization exists amongst the Western nations, under the sign of Atlanticism.[253] But this incipient order has a merely exterior and formal character, it lacks the counterpart of an idea. If one speaks here of order and of liberty, one does not say for what this order and this liberty in the end ought to serve; and when one speaks of the value of man, one does not indicate in what not merely material framework this value should be defined.

Heinrich is associated with another writer, A. von Schelting,[254] who, following the same order of ideas, has concluded by saying that if the world of the "West" does not know how to regain its historical idea, or what might be called the eternal spiritual content of Europe—if in the nations of Europe such an idea does not reawaken sufficiently to unite them under its sign, without confounding them—then it will not long be able to maintain its due place in history, or even to defend its own existence.

Another important point has been highlighted by H. Freyer,[255] who notes that today Europe no longer has to protect itself from foreign invasions, as it did in the time of the Persians, the Cathaginians, the Saracens and the Tartars, but against degraded derivations of its own

---

253 A term signifying the close economic, military, or diplomatic ties between Europe, Canada, and the United States, either for the purposes of mutual defense or for the goal of "prosperity."

254 Alexander von Schelting (1894-1963), a German sociologist.

255 Hans Freyer (1887-1969), German sociologist of conservative bent, and the author of various works in that spirit.

civilization, namely Russia and America. We find ourselves surrounded by external enemies, only because there exists a second internal enemy.

The same idea was expressed, already some time ago, by Franscesco Coppola, on occasion of the Volta Conference,[256] when he spoke of the "bad conscience of Europe": on the brink of betraying itself, Europe took responsibility for the creation of those ideologies and those forms of life which today constitute the gravest of its menaces, insofar as they are absorbed and developed to the hilt by non-European powers. This menace is all the greater precisely because Europe continues to import into itself the germs of the same evil. Heinrich sees these matters no differently. He observes, however, and rightly, that it is perhaps a good thing that the internal enemy is, so to speak, objectivized and macroscopized into an external enemy, because otherwise, there might have been the danger of not recognizing it internally, of not being able therefore to take a stance in the face of it.

Once all of this has been clarified, the problem that naturally presents itself is to identify the point of the fracture—the point, that is, in which the deviation commenced within Europe itself. This would require an ample historical examination, of which Heinrich wished to indicate only the most essential terms.

According to Heinrich, the European idea corresponded to an organic order, that of a civilization and of a society articulated in particular bodies or unities which were well differentiated and hierarchical, and to which the single individual pertained in a living and direct way. The whole maintained transcendental references, because there was a varied connection between temporal reality and the spiritual, the sacred, the

---

256 Coppola (1878-1957) was a prominent Italian journalist and politician, and an unrepentant supporter of Mussolini's fascism. The Volta Conferences were a series of four international conferences held in Rome by the Royal Academy of science, which took as its point of departure various themes in the humanities and the sciences. The Conference here referenced was the second; its theme was precisely the question of Europe. A number of fascists took part. Evola mentions this event also in Chapter 16 of *Men Among the Ruins*.

super-mundane, in the positive forms of a grand tradition which was singular in essence, but rich and multicolored in its diverse expressions.

Heinrich holds that the point of crisis of the European idea manifested itself when this organic order entered into crisis, and the simple individual was brought ever more to the foreground, divorced from his connections to the particular and well-differentiated unities in which he carried out his life and his activities. This is the dissolving principle of individualism in its broadest sense: individualism which, in the end, would give birth, against itself, to its opposite. As the regime of particular unities has ceased, a new power had to take form, the so-called *modern State*, which knows only the amorphous and more or less leveled mass of the *citizens*. It seeks to keep these together and to control them with a centralized apparatus based on public powers, on bureaucracy, on the regime of the police and so forth, up to the ultimate rigid, soulless and hypertrophic forms of statolatry[257] and totalitarianism. The so-called *national States*—as Heinrich justly observes—have precisely this historical origin, and arose in the course of the dissolving process in the previous organic system. And the concept of *nationalistic sovereignty* is the exact counterpart on the international plane of the individualistic principle within a State: through it one negates every

---

257 Meaning "worship of the state." This term has an interesting heritage, coming, as it does, from a work (*Doctrine of Fascism*) by none other than the "philosopher of fascism" himself, Giovanni Gentile (see note 6 to Chapter 1 above and the entirety of Chapter 34 below). Evola's derogatory use of the word here is enlightening for his critique of Gentile and the various Gentilian currents within fascism.

higher idea which is apt to bring about a sensible order, an organic unity of diverse peoples, in what might call itself a European ecumene.[258]

Materialism runs parallel to this negation of everything which transcends the particular—an anti-metaphysical vision of existence, negator of every higher interest, every spiritual form of authority, every sensibility for what transcends concrete reality and the reign of material realizations.

Along this road Europe has betrayed itself, and through a specific dialectic its dismembering individualism has produced precisely those currents—"social" in their mitigated form, collectivist and communistic in their radical forms—which, as we have noted, characterize the world powers of today. And these are the same powers which on the international plane most menace Europe and whatever remains in Europe of a healthy and normal order.

It would be difficult to contest the justice of these ideas. We ourselves have had many occasions to emphasize such things, observing how nothing serious can be achieved if we stop ourselves halfway, taking up as remedy principles and ideologies which present the same evil, only in a more diluted and less visible form. This is also the illusion of those who let themselves be seduced by certain feeble ideological appendices of Atlanticism—that is of those democratic and liberal principles which, genetically and historically, are derived precisely from individualism, and which despite all their talk of values of personality and of "humanity" really take as their unique background a materialistic, empirical and pragmatic vision of existence.

---

258 From Ancient Greek οἰκουμένη, meaning "the entirety of the inhabited world," the same origin of our word "ecumenical." The idea of a European ecumene would then be a "European Union" which consists, however, not of a single undifferentiated people, but of various related groups, nations, communities, societies, etc.; precisely as the "inhabited world" is identified by the presence of human beings in various nations, not by their perfect uniformity or by any shared and overarching political structure.

On this plane, the "West" is effectively devoid of any idea what-soever worthy of the name—any idea capable of making appeal to something super-individual, capable of truly animating and uniting its parts beyond every petty interest and beyond the simple physical fear of worse things to come. Heinrich is also right when he, citing Caneval,[259] speaks of the difference in collective climate between the "Orient" and the "Occident": the practical materialism of the "Occident" brings us, he says, to a condition of inferiority, by way of its individualistic, hedonistic, and bourgeois aspects. On the other hand, the ideological materialism proper to Marxism and to communism has the character—even if it be distorted—of an idea or a super-individual ideal; and Moscow has the sinister power of deploying fanaticism and dedication for any aim whatever, to a degree which no democracy of the Occidental, liberal or social type, is capable of attaining.

Having clarified all this, the way toward a theoretical European reintegration would appear clear enough: in every sphere, including that of the economy, one must carry oneself beyond the regime both of individualism, as well as of the amorphous and collectivized mass. So far as the ideas of Heinrich go, certain reservations should be expressed about one point in particular: Heinrich, following Spann, proposes the principle that man can be a person only in function of a given collective or community, understood as a preexisting reality, anterior and superior to him. This is a dangerous idea, which might lead the organic conception to end in naturalism, thereby furnishing a justification for collectivizing forms. The human persona should be considered as the primary element in being, formed in itself. That which can carry it beyond itself into a vaster order and into a unity of action can only be an idea freely chosen, not the binding obligations of a given community. It is in these terms—that is in the terms of an essential internal liberty—that we must understand the fundamental

---

259 I have been unable to find information on anyone of this surname.

exigencies formulated by Heinrich for a reaction against the current practical materialism: namely, that the profession makes itself vocation, economy becomes service, property has that conditioned functionality which in other times was connected to the idea of the fief.

More, Heinrich proposes four principles as the basis for a "conservative revolution" in the sign of the European idea. Above all, a non-individualistic liberty, obedient to an internal law. In the second place, an organic order with a large margin of decentralization and of partial autonomy, so as to favor the formation of new intermediate unities capable of rearticulating whatever has adopted atomistic, leveling and mechanical characteristics in modern society. In the third place, full reestablishment of the personality in all its directive functions, with a recovery of the principle of true authority and of direct responsibility. Finally, and, indeed, as background to all the rest, an interior steadfastness, an indestructibility, and the elimination of every fear with regard to the world surrounding—disposition which can be expected from a reconnection of the person with the super-mundane reality, and with that which in the most severe, virile and positive terms might be called spirituality.

It is on this basis that, according to Heinrich, one can speak of an idea of the "West." It will be the task of the living European forces to work in such a direction. There is little to object to in all of this, and one can recognize the opportunity which such ideas bring into relief. Heinrich has succeeded in gathering about himself a group of valid individuals who keep themselves to their posts by conducting what is in many respects an interesting activity. However, so far as the present practical possibilities go, one should not tarry in optimism.

Since the European collapse which concluded the Second World War, no important foundation can be found upon which one can leverage any important modifications of the general situation. Politically, the game of garrulous democracy continues in Europe, and it is capable only of creating the unstable forms of a badly organized disorder.

And in Italy, this democracy cedes ever more ground to the pressure of the left, due to the pusillanimity, the irresponsibility, and the insipidity of the rulers.

What might come from the French experiment is not yet clear. Western Germany, it is true, has been able to regain its feet economically and materially, but its fall in tension and spiritual level, its intolerance for any idea worthy of the name, its indiscriminate flinging of its entire most recent past into the sea, are worrying symptoms.

From England it is difficult to expect a European conscience today, given that in all its history it has acted in the opposite direction, in obedience to its own merest profit. Spain's sphere of influence is quite limited. In general, practical Americanization is in full gallop in all the European West, with deleterious and often irreversible effects, as the counterpart of its not irrelevant financial and military gravitation around the United States.

In the end the monarchies have passed away, or have lost their prestige, and even from the predominant religion in the West one can scarcely expect a decided counter-current stance, as in other times it was able to offer valid elements to the organic and hierarchical European idea.

Thus one must not fail to recognize the great distance standing between the exigencies for which Heinrich has acted as spokesman (which it is difficult not to perceive), and any practical possibility for an efficacious action, beyond whatever might come from small groups. This is not to deny that it is good that there exist today some who maintain a precise consciousness of higher tasks, who do that which is given to them to do, acting from freedom of spirit and impersonality, and who do not expect immediate and tangible effects from everything they do.

24. AT THE "WALL OF TIME"

Ernst Jünger[260] is considered one of the greatest living German writers, and in Italy several of his works have already been published by some of what are considered our foremost editors (*On the Marble Cliffs* by Mondadori, *Gardens and Streets*[261] by Bombiani, *Radiations*[262] by Longanesi). He has elicited interest here, however, above all well-known cliques of literary critics and dilettante intellectuals, who have in view those aspects of Jünger's works which remain within their horizons and which accord with their tastes—aspects which for us are rather less relevant.

For some time, it has not been the literary Jünger to attract our attention—the essayist, the writer of a refined and exceptionally personal style—but rather the author of the early works, which reflect directly on the experiences he lived at the front during the War. Jünger had just finished middle school when, for his intolerance of the bourgeois and stagnant climate of the ambient in which he lived, he fled his

---

260 Ernst Jünger (1895-1998) was a German soldier and writer. Few of his many books have been translated in English; in all references which follow, if the book has not been translated, I provide the original German title in footnote. The present chapter contains many relevant details of Jünger's life.

261 *Gärten und Straßen*, 1942.

262 *Strahlungen*, 1949.

paternal home to enter the Foreign Legion.[263] When the First World War erupted, he voluntarily enlisted; he was injured various times and earned the highest decorations of valor. His books of this early period treat of the war. One might call Jünger the "anti-Remarque":[264] in contrast to the defeatist and pacifist literature of the first post-war period, he emphasized the spiritual, nay, the transcendental dimensions which the war might present to these technologized modern forms most destructive for a determinate human type.

After the books of war comes the work which for us remains this author's most important, *The Worker—His Figure, his Sovereignty*.[265] This work produced a vast echo, and it is really fundamental for the problem of the vision and the sense of life in the modern epoch. We will give an overview of its content: only an overview, because we have published a book on it, to which we will redirect the reader. That work of ours substitutes a translation of the book (which was for various reasons found to be impossible).

There is a continuity between Jünger's books of war and *The Worker*, in the following way: in modern war man must challenge not so much other men (the enemy) as the unleashing of technology (the "battles of materiel," the "mechanized death") and with it the destruc-

---

263 The French Foreign Legion was founded in 1831. It is an official part of the French military, but as its name suggests it recruits individuals from other countries than France. Those who enlist can do so under pseudonyms, thus historically rendering the Legion a magnet for individuals with criminal or troubled backgrounds. It presently has about 7,700 men in its regiments.

264 Erich Maria Remarque (1898-1970) was a German novelist best known for his novel *All Quiet on the Western Front*. In that book as well as in others that he wrote, Remarque penned descriptions of war in its harshness and terror, and for this he is often taken to be a spokesperson for the pacifist cause.

265 German title: *Der Arbeiter. Herrschaft und Gestalt*. This work has been translated into English by Greg Johnson. Evola dedicated a book to the analysis of the idea of the Worker, *L'Operaio nel pensiero di Ernst Juenger* (*The Worker in the Thought of Ernst Jünger*, 1960; yet to be translated into English).

tive forces of a non-human, "elemental" character (the "emergence of the elemental," just as the forces of nature are "elemental"). Whoever can keep his feet, whoever can survive not only physically but above all spiritually in these events into which he has been flung, will be a new human type, one which knows how to leave behind himself everything tied to his particular person and his own instincts, his way of thinking and of acting, his "idealisms" and the values of bourgeois life. He will be a type capable of an absolute and impersonal effort, of love of action for itself; a type lucid and cold and, at the same time, ready for an elemental leap—such a one as knows in the end how to foresee and seize a higher meaning in existence in the marriage between life and danger, between life and destruction. Jünger believed he had observed the incipient appearance of a kind of new humanity, almost a new race, recognizable even in its very physical traits, in those who were not broken by the experience of modern war, who were, internally, its conquerors, quite beyond the opposition of fronts and ideologies, quite beyond the outcome of the war.

The *Worker* develops analogous motifs in relation to the general climate of the latest civilization. The choice of the term "worker" is an unhappy one. As Jünger conceives him, the "Worker" does not correspond to a social class. He is a new human type capable of actively adapting himself to everything in the modern world which, from the point of view of the previous civilization, has a destructive character. Not only in war but also in peace the forces which man has set into motion through technology and mechanization turn against him. They destroy the ancient orders and the ancient values, and above all that which the bourgeois epoch had sought to create through its conception of "society," with the cult of the individual, of reason, of "humanity." All of this has entered into crisis due to the appearance, here too, of "elemental" forces in mechanical forms, in general objective processes, in a "total mobilization" of existence. Just as in war, it is not given to modern man to withdraw from modernity. The same alternative is posed to him: to be destroyed—not physically but internally (modern nihilism, "the death of God," materialization, leveling, regime of the masses)—or else to transform himself, to become a new being.

Jünger's "Worker" is a symbol and corresponds to this new type. Technology is the instrument with which he "mobilizes" the world, awakens, activates, and dominates elemental forces. He confronts all the processes which seem to entail a mortal impoverishment, a discouragement of the entirety of existence, through their striking of the individual, through the destruction of all that subsists of the bourgeois, traditional "museum" world, through dissolving the ancient social nexuses and the ancient habits, through the ever greater abolition of all color, variety, particularity, subjectivity, through emphasis rather on the mechanic, the mathematical, the objective. The "Worker" adopts all this toward the end, so to speak, of an essentialization or a purification ("the way of the salamander,[266] which passes through the flame"). It is an existential challenge which puts him to the test and which, if the test is overcome, carries him to affirm himself in a new dimension of being.

And also in this sphere Jünger believes he is harbinger of a new type, with uniform recognizable characteristics which are even physical. This type is marked by impersonality, by lucid, active adaptation toward his ends, by contempt for all that which is merely individual, by the total severance from values of the past, by the natural disposition to command and to obedience, to a "heroic realism," to a new posi-

---

266 According to numerous legends of antiquity, salamanders were gifted the power to pass unscathed through the flames. Pliny reduces this to the cold, humid quality of the salamander's skin. The idea persisted throughout the Renaissance: Leonardo da Vinci ascribes the same qualities to salamanders, and Benvenuto Cellini, the sculptor of the magnificent *Perseus* in Florence, reports seeing a salamander crawl out of the flames in his fireplace as a boy (see his extremely diverting *Autobiography*, Chapter IV).

tive anonymity (symbol of the "unknown soldier,"[267] to be integrated however with that of the "unknown captain"). Jünger here had spoken of a style which might call itself as much "Spartan" as "Prussian" or "Bolshevik" (with reference to the "ascetic" type of early communism). He had foreseen new hierarchies establishing themselves *de facto*, essentially with the differentiation of those who undergo the processes of intrinsic dissolution in a transitory phase and who still engage these in an active way. In particular (and this is interesting) he spoke of a "metaphysics" closed within the mechanized world. In the supreme grades of the new hierarchy the "Worker" would incarnate such metaphysics in the form of a new existential unity, beyond the antitheses of blood and spirit, of power and right, of liberty and necessity, of servitude and command. On such a basis, the ideal of the Orders was proposed once again, as those differentiated unities of life from out of which a severe discipline might impress precise forms on the being and the action of the single individual. The new State, the state of the "Worker," would base itself upon a number of such Orders. Finally, beyond the phase of transition—the dynamic, revolutionary and destructive phase of a world mobilized and transformed by technology—Jünger foresaw a "classic" phase, so to speak, with finished and stable symbolic forms, almost like the impersonal and sacral civilizations of the origins, but now with planetary extension. For even as technology irresistibly embraces all the world and stops at no frontier, so no final stage can be conceived except as a likewise global system, in which the figure and the sovereignty of the "Worker" would be affirmed, after possible final collisions between the antagonistic power blocs.

---

267 Reference to the practice in many countries of establishing a "tomb of the unknown soldier," in commemoration of those who have fallen in war without being identified. The same tomb can serve as a symbol of the soldier as such in his quality as soldier—his impersonal dedication to a cause, his discipline and obedience, his willingness to die for his country. The suggestion here is that a similar ethic might come to apply as well to the captain, or the commander.

In synthesis (and for the rest we must redirect the reader to our book on the Worker) these were the views of the *The Worker*. They exerted a noteworthy influence on the nationalistic and combative German currents of the first postwar period and anticipated several essential orientations of the corresponding revolution, and subsequently of national socialism. Except that precisely at the advent of this regime, Jünger underwent a sudden change of orientation and of level. It seems that in national socialism he had detected a species of distortion or of *reductio ad absurdum* for various positions of *The Worker*. Personally, he withdrew (when he was called back to the Second World War, he did not particularly distinguish himself). As a writer, his new production, when it did not have a character of simple literature or of compendia (notes, psychological observations, essays, the futuristic fantastical novel *Heliopolis*[268]—also, at a higher level and with a symbolic content, *On the Marble Cliffs*), he demonstrated a perceptible spiritual shattering. This accounts above all for certain minor writings of ideological pretensions, such as *The Peace, The Gordian Knot*[269] and *The Forest Passage*. One would almost say that, as had happened to not a few of his compatriots, the defeat provoked a shock in him and surprisingly opened him even to motivations related to that "democratic," or at least "humanistic," reeducation which was conducted in Germany in the new postwar period. This was in open contrast to those motivations he formerly had defended in the precedent period. Let it suffice to say that while he had coined the watchword of attack rather than defense, and also that of challenging the "elemental," *The Forest Passage* in the French edition was defined as a kind of manual "for the man of resistance," to whom are indicated the means for concealing himself and withdrawing himself from the era of "totalitarianism." Also *The Gordian Knot*, which treats supposedly of the relations between "European" ideals

---

268 *Heliopolis. Rückblick auf eine Stadt*, 1949.

269 The Peace: *Der Friede. Ein Wort an die Jugend Europas und an die Jugend der Welt* (1945). The Gordian Knot: *Der gordische Knoten* (1953).

and the "Orient," betrays in more than a single respect the political watchwords of the new German climate.

Jünger's new book, *At the Wall of Time* (*An der Zeitmauer*, Glett-Verlag, Stuttgart, 1959), signals anew a change of direction and brings one back in a certain measure to the field of problems treated in *The Worker*. Spiritually, with respect to the production just now mentioned, it represents therefore a re-elevation. From an objective point of view, however, it does not add much to whatever was valid in his previous positions, which was the most interesting part of his first period. The treatment is not systematic; and instead of deepening the analysis of the immanent problems of interior formation and of the super-ordered meanings of existence in the "era of the Worker," it carries us in large part into a different sphere, that of eschatology and of the metaphysics of history.

Now, when one wishes to enter such a sphere, one can no longer proceed through personal intuitions, but one must take one's bearings precisely from traditional teachings, as for example René Guénon and his school have done, and as we ourselves have sought to do. Such references are lacking in Jünger; he goes it alone, or else he takes his bearings by the current culture, from which he picks out the right things here and there, almost by accident, and intermixes them with many tangents and much dross.

The expression "wall of time" is to be taken in an analogous sense to the "sound barrier": a limit, whose surpassing is followed by new forms of movement. The confused sensation of a world about to end is analogously taken as a limit to be overcome. There is a certain reference to the "civilization of the Worker," which is now presented as a "cosmic civilization," insofar as man's forces within it begin to profoundly affect the substrate of reality and of nature, and to activate this substrate (the atomic era, new horizons for technology). Moreover, according to Jünger, something will begin to move even in the foundation of the universe, over and above the foundation of man, almost as the painful and presently destructive gestation of a new reality. The ideas of the *Worker* return as presentiments of certain "metaphysical" potencies behind the façade of this entire modern mechanized and disanimated world. And all the sufferings, the crises, the sacrifices of the latest humanity (in "greater number than those that Moloch[270] ever demanded, in greater number than the victims ever reaped by the Inquisition") will be obscurely ordered in this new era, somewhere beyond the "wall of time."

In all frankness, it would be fitting to speak here of a certain kind of "historical epoch," rather than of "time." Indeed Jünger commences from the observation, which is in itself correct (beyond writers of the "traditional" school and in ethnology itself, this observation can be found already in Schelling[271]), that what is habitually called the period of prehistory, or "mythic" time (to be clear, the time before Herodotus[272]), does not correspond to a simple portion of that "historical time" which we know, but rather to a different time, to a different spiritual, human, and existential clime, unknown to us. After this, the "historical epoch" in the proper sense arose as a cycle which, with all its values, its institutions, and its ideas, is about to be exhausted: whence the feeling of the "wall of time," beyond which, as beyond a hiatus or a "solution of continuity," powers and processes will begin again to act which are not simply human, but in a certain sense are "metaphysical," even as they were in the "mythical" age (the "trans-historical world"). We cannot

---

270 A Canaanite god associated with human sacrifice. He is referenced several times in the Hebrew Bible (see 2 Kings 23:10 and Isaiah 57:5-9).

271 For Schelling, see note 15 to Chapter 1 above.

272 Herodotus (c. 484-c. 425 BCE) was a Greek historian of such importance that Cicero called him the Father of History. The name has rightly stuck. His wide-ranging *Histories* (Greek ἱστορία, meaning an investigation or an inquiry) were perhaps not the first of their kind, but certainly the first major work in the direction of history as we understand it today, and it is no accident that we take the word itself from Herodotus' title.

linger here on such ideas, which belong to a special field. It is important for Jünger however that that boundary be actively superseded. Here an alternative arises, analogous to that already considered in other fields, for the war, for the world of the "Worker." Beyond that boundary, come what may, some men at least must salvage "human freedom."

Before Jünger's new book came out, in our examination of *The Worker* we had already indicated the necessity of considering two possible outcomes of the entire process of the last civilization, one positive, the other negative. Indeed, due to the emergence of the "elemental" and the entire technological, mechanical, discouraged world, which is the enemy of the individual and human, one can also conceive a negative, regressive, barbaric ("Ahrimanic"[273]) outcome—and in the same way, as we have seen, Jünger was able to match the new type to the Spartan type, the Prussian type, the "Bolshevik" type, in the name of a unique active and anti-personal realism. This was already significant. Also in his new book Jünger comes to recognize the danger of the negative outcome, which would lead toward "zoological, magical or titanic orders." This book is not lacking even in references to a possible catastrophe of planetary proportions, corresponding to our contemporaries' well-known anguish at the possibility of war—the counterpart of their euphoria at the atomic era, with its incipient "second industrial revolution," which is supposed to bring us every good and every happiness. But the prevalent tone of Jünger's book seems to be optimistic. We are made to understand that the nihilistic phase can be overcome. The dissolution and the leveling are compared to the whitewashing of a house which awaits new tenets. The void is recognized; one is made to think however that it is the void of a new form, like a mold, created by a higher force to be filled. The old motif reappears, as a species of faith, with reference to the type of the "Worker." Considering all that

---

273 That is, an outcome favoring Ahriman, the Zoroastrian anti-god. See note 144 of Chapter 13 above.

which has happened and which might yet happen, Jünger says, "From that fire, we see rising only the figure of the Worker, become mightier. We may therefore suppose that the most igneous elements are hidden in him, and that they have not yet had a pure fusion. There are yet many empty molds."

But with this one encounters also the essential problem, which cannot be resolved by means of mere imagery. Indeed, there are in fact two problems. Before all one must ask oneself if, beyond the bourgeois era and its subsequent nihilism, there will really come a climate of high tension (of "extreme temperatures") which characterizes the horizons of the world of the "Worker" and of "heroic realism": for such a world might even seem anachronistic and fanatical to many, given the ideals of a life which is safer, easier, more "social," in which science and technology are at the service of this duly bridled and normalized human animal. Such are the ideals today predominately cultivated in various parts of the world, especially in the democratic Occident and in consumer society. In the second place, even supposing that the world of the "Worker" should be formed, there is the problem of a necessary, essential internal mutation, capable of making Jünger's metaphysics something more than an empty word and an optimistic assumption—that "metaphysics" to which Jünger so often refers, as to the invisible counterpart and the justification of the world, and so also of the new type, or, at least, its superior exponents.

Jünger had already perceived both these lacunae as well as the problem itself when he compared the type of the "Worker" to a coin which on one side is strongly minted but on the reverse side is formless. And here, by hypothesis (that is, by the fact that the nihilism of the transitory phase excludes the contribution offered by values of the precedent tradition) everything remains at the fluid and problematic state; nothing external can indicate a direction and furnish a support. Jünger in his last book mentions two possibilities as regards the problem of "spiritualization" of the new type (spiritualization in a profound, ontological, existential sense, beyond all theories, morals and religious confessions) and so also for the whole new civilization and of the world controlled by the "Worker." The first is that everything will emerge from a cosmic process, which employs man as a means and as a collaborator armed with responsibility and a faculty of direction. But here one rests in the field of pure hypotheses, and it does not seem to us that such hypotheses today are confirmed by anything even remotely positive or tangible. The second possibility is that man himself will originate the initiative, that he with an ever more precise consciousness will penetrate ever deeper strata of reality, beyond the "historical" (one does not know precisely what Jünger here wishes to say), mobilizing and spiritualizing these strata. But this is evidently a vicious circle, because in order to spiritualize and transform these strata, it is necessary to commence from spiritualizing and transforming oneself. That is, "mutation" would be necessary ("mutation" here meant precisely in the biological and genetic sense, designating the rude and non-deducible origin of species and new forms). This mutation itself constitutes the problem. In this respect there is nothing in Jünger but vague and optimistic "cosmic" perspectives on a general process, which is attributed a meaning by his interpretation alone. Yet the center of gravity and the justification of the whole are connected precisely to this point.

Given the asystematic character of *At the Wall of Time* which we have already mentioned, it is not necessary here to develop a more detailed analysis of the book's contents. Through the references we have made, it is already possible to note how, from the time of the "Worker," the plane appears to have perceptibly moved toward a sphere wherein—let us repeat it—it is difficult to avoid wandering amidst merely personal ideas, unless one takes one's bearings by a firm traditional doctrine. Instead, Jünger has added almost nothing to the valid positions of his first book on the Worker, nothing which might be of interest to us. As we have said, this valid and important part is relevant to the problem of a new human type, kin to the unbroken man formed by selection in the Great War, which would be capable of overturning the most corrosive and nihilistic processes of the current technologized epoch (itself often brought out of new elemental forces), and of making them serve his spiritual formation—quite beyond the entire bourgeois world, but also beyond the discouraged and chaotic phase of transition. All of this toward the end of positive developments, the which however presuppose an internal mutation of the human substance, the possession of a spiritual core—spiritual because it is connected essentially with something transcendent (we express ourselves approximately, because otherwise our discourse here should become long indeed). In this connection we have often employed the formula and the symbol of "riding the tiger."[274]

---

274 See Evola's 1961 book *Ride the Tiger.*

25. POTENCY AND INFANTILISM

Werner Sombart is an author worthy of more study than he is generally afforded. One could draw from Sombart the example of a serious method of investigation into socio-economic phenomena which is distant from partiality and from the deformations of materialistic, and especially Marxist, sociology. For Sombart, economic life itself is composed of a body and a soul. There exists, that is, an *economic spirit* distinct from the forms of production, distribution and organization; this spirit varies so as to give direction, sense, and foundation to these forms, differing from case to case and epoch to epoch. His work on modern capitalism stands out among his writings as a classic; in this work, Sombart has brought into relief precisely the search for the spiritual factors of economic life, and the significance that these in the end have conferred on the West.

It is not our intent here to give a framework for such research. We will instead touch upon one particular point, emphasized by Sombart in a book which has been published also in Italian.[275]

We are speaking of the form that the economic process has assumed in the period of high capitalism; we are referring therefore essentially to America. This is a development which tends toward unlimited expansion, because every stopping up or slowing down

---

275 Evola works from Sombart's *Der Bourgeois* (1913), which is yet to be translated into English. The Latin quotation below ("let there be production, though man should perish") comes from the same work.

194

signifies falling behind or being crushed. The immediate and natural ends of the productive process become subordinate. *Fiat productio et pereat homo!* And this process, from which the capitalistic entrepreneur cannot any longer detach himself, seizes him soul and body; he comes to love it, to want it in and of itself, for it begins to constitute the very sense of his existence; he "does not have time" for anything else. We find here a type therefore which no longer even asks itself why it should be racing to infinity, why there should be such a febrile agitation of these chain-like structures which drag the masses along and dictate laws to global politics, and in which the masters are no freer than the last of their laborers. Such a situation in the end appears natural, evident. One believes that the prosperity of economic life, the progress of modern civilization itself, requires it.

Sombart holds however that such a state of things would never have been consolidated if certain internal factors in the current epoch had not gained the upper hand. These factors belong to the infantile psyche more than to that of a true man; for which the soul hidden by this entire process is, at bottom, nothing but a regression. He indicates the correspondences through certain characteristic points.

In the first place, Sombart speaks of the splendor exuded by all that which is great in the sense of material grandiosity, of the gigantic, of great quantity. The fascination that this exercises on the child is no different from that which it typically has also exerted on the great entrepreneurs of an Americanized economy. In general, the tendency, as Bryce[276] says, "to mistake bigness for greatness"—that is, to confound true, interior greatness, with external greatness—has become

---

276 Viscount James Bryce (1838-1922) was a British jurist and historian who worked as ambassador to the United States from 1907-1913. He was well-travelled in the United States, and he wrote a very thorough and influential three-volume work on American institutions entitled *The American Commonwealth*, from whose Third Volume (Chapter CX) the present quotation "to mistake bigness for greatness" is taken. Evola leaves this quotation in the original English.

the insignia of an entire civilization. The which is nothing if it is not primitivism.

In the last analysis, the very mania for records[277] in every field leads us back to the same point: it is the search for something which in tangible, measurable terms, that is in merely quantitative terms, beats something else, without regard for any other subtler factor or characteristic. At the same time this is, according to Sombart, one of the forms in which we can perceive another infantile characteristic— pleasure in the speed of things, from the spinning top to the carousel. This pleasure changes plane and proportion, but in intensifying and multiplying itself in the world of technology and in many other spheres of materialized modern life, it never loses its original puerile character.

In the third place, we must consider the love of novelty. As the child is immediately attracted to whatever presents itself as new, as he immediately abandons the toy he knows and is carried away by an- other, leaving halfway one thing when another attracts him, similarly modern man is attracted by novelty as such, by all that which has the character of something never before seen. The *sensation* reduces itself, in essence, to the impression that one feels in seeing a novelty. But precisely the avidity for this sensation is one of the most characteristic traits of the current epoch.

Finally comes, according to Sombart, the feeling of power, in situations which would be referred to by psychoanalysis as "overcompensation."[278] This is the joy, again basically puerile, which one experiences in feeling oneself superior to others on an entirely external plane. Our author quite justly remarks, "Analyzing this sentiment, one verifies that, at bottom, it is nothing other than an involuntary and unconscious confession of weakness: for the which it constitutes also

---

277 Evola puts "records" in English in the original.

278 In psychoanalysis, overcompensation refers to unconscious process by which a human being, to compensate for his own weaknesses and deficiencies, seeks out power, authority, or dominance.

one of the attributes of the infantile soul. A man who is truly great, naturally and internally, never attributes a special value to exterior power."

Sombart here considers a yet wider sphere, and his considerations are worth reporting. "A capitalistic entrepreneur," he says, "who commands ten thousand men and enjoys this power resembles a child, happy to see his dog obey his smallest gesture. And when it is no longer money or any exterior constraint which assures us direct power over men, we feel proud to have subjugated the elements of nature. From which the joy that 'great' inventions or discoveries provoke in us." Our author adds, "A man gifted with profound and elevated sentiments, a truly great generation engrossed with the gravest problems of the human soul, does not feel itself enlarged for the success of some technological invention. It attributes nothing but a secondary importance to these instruments of external power. Yet our epoch, inaccessible to whatever is truly great, does not appreciate anything at all *but* this external power, rejoices in it like a child and dedicates a true cult to whomever possesses it. Here is the reason why the inventors and the millionaires inspire an unlimited admiration in the masses."

These factors, as is evident, have efficacy in the modern world generally. Yet they take particular manifestations in the economic-productive field which, at bottom, constitutes their point of departure. And it is easy to follow their development not only in the sphere of the great capitalistic structures, but also beyond them, when one tends to confer to the very State the degrading character of a species of trust,[279] of a pure centralized system of work and of production which must continue to the bitter end.

As for these last considerations of Sombart, it goes without saying that they would be badly understood if one interpreted them as some attack, in the name of an abstract idealism, on the ideas of activity and

---

279 "Trust" obviously in the economic sense. Evola here uses the English word.

of human affirmation in general. It is not activity which one attacks, but *agitation*; not true affirmation, but mistaken affirmation. There is a limit, beyond which a man who is turned exclusively toward the external loses all control over the forces and the processes to which he has given life; and then he finds himself standing before an apparatus over which he might exercise a certain power of direction only by remaining chained to it and enlarging his dependency on it day by day, simultaneously as he entangles the masses and, in the end, even certain nations in its vortex-like, chain-like motion. That which Sombart has called the "economic era" has precisely this sense.

It is worth adding that, so far as power in particular goes, there might exist a power which can be reduced neither to external greatness nor to "records,"[280] which does not aim at matter and at quantity, but which presents itself as sign and sigil of an interior greatness, of an effective superiority. We of today seem ever more to misplace the tracks of such a power—nay, even the very notion of it. One might rediscover it, perhaps, precisely when one looks in the first place toward the internal, when one desists in this agitation, this fever to get ever beyond without a precise sense of where or why, without a precise sense of what is truly worthy of human effort and what is not worthy of it. Perhaps at such a point as that, everything which modern man has created will discover one that can truly dominate it—even if today the paths by which we might reach such an end remain yet inscrutable.

---

280 Once more, Evola uses the English word "records."

26. EMPEROR JULIAN

One is cheered by every encounter with scholars who are capable of carrying themselves beyond prejudices and the deformations of many current historical views. Raffaello Prati[281] is such a one, as he demonstrates in his translation and presentation of the speculative writings of Emperor Julian Flavius, entitled *On the Gods and Men.*

It is already significant that Prati prefers the term "Emperor Julian" to the commoner "Julian the Apostate."[282] This last is an unhappy term, because, rigorously speaking, "apostate"[283] should be reserved for

---

281 I have been unable to find much information on this scholar. He has penned several books and translations, many of which are dedicated to the subject or the works of Emperor Julian—including, for instance, Julian's ironical polemic against beards. (Julian himself wore a beard, for which he was mocked by the Christians of Antiochia; his polemic in reality is against this same community. See Julian's 363 work *Misopogon*, meaning "Beard-Hater.")

282 Julian, who was emperor after Constantine's conversion, was the last non-Christian emperor of Rome. He dedicated much of his life to the attempted reintroduction of the pagan cults into Rome against the growing Christian presence, but he was not successful in his efforts; and in consequence, the subsequent Christian or crypto-Christian historiography has nominated him the Apostate. Evola's point here is that Prati's neglect of this epithet reveals a somewhat wider and more objective perspective than is generally to be expected from our scholars.

283 The word comes from the Ancient Greek ἀποστασία meaning literally "standing away," and originally signified "rebellion, revolt, defection." It came to be used in its religious sense especially after the Justinian Code of the sixth century identified it as a punishable offense.

whomever has abandoned the sacred traditions and the cults which formerly made the greatness of soul of Ancient Rome in order to adopt the new faith which was of neither Roman lineage nor Latin, but of Asiatic and Judaic. It is inappropriate to apply such a term to that man who had the courage of his traditions, and who attempted to reaffirm the "solar" and sacral ideal of the empire, as was Julian Flavius' intent.

Julian composed these texts in his tent, between march and battle, almost as if to draw upon new spiritual forces for the confrontation of harsh vicissitudes. The reading of these texts would be useful for those who follow the current opinion according to which paganism in its religious aspects is more or less synonymous with superstition. Indeed, Julian, in his attempt at traditional restoration, opposed a metaphysical vision to Christianity. He forces us to recognize a content of superior character behind the allegorical clothing of the pagan myths.

He indicates the fundamental point when he writes, "When the myths of sacred subjects are presented as irrational in their content, precisely for this it is as if they were telling us with voice stentorian, not to keep ourselves to the words, but to investigate and inspect the secret sense... Through this absurd disguise there is hope that, by surpassing the current and manifest significance of the words, one might arrive at perception of the absolute substance of the gods and their pure intelligence, which transcends all existent things here below."

This is moreover the general rule that one should follow whenever one approaches the ancient mythologies and theologies. To speak definitively of superstition and of idolatry here, is to confess one's mental obtusity and bad faith.

So in this revaluation of the ancient sacred Roman tradition which Julian attempted, what matters is the "esoteric" idea of nature of the "gods" and "knowledge" of them. Such knowledge signifies interior realization. From such a vantage the gods appear to be not poetic fictions or theologico-philosophastic abstractions, but rather symbols and projections of transcendental states of consciousness.

Thus Julian, who was himself an initiate of the Mithraic Mysteries, strictly associates a superior self-knowledge with the path which conducts to "knowledge of the gods"—an end so high, that he does not hesitate to say that dominion over all the lands, both Roman and barbarian, is nothing compared to it.

He carries us back to the tradition of a secret discipline, thanks to which the self-consciousness is radically transmutated, and new potentials and new interior states come to constitute it, first of all by preparation through a life of purity and of ascesis, then by confronting determinate special experiences of the initiatic rites. The interior states thus brought about are precisely those which in the ancient theology were adumbrated in the symbolic figures of the various Numina.[284]

The power to which Julian principally consigns his hymn—the same hymn that he repeats with the last words of his life, as he expires at dawn on a field of battle[285]—is Helios. Helios is the Sun, not as a

---

284 Numina (consider our English word "numinous") is Latin for "divinities or divine wills." They were held to be, among other things, the guardian divinities of the emperors.

285 Julian was killed by a Sassanid spear which struck him as he and his army were retreating. The wound was not immediately fatal, and in the coming days he had ample time to deliver his last words. Evola is certainly not referring here to the almost surely apocryphal utterance which the historian Theodoret ascribed to Julian at his death: "You have won, Galilean!" Evola alludes most likely to the account given by the historian Marcellinus of Julian's demise, with its lengthy record of his final address. The most relevant part for the present context is this: "Nor am I ashamed to confess that I have long known, from prophecy, that I should fall by the sword. And therefore do I venerate the everlasting God that I now die, not by any secret treachery, nor by a long or severe disease, or like a condemned criminal, but I quit the world with honour, fairly earned, in the midst of a career of flourishing glory. For, to any impartial judge, that man is base and cowardly who seeks to die when he ought not, or who avoids death when it is seasonable for him" (translation C.D. Yonge). The complete address can be found in Book XXV of Marcellinus's Roman History, Part III, Sections 15-21.

divinized physical star but as the symbol of metaphysical light and of power in a transcendent sense, manifesting itself in man and in those who are regenerated as sovereign mind and as that mystical force "from the heights" which in antiquity, and in Rome itself by way of an Iranian influence, stood in intimate rapport with the dignity of the sovereign.

It is in this framework that Julian defines the significance of the imperial Roman cult which he wished to restore institutionally against Christianity. The central ideal is precisely that the true, legitimate master can only be he who possesses an almost supernatural superiority, he who is almost an image of Helios himself, the king of the sky. Only then are authority and hierarchy justified, only then is the Kingdom sanctified, only then does there exist a luminous center of gravity for a complex of human and natural forces.

Julian yearned for the realization of this "pagan" ideal in a sturdy unitary imperial hierarchy furnished with a dogmatic fundament, complete with disciples and laws. The emperor would be the summit of its priestly cast—he who, regenerated and made more than a mere man by the Mysteries, incarnates simultaneously spiritual authority and temporal power, and is *Pontifex Maximus*,[286] ancient dignity which Augustus had renovated. It presupposed the sense of nature as a harmonious whole permeated with invisible living forces; also a monotheism of the State through a group of "philosophers" (better say, "sages") capable of intellectually penetrating and, to the degree it is possible, of initiatically realizing the traditional theology of the Roman world.

There is an evident antithesis here in respect to the dualism of original Christianity, with its "give to Caesar that which is Caesar's,

---

286 Latin: "greatest builder of bridges." After Augustus it referred to the emperor himself until Gratian rejected it. It was later absorbed by the Christians, and remains to this day as one of the official titles of the Pope (*Summus Pontifex*).

to God that which is God's,"[287] with its consequent refusal to render homage to the emperor other than as a temporal head (refusal, which judged as a manifestation of anarchy and of subversion, brought statal persecutions against the Christians).

But by then the epoch was of such a quality as to impede the realization of Julian's idea. There was need of a living adherence to the tradition for its realization, as well as a synergy of the various social strata, the subsistence of the ancient conception of the world in still-living terms. Instead, a scission had entered irremediably between the content and the form of the pagan society.

The very success which Christianity had obtained appeared to be a fatal symptom. For many, to speak yet of the gods as of interior experiences and to consider the above-mentioned transcendental and "solar" presuppositions for true sovereignty, could be nothing other than fiction, mere "philosophy." In other words, the "existential" basis was lacking. Moreover, Julian deluded himself that he could translate these teachings into formatory forces on the political, cultural, and social plane—teachings which for their very nature were destined more than ever to pertain only to very restricted spheres.

Not to say that there was a contradiction, in principle, between Julian's ideas and the ideal of a governmental application of those spiritual and, in a certain measure, transcendental contents. That this contradiction does not exist is demonstrated by the historical reality of an entire series of civilizations centered on "solar" spirituality—from Ancient Egypt to Iran, up to the Japan of just yesterday. In the Roman world in the time of Julian however there no longer existed a human and spiritual substance capable of building the nexuses and the relations of participation proper to a new living hierarchy, in the sense of a totalitarian imperial organization oriented sacredly on a pagan basis.

---

287 Jesus' words to the agents of the Pharisees, who were attempting to entrap him into speaking against Caesar. Matthew 22:21.

A well-known book of Dmitry Merezhkovsky, *The Death of the Gods*,[288] paints in an admirable and ever so evocative way the climate of the world in which Emperor Julian lived, in the shadows of a true "twilight of the gods."

After a long hiatus, something of the ancient tradition ought to have risen again with the appearance of the Germanic races on the scene of great European history, when one could speak of a "*Restauratio Imperii*" under the sign of the Medieval Sacred Roman Empire. This is true above all if one considers the Ghibelline tradition, understood as a reclaiming of the Empire against the hegemonistic presumptions of the Church, to be nothing less than a supernatural dignity on par with the Church itself.

In this respect it is important to consider also that which was contained in almost hidden form in the chivalric literature, in the so-called "imperial legend"[289] and in other documents.

We have sought to gather and to adequately interpret all this material in one of our works entitled, *The Mystery of the Grail: Initiation and Magic in the Quest for the Spirit*.

---

288 Dmitry Sergeyevich Merezhkovsky (1865-1941) was a Russian writer and critic, and one of the founders of the Symbolist movement. His book *The Death of the Gods* (1895) was a novel which treated of the times of Julian as a vehicle for investigating Christianity and paganism. It had a troubled history with the censors and the authorities, but was a popular success.

289 I do not know what text Evola is referencing in particular, but he is clearly alluding to the standard Medieval legend surrounding multiple emperors, by which the emperor, rather than dying, withdraws to an unreachable place, and remains there slumbering until some final battle to determine the rule of good or evil in the world. (See Chapter 13 above.) This was later absorbed, in Christian key, by the hagiographical *Golden Legend* of Jacobus da Varagine (c. 1230-1298), and it might be that Evola has this text in mind, though the *Golden Legend* focused much more exclusively on the lives of the saints.

27. METTERNICH

The climate today in Italy is not naturally favorable for an adequate appraisal of the figure of Metternich. Metternich was the *bête noire* of the Risorgimento, and today one likes to believe that Italy has been reborn after a new "Risorgimento," taking that movement in its most dubious aspects. But even for those who do not hold to such a view, it is not easy to overcome certain rooted prejudices, nor to acquire that free and wide vision which certain foreign historians have already made their own. Nor have they done so without reference to the problems and the crises of contemporary Europe.

As the first among these historians, one might cite Malynski and Poncins, who in their exceedingly interesting book *The Occult War* (published also in Italian in 1938)[290] presented Metternich as the "last great European"—the man who, elevating himself beyond every particularist point of view, was able to recognize the evil which menaced the whole European civilization, and intended to prevent it under the sign of a solidarity of the traditional and dynastic, and therefore supernational, forces. For he knew that the solidarity of the forces of subversion themselves were supernational.

---

290 *The Occult War* is the French work of Viscount Léon de Poncins (1897-1975) and Emmanuel Malynski (?-1938). It proposed that the revolutionary movements of modernity can be traced back to the influence of the Jews on the one hand and the Masons on the other, and it gave its overview of recent history from that perspective. It was translated into Italian by Evola himself in 1939.

A. Cecil's *Metternich*[291] is a more recent work along these lines, and it is interesting not only for the nationality of the author—he is English—but also because in the latest edition of the book Cecil, reacting against those who have interpreted his work as a provocation, emphasizes the overall meaning of the European intention and action of Metternich after his times and up to the Second World War. Cecil writes: "Metternich's methods deserve closer study on the part of all who are interested in the avoidance of complete European disintegration." Thus Cecil considers above all the European idea. It is interesting that he sees in Metternich a reaffirmation of a tradition of classical, Roman spirit. This is a tradition which understands itself as comprising divers peoples in a supernatural unity, all the while respecting their differences—a tradition which understands that true liberty is realized under the sign of a super-elevated law of order and of the hierarchical idea, not in democratic and Jacobin ideologies. And it is Metternich himself who said that "every despotism is sign of weakness."[292]

Cecil justly remarks that "to sign the death warrant of Austria was to provide a formula for the destruction of Europe." This because Austria still incorporated, at least in principle, the idea of the Holy Roman Empire—namely, that of a regime which might contain various and diverse nationalities without oppressing them and denaturalizing them. Now, without a formula of the kind, it is impossible to think that Europe will one day rediscover, in this world of exasperated nationalisms and devastating internationalisms, that unity which appears by now to be the essential condition for Europe's very existence as an autonomous civilization.

Metternich knew rightly to see in democracy and in nationalism the principle forces which would overwhelm traditional Europe,

---

291 *Metternich, 1773-1859: A Study of his Period and Personality* is the work of Algernon Cecil (1879-1953).

292 The quotation is taken from Metternich's "Political Testament," written from the period of 1849-1855.

barring some radical action. He understood the internal nexus of the various forms of subversion which, commencing from liberalism and constitutionalism, lead up to collectivism and communism. And he thought that every concession in this connection would be fatal. Cecil here rightly says that even as Robespierre carries a Napoleon in his wake, Napoleon, in his turn, carries a Stalin:[293] because Bonapartism and totalitarianism itself are not democracy's antithesis but rather—as Michels and Burnham[294] have demonstrated—its extreme consequence.

For Metternich the remedy was the idea of the State as a super-elevated reality founded on the principle of a true sovereignty and

---

293 Maximilien Robespierre (1758-1794) rose to power in France after the Revolution, in which position he became one of the foremost figures during the Reign of Terror. He himself identified "terror" with justice and virtue, and his theory led to the death of many aristocrats as presumed enemies of the state were imprisoned and executed at the guillotine. His consolidation of power is often seen as the road by which Napoleon Bonaparte (1769-1821) was able to attain his preeminence. The connection between Bonaparte and the General Secretary of the Soviets, Joseph Stalin (1878-1953), is certainly less clear, not least of all for temporal and geographical distance between the one and the other. The point here seems to be that all these figures are but various instances of one and the same historical tendency, one and the same historical "flow."

294 I believe the reference here is to the Italian Robert Michels (1876-1936) and the American James Burnham (1905-1987). Michels was a sociologist who formulated what is known as the "iron law of oligarchy," stating in effect that no matter how democratic a state is to begin with it will always end with the formation of oligarchical power. Burnham wrote about Michels in his 1943 book *The Machiavellians*. Burnham began as a revolutionary activist of the left, and ended up as an American conservative (he was, for instance, a regular contributor to *National Review*). A common theme of Burnham's writings is that best explicated in his *The Managerial Revolution*, in which he proposed that all modern societies of all kinds are moving toward the elitest control of a minority of "managers," who will have primary control over the means of production. Though he recommended that these elites maintain a façade of democratic appearances, it is evident that this would be only a cover for the true workings of power.

authority, rather than on the mere expression of the *demos*.[295] He did
not believe in "nations," for he saw in them only a mask of the revolution, an anti-dynastic myth. As for his creature, the Holy Alliance[296]—
that was an extreme attempt which, even if it was able to guarantee
Europe a fecund peace for an entire generation, yet still was not up to
the heights of its informing principle. At bottom, it lacked a true idea,
something that could make it truly sacred and which could, moreover,
make it a constructive unity rather than a merely defensive one. Cecil
recalls how Maistre had already rightly indicated the point, when he
said that one should make not a "counter-revolution," so much as "the
contrary of a revolution"—that is to say, one should proceed to positive political action, commencing from strong spiritual and traditional
bases, and only as the natural consequence of this should one sweep
away all subversion and usurpation on part of the lower powers.

---

295 From Ancient Greek δῆμος, the evident root of our word "democracy," meaning
the "force or rule of the people." The use of the Greek is significant, as the word
demos had to the Greek ear quite another sense than "people" does to ours. It
was above all an equivocal term, and in some cases was used in a derogatory
way, as the "commoners" was once used by the aristocracies to delineate those
who were ruled and who were incapable of ruling. This sense is preserved in
our word "demagogue," one who manipulates the simplicity and selfishness of
the *demos*. This is complicated by the higher use of *demos* in antiquity, in certain
specific contexts where it indicated something like a free people; it often had
this sense, for instance, in democratic Athens. But even here it is important to
remember that it was used as a term of distinction; if the Athenian *demos* was a
free people, the same could not be said of other *demoi* in other places.

296 The Holy Alliance formed after the defeat of Napoleon in 1815. Its signatories
were Russia, Austria, and Prussia, monarchical powers all, and its explicit intent
was to stem the rising tide of liberalism and secularism. The nations involved
promised each other mutual support against revolution and the influences of
democracy. Though its principles seemed to gain in power in its first decades,
leading even to similar alliances with France and Britain, it began to disintegrate
soon after, and broke apart altogether during the Revolutions of 1848.

Now, there is no doubt that we need an idea of this kind, associated with a combative solidarity of all the forces that in our Europe yet keep firm and brings us to react against the virus of the so-called "immortal principles" (the "French evil," as Cecil calls it, which is now no longer physical so much as spiritual). There is no doubt that only this idea, assuming it finds men up to its height—and, if possible, even *sovereigns*—can save whatever in our civilization is still salvageable.

28. DONOSO CORTÉS

Together with Count de Maistre and Viscount De Bonald,[297] Donoso Cortés, Marquis of Valdegamas, constitutes one of the triad of the nineteenth century's great counter-revolutionary thinkers, and his message even today has not lost its topicality. In Italy Donoso Cortés' doctrines are not well known in what seem to us their most important aspects. There has been a recent reprinting of the Italian translation of his work on Catholicism, liberalism and socialism. Although this has been taken as his principle work, it is not therein that one must seek the most valid points of reference; the work is too full of often boring meditations on "secular theology" which rest heavily on the dogmas, ideas and myths of the Catholic religion, sufficiently so as to prejudice the validity which various of its positions might have in a larger and more "traditional" view—"traditional," that is, in a higher sense. One should glean from this book essentially the idea of a "theology of the current politics"; Cortés affirms, that is, the inevitable presence, beyond certain of their exterior and merely social aspects, of a religious (or anti-religious, "diabolic") foundation to the various ideologies which today have a kind of primacy in the general consideration.

Apart from that which Cortés says about Catholicism, in his treatment of liberalism he more or less reproduces that which the men of

---

297 Louis de Bonald (1754-1840) was a French conservative thinker and politician, known for his strongly traditionalistic and counter-revolutionary stance. For Cortés, apart from this entire chapter, see also note 161 to Chapter 14 above.

the conservative and counter-revolutionary Right, with Metternich (who was an admirer of Cortés) at their head, had glimpsed: namely, an inevitable concatenation of causes and effects.

The liberalism of the time, which was *bête noire* in all the conservative regimes of the continent, paved the way for further decline. For this Marx and Engels had already applauded its instrumental function in the destruction of the previous traditional institutions—all the while warning cynically that "the rope had been measured," that the "executioner stood waiting behind the door."[298] The executioner corresponded to the successive stage of subversion, to socialism and to communism, which, in supplanting liberalism, would have continued its work and brought it to term. Cortés recognized socialism's aspect of being an inverted religion; its force, he wrote, is due to its contain-

---

298 I have been unable to source the first quotation, though it might be a reference to a famous statement which is variously attributed to Stalin, Lenin, and Marx, namely: "The last capitalist will be hung with the rope that he himself has sold us." The second quotation comes from an article which Engels wrote for the German journal *Deutsche-Brüsseler Zeitung*, January 23, 1848, entitled "The Movements of 1847," which could not more clearly underline Evola's point. Here is the last paragraph of this article, in full, from which Evola takes his citation: "So just fight bravely on, most gracious masters of capital! We need you for the present; here and there we even need you as rulers. You have to clear the vestiges of the Middle Ages and of absolute monarchy out of our path; you have to annihilate patriarchalism; you have to carry out centralisation; you have to convert the more or less propertyless classes into genuine proletarians, into recruits for us; by your factories and your commercial relationships you must create for us the basis of the material means which the proletariat needs for the attainment of freedom. In recompense whereof you shall be allowed to rule for a short time. You shall be allowed to dictate your laws, to bask in the rays of the majesty you have created, to spread your banquets in the halls of kings, and to take the beautiful princess to wife — but do not forget that 'The hangman stands at the door!'" The last quotation is taken from the poem "Ritter Olaf" by Heinrich Heine.

ing a theology, and it is destructive because one is dealing here with a "Satanic theology."

But whatever might be harvested from this work is less important than that which one finds in various others of Cortés' writings, and above all in the two famous speeches he made to the Spanish Parliament, which contained a diagnosis and an historical prophecy of almost visionary lucidity. The revolutionary movements of 1848 and of 1849[299] were sounded by Cortés as an alarm. And he foresaw the fatal process of the leveling and the massifying of society, brought about by the progress of technology and by the development of communications. He says that not England (which one indicted with the subversion inherent in liberalism) but rather Russia (which then was Tsarist) was to be the center of the subversion, through the connection of revolutionary socialism to Russian politics (precisely as has occurred in our epoch, with the advent of Soviet communism). This is a singular forecast if one considers the period in which it was formulated. Cortés here meets the great historian Alexis de Tocqueville who in his work on *Démocratie en Amérique*[300] had seen in Russia and in America together the principle forcing bed of such subversive processes.

Cortés warned of the acceleration of the rhythm, the approaching moment of "radical negation or of sovereign affirmation (*llega el dia de las negaciones radicales y de las afirmaciones sobranas*)"; and the whole of presumed progress in the technological and social camp would only

---

299 For these revolutions, see note 109 to Chapter 10 above.

300 French: "Democracy in America." *Democracy in America* is the magisterial and nigh peerless analysis of American society by Alexis de Tocqueville (1805-1859), a French diplomat and historian who had travelled America extensively. His keen and myriad observations, as well as a startling array of deep critiques and remarkable predictions about the near and distant future, were published in his two-volume work *Democracy in America* in 1835 and 1840, which to this day remains one of the finest and most thorough investigations into America, and indeed into modern politics, ever penned. The prophecy here in reference can be found in Volume I of *Democracy in America*, Part II, Chapter 10, Conclusion.

bring that moment nearer. He foresaw that the massification and the destruction of the previous organic articulations would lead to forms of totalitarian centralization.

He could glimpse but few paths of escape from this situation. He recognized that the epoch of monarchical legitimism had waned, because "there no longer exist kings; not one of them would have the courage to be king other than by the will of the people." On the other hand he recognized with Maistre that the absolute decision is essential to sovereignty, to statal authority—a decision without any appeal to anything superior, analogous almost to papal infallibility. For which he took a stance against parliamentarianism and bourgeois liberalism, against the "class which discusses"—for in the decisive moment, this class would not be up to the heights of the situation.

In this context, Cortés recognizes however also the peril of a new Caesarism, in the pejorative sense of a formless power in the hands of individuals who are deprived of every higher anointment—a power exercised not on people but on simple gray masses. He spoke of "plebeians of Satanic greatness," which seem to act in the name of and for the good of an other-worldly sovereign. Given however that every legitimistic conservatism seemed to him emptied of every vital force, he sought a surrogate to bar the way to those forces and powers which arise from beneath. So he defended dictatorship as a counter-revolutionary idea, an antithesis to anarchy, to chaos and to subversion—if nothing else, as a *pis aller* or a *faute de mieux*.[301] But he spoke also of a *dictadura coronada*.[302] The expression is certainly suggestive; it includes the "decisionistic" anti-democratic idea, it recognizes the necessity in a power which decides absolutely (that which counted for Maistre as the essential attribute of the State), but at a higher level of dignity, indicated by the adjective *coronada*.

---

301 French. *Pis aller*: "a last resort," lit. "to go worse," in the sense "should the worst come." *Faut de mieux*: "for want of something better."

302 Spanish: "crowned dictatorship."

But every concretization of this formula encounters manifest difficulties. In the time of Cortés there yet existed dynastic traditions on the European soil, and the formula might have been realized if one of their representatives had but taken ownership of the ancient maxim *rex est qui nihil metuit* (he is king who fears nothing).[303] Certain forms of so-called authoritarian constitutionalism might have counted as an approximation of this, and signally that which Bismarck[304] realized in Germany. But in a system wherein the dynastic traditions have deteriorated or have disappeared, it is not easy to find a concrete point of reference for the dignifying attribute of *dictadura* which Cortés so decidedly patronized as the political solution.

Today all of this seems very clear, because certain authoritarian regimes have effectively arisen to stem the disorder and anarchy, but they are of the genera of the so-called "Colonel's regime"[305] which, at best, lacks the above-mentioned higher dimension of counter-revolution.

Donoso Cortés knew how to formulate a problem of fundamental importance in a pregnant way, and he made exact forecasts of the situations which would mature from it. The problem he formulated seems in the course of the times ever less susceptible of true solutions—that is, solutions corresponding to the *affirmaciones sobranas* opposed to the *negaciones radicales*. Cortés died at only forty-four years of age, in 1853. He was able however to garner the entire meaning of certain

---

303 The expression is Latin, and comes from Seneca the Younger (c. 4 BCE-65 CE): *Rex est qui metuit nihil, rex est quique cupiet nihil, hoc regnum sibi quisque dat* ("He is king who fears nothing; he is king who wants nothing. Each may give himself such a kingdom." Translation mine). *Thyestes* 388-390.

304 Otto von Bismarck (1815-1898), Prussian statesman and Chancellor of the German Empire. His name is often associated with the policy of *Realpolitik*, which emphasized the practical side of diplomatic and state affairs, rather than the ideological or moralistic side. He was famous for ruling with a firm hand, and was known by the name "the Iron Chancellor."

305 That is, a military junta in which high-ranking members of the military rule.

precursory ill-omened signs, constituted in the first crises of the European world which manifested in 1848 and 1849, even before their general consequences had been rendered very visible.

Notwithstanding the interest he awakened, a few years after 1848 Donoso Cortés was almost forgotten in Europe and his name passed into the superb ranks of the isolated, of the ignored, of those who suffered the conspiracy of silence of the nineteenth century. Only the most recent events have newly attracted attention to him. In an excellent work (*Donoso Cortés in gesamteuropdischer Interpretation*) Carl Schmitt[306] observed that of the two antagonistic currents, the socialistic revolutionary current on the one hand and the counter-revolutionary current of the times of Cortés on the other, the first has subsequently enjoyed systematic developments while the second has been arrested. Schmitt wrote these words in 1950. But in the meantime the situation has fortunately changed, with the formation of a thought of the Right and with the revival of the idea of Tradition. So in our days we can enumerate Donoso Cortés amongst those from whom one can ever draw useful indications—particularly should that moment of absolute decision come, of which Cortés had spoken.

---

306 Schmitt (1888-1985) was a German political thinker often remembered for his keen analyses of sovereignty and his theory that the distinction between "friend" and "enemy" lies at the root of political forms. His relationship to Nazism (though atimes strained) has rendered him anathema to certain segments of contemporary scholarship, and most of his works have yet to be translated. This notwithstanding, he has enjoyed a lasting influence. His work on Cortés, which has not been translated into English, was published in 1950.

29. THE HENRY MILLER PHENOMENON

Henry Miller[307] has been attributed a peculiar significance in the gallery of figures representative of our times. Miller enjoys what is by now an almost unanimous recognition in the international literary world, while conserving for many the infamy of being a pornographic, scandalous and anarchic writer. We ourselves have had a certain interest in him, above all on the basis of the books of his earliest period, such as *Tropic of Cancer* and *Tropic of Capricorn*, which are prohibited in various countries.[308] Works of the kind could indeed be taken as the testimonies of a world in dissolution, a desperate world in revolt. Thus certain members of the latest generations, and especially those overseas, who have gambled everything—hipsters, beats and such like—have seen in Miller one of their masters and standard bearers.

So far as we are concerned, the Miller's negative aspect is precisely his valid aspect: the Miller who attacks the entirety of modern civilization ("stone forests" in which chaos moves) and, especially, American civilization (the America "which harvests the most degenerate parts of

---

307 Miller (1891-1980) was an American writer of some notoriety who passed a number of years in Europe. The following chapter provides a deal of relevant biographical information. The citations to his work found in this chapter are all taken from *Tropic of Cancer* or *Tropic of Capricorn*, unless otherwise noted.

308 As, for instance, the United States until a 1961 court ruling. Also in Norway; see below in the present chapter.

Europe"[309]) and its culture ("gurgling like a sewer"); the anti-conformist Miller who writes, "Who that has a desperate, hungry eye can have the slightest regard for these existent governments, laws, codes, principles, ideals, ideas, totems, and taboos?" and who speaks of existential situations "that make one think of murder or suicide, anything that might create a vestige of human drama."

In general, the better part of Miller's books present themselves as a continuous (more or less manipulated) autobiography, constellated with reflections, with descriptions of the most various characters and with every kind of episode. Beyond which there are intriguing points at which, as if due to some trauma, we are presented with moments almost of illumination and superior lucidity in the midst of a chaotic and muddled event: almost flashes of higher certainties amidst extreme chaos, or the perception of nearly magical appearance of a reality of things existing in their essence and purity ("In that moment I lost completely the illusion of time and space: the world unfurled its drama simultaneously along a meridian which had no axis. In this sort of hair-trigger eternity I felt that everything was justified, supremely justified"), lacerating that species of trance-like stupefaction in which modern men habitually live, without ever becoming aware of it. In the middle of the mayhem and the most absurd situations, almost some confused tendency toward self-liberation acts up, the search for "one's own authenticity" ("Every time you come to the limit of what is demanded of you, you are faced with the same problem—to be yourself! And with the first step you make in this direction you realize that there is neither plus nor minus; you throw the skates away and swim. There is no suffering any more because there is nothing which can threaten your security." Also, "I

---

309 I have been unable to find the original English for this reference, but it surely occurs, as all the present cluster of quotations, somewhere in *Tropic of Cancer* or *Tropic of Capricorn*. This quotation has been translated directly from Evola's Italian.

had to grow foul with knowledge, realize the futility of everything, smash everything, grow desperate, then humble, then sponge myself off the slate, as it were, in order to recover my authenticity."[310]). These are the very motifs of a certain kind of existentialism. The line of thought, however, if seriously deepened, might also not be without analogies to Zen, the ancient school of the Far East, which moreover even Miller knew something about (confusedly: he read every sort of thing) and for this he has recently attracted the attention of the "burnt" generations.

It is arduous enough to retrace this line of thought through the books of Miller, so great is the disorderly affluence of divergent motifs, of contradictory impressions and also—in notable measure—of tangents, now literary, now philosophastic and introspective. So far as the much-decried "obscenity" of Miller goes, it is really the least of these motifs. In the first place, it is confined almost entirely to the first books, *Tropic of Cancer* and *Tropic of Capricorn*, and appear ever less in his other writings. There is nothing exciting about it; he speaks of some of the most salacious sexual things as of pure facts, without any kind of eroticizing atmosphere apt to inflame the reader's imagination: he speaks of them rather with almost grotesque rawness. It is the triviality of his expressions if anything which is bothersome. Unfortunately, Miller is among those who gratify themselves with that vulgar language which until yesterday was the prerogative of the plebes, a bad usance which today has gained a foothold both in literature as well as in the speech of persons who would like to prove themselves "open-minded," when they are only stupid. At the bottom of this is a self-contamination which a psychoanalyst would trace back to a "guilt complex" or else to a deviated compensation of an

---

310 This last quotation is from Miller's essay "Reflections on Writing," from *The Wisdom of the Heart*.

"inferiority complex."[311] It might also be for this that the "obscenity" of Miller loses its bite and becomes banal; it reduces itself to bad taste. We are reminded how the renowned poet Alfred De Musset[312] won a bet by writing an absolutely "pornographic" book—*Gamiani*—without using even a single indecent word.

But leaving this aside, the value of the testimony of Miller's work is found in the terms indicated above; and this value has proved considerably diminished in that part of him which has a different, and at bottom uninteresting, orientation: not the nihilism and the effort to grasp something absolute beyond the "ground zero of values," but rather a primitivistic attachment to "life" in all its aspects—not devoid, even, of faith and enthusiasm (these are the "euphoric" moments which in Miller alternate with the depressive ones). All things considered, Miller proves for this far enough from being really "burnt." In his books we see him even too often carried away in the most infantile and fleeting manner by some idea or other, some author or other. He goes so far as to say that Dostoevsky "changed the whole face of the world." He "discovers" Spengler (!!). He exalts D. H. Lawrence, with his suspect philosophy of life and of the flesh. He is fascinated by Joyce. He feels himself in profound debt to Swami Vivekananda, the mediocre, strongly Europeanized popularizer of Oriental doctrines. He goes into ecstasies over an art historian such as Elie Faure. He is gratified by the recognition bestowed on him by the narcissistic parlor philosopher H. Keyserling. He becomes aware of Dadaism more than fifteen years

---

311 A "guilt complex" in psychology refers to an inability to get over feelings of guilt or shame, resulting in excessive self-blame. An "inferiority complex" refers to the subconscious feeling of uncertainty in oneself or lack of self-regard, which leads afflicted individuals to overcompensate in unusual ways.

312 Musset (1810-1857) was a French dramatist, poet, and novelist. The full title of the work referenced here is *Gamiani, or Two Nights of Excess*.

too late.[313] And all this, even as he writes words like these: "*Be still, and wait the coming of the Lord!...*That was the sort of message I should have liked to dispatch at intervals to the god of the literary realm so that I might be delivered from confusion, rescued from chaos, freed of obsessive admiration for authors living and dead whose words, phrases, images barricaded my way."[314] On the whole, the highs and lows in this interminable narrative monologue continue to alternate (the manic phase and the depressive phase, as a psychiatrist would say), and nothing acquires a precise form.

From a personal, human point of view, matters stand no differently. Miller confesses, "I'm enthusiastic and I exaggerate, I adore and worship." He expresses the desperation of a Romantic for the departure of "Mona" (one of his wives). He does not shun utopian hopes for a civilization to come (in which, moreover, an essential part would bear the "dark feminine" or "maternal background" of existence). The

---

313 Fyodor Mikhailovich Dostoevsky (1821-1881), author of *Crime and Punishment* and *The Brothers Karamazov*, is considered one of the greatest Russian novelists of all time. For Spengler, see note 3 to Chapter 1 above. D.H. Lawrence (1885-1930) was an English poet and novelist famous for his untimely (he was often censored) investigation into themes of sexuality. James Joyce (1882-1941) was an Irish novelist who revolutionized his art with his groundbreaking modern work *Ulysses*, composed in a rococo multitude of literary styles. Swami Vivekananda (1863-1902) was an Indian Hindu who was in large part responsible for the introduction of certain Oriental philosophies into the West. Jacques Élie Faure (1873-1937) was a French art historian. Hermann von Keyserling was a German intellectual who interested himself in natural science and adopted a form of social Darwinism as his guiding political principle. He and Miller were correspondents for a time. Dadaism was an avant-garde art movement which emerged in response to "capitalistic culture." It began to appear in Europe toward the beginning of the twentieth century, and arrived notably in New York and subsequently in Paris around 1915. Miller was introduced to it when he moved to Paris in 1930, and he himself described his response to it as "infatuated, intoxicated."

314 From "Not I, But the Father within Me," in *Henry Miller on Writing*, selections of Thomas H. Moore.

counterpart of this, on the other hand, seems to be his charge against the "criminal aspect of the mind," that is of the rational *I*—see Klages (in part Bergson, Spengler and the like)[315]; likewise he holds out hope for an art of the future. He is capable of the most ingenuous and, for us Europeans, the most provincial forms of admiration (for example, for the whole of French culture). He accuses men of not knowing love, "the love that asks nothing in return," and sees in this love a species of universal remedy, with the adjunct of pacifistic themes together with the deprecation of the entirety of war and combat. There are as many other facets which reveal, in this nihilist Miller, the foundation even of a "good man," a man who, far from being "burnt," is but merely deluded.

As for the rest, even in practical life Miller the man seems to have little by little normalized himself. His anti-Americanism and his existential restlessness must have been attenuated if he wound up settling in California, in an orderly *ménage*.[316] He long since paid the piper of conformism, for he married—four times: the which indicates the purely exterior and frivolous side of the matter.

---

315 Ludwig Klages (1872-1956) was a German psychologist and nominee for the Nobel Prize in Literature. In his philosophy he advocated an extreme version of Nietzschean "life philosophy." Henri Bergson (1859–1941) was a prominent French philosopher whose work concentrated on the centrality of experience over rationality. He is often remembered in the context of his 1907 work *Creative Evolution*, in which he proposed an *élan vital*, a vital urge, at the basis of all life and hence all evolution. Evola mentions him in one of his footnotes to Chapter 12 of this work (see note 124 of that chapter).

316 French: "household," understood mainly as the members of a household.

In a letter sent to the courthouse of Oslo on occasion of the proceedings made against one of his books,[317] he writes, "Would it please
the Court to know that...I am not regarded as a 'sex addict,' a pervert,
or even a neurotic? That, as a husband, a father, a neighbor, I am
looked upon as 'an asset' to the community? Sounds a trifle ludicrous,
does it not?"—for which, he himself asks if the author of those lecher-
ous books, which are autobiographical in nature, and this man Miller
can be the same person. He states that they are. So either one must
posit Miller's dotage due to age and literary success, or else one must
perceive a contradiction which quite cripples Miller's symbolic and
representative value. With this on top of all the other aspects that we
have indicated, however, we quite lose steam, and we must recognize
that as witness of the epoch and of the liminal experiences of the epoch, only the "negative" Miller is interesting.

Regarding his books, which have been issued also in Italian translation, there is little enough in particular to say about *Nexus*, which he
finished writing in 1959.

At first sight we are presented with a nice *ménage à troi*,[318] with
Miller, Mona (who seems to be his second wife) and Stasia, the lesbian
friend of Mona (this cohabitation, this combination, is explained in
these words by Mona: "The more I love you [Miller], the more I love
Stasia"). This is the period in which Miller almost found fame, during
which he called himself a writer but made few attempts at writing. In

---

317 In 1957 Miller's work *Sextus* was deemed obscene by the Norwegian government, and its seizure was ordered throughout the country. This case had the
dubious distinction of being the first of its kind in Norway in over seventy years.
An initial court ruling upheld the banning and confiscation of Miller's work, but
an appeal to the Supreme Court resulted in the clearing of all charges. Miller
wrote two open letters to the court; the quotation in this paragraph comes from
the second of these.

318 French: "household of three," in particular a household in which a "couple of
three persons" lives.

the meantime Mona above all supported him; and she did not have too many scruples, toward that end, of demonstrating herself "obliging" in a nocturnal locale of the artist village where she worked. Stasia is a Russian artist with the befuddlement typical of the Slavs. While on one page we see her working on the same lines as Miller in her revolt against the petrified and empty world of the "beehive"[319] skyscrapers inhabited not by "poets" but by "monsters" two pages afterward we hear her say that once she sought to make a dog mount her, whereupon she confesses, "It was so ludicrous. He finally bit me in the thigh." But after this enticing beginning the book passes to the carousel of various characters, of various impressions and meditations, according to the confused succession of the motifs hereabove mentioned.

The Best of Henry Miller is the title of a translation of "purged" selections, edited by L. Durrell, of passages of Miller's fiction and non-fiction writings. Parts of his work are presented, that is, which are acceptable even to the current and puritanical public: this is Miller essentially as *literatus*, describer of types, man of a particular sensibility, writer of excellent style. Almost a third of the selections is made up of non-fiction or excerpts of simple literary criticism or the like: the which might be of interest to many, but to us seems secondary and of current consumption. Thus it cannot be said to pertain to the "best." In this respect, however, if we ourselves were to render judgement, we would have to put ourselves to doing literary criticism, the which is foreign to us. Here we wished only to bring to attention above all to the "Miller phenomenon," not so much as an artistic phenomenon, but as an expression of the times.

---

319 I am inferring that this is the passage Evola has in mind. His citation in Italian is "*tutti saltellano come pazzi*," or "everyone hops along like madmen," but there is nothing quite like this in Miller's original English, at least at this point in *Nexus*. The following quotations taken from Miller in this paragraph are also from *Nexus*.

30. VILFREDO PARETO, ANTI-CONFORMIST AND ANTI-DEMOCRAT

Even leaving aside his system of sociology, upon which judgements might vary, one reads and rereads Vilfredo Pareto[320] ever with pleasure, first for his clear and lively style, but beyond all for his anti-conformism, for his courageous love of the truth and for his intolerance toward the ideologies, the myths and the mendacities of that bourgeois and democratic pre-fascist world, in whose epoch he conceived his principal works. Since such a world has been resuscitated in our days, yet more virulently than ever, many of Pareto's considerations retain a character of surprising topicality.

Apart from his congenital aversion for every form of democracy, Pareto has made an important contribution to the antidemocratic principle in the field of positive sociology by demonstrating the law of the "circulation of elites," which validates that principle on a general plane. Pareto has, that is, confirmed the constancy of the phenomenon

---

320 Pareto (1848-1923) was an Italian political scientist and sociologist, but also an engineer. The Pareto Principle, which states that about 80% of the effects for most events come from about 20% of the causes, was his discovery—a most curious principle with a wide variety of applications. Pareto himself noted, for instance, that in Italy about 20% of the population owned about 80% of the land, and that in a garden about 20% of the pea-pods will contain about 80% of the peas. The idea has been put to valid work in economics, management, science, and sports, and it is entertaining, and often fruitful, to try to put it to use in other fields as well.

of the existence of an elite, that is of a minority which dominates, in every society. Thus a more or less elaborated hierarchy is an ever-present sociological datum, even in those cases wherein one negates such in speech. But the elites can be traded out; different social groups can, by "circulating," substitute one another, possibly undermining one another, so as to form up a new elite. Pareto limits himself to demonstrating the general sociological structural phenomenon of the elite; he does not develop a philosophy of history so as to discover what *qualities* of elites have followed one another in the course of the times known to us. From the traditional point of view, naturally, we are witness to a process of regression which in our days is reaching its limit.

Pareto spares no jibes when he comes across those myths which he calls "the secular religions of the bourgeois world," myths which have substituted the truth and the values of other times. Humanity, Democracy, Progress, Liberty, Popular Will, Equality, puritanical moralism and so for and so on—words all frequently written in the upper case, as before one wrote the name of God; the objects now of a new cult and a new fanaticism. Above all some quotations gleaned from the principle work of Pareto, *Treatise of General Sociology*,[321] might be of interest to us.

Let us commence from egalitarianism. Objectively speaking, equality is absurd. Pareto (§ 1227) says that if the sentiments of equality might sometimes be strong, this is owed to the fact that they have nothing to do with true equality, because they refer not "to an abstract value, as certain ingenuous intellectuals still believe, but rather to the direct interests of persons who wish to withdraw themselves from an inequality which is against them, and to institute another favorable to them—the last aim being, for them, their principle aim." In other words, every egalitarian ideology is only an instrument, hypocritically

---

321 Pareto's four-volume 1916 work *Trattato Di Sociologia Generale*, which was translated into English by Arthur Livingston in 1935.

used for subversive ends. An analogous evaluation had already been made by Tacitus,[322] and Vico after him noted that equality is exalted and proclaimed first to overturn one's superiors, then to draw alongside them, and finally to put them under oneself as inferiors, instituting new inequalities through a hierarchy which has been turned on its head. Referring to Sparta, to the ancient Nordic races and also to England, Pareto reminds us that only the members of an exceedingly restricted aristocracy counted *de facto* as effectively "equal" or "peers" (in Greek, *omoioi*),[323] the which imposed on themselves the rigorous observance of difficult duties of caste. Nothing at all, therefore, which corresponds to a leveling egalitarianism.

Among other things, Pareto attacks the slanderous interpretation of the feudal regime as a regime of violence and subjugation, which is presented by the "progressive" historiography. He writes (§ 1154), "It is an absurd thing to imagine that ancient feudalism in Europe was imposed exclusively by means of force. It maintained itself rather in part by sentiments of mutual affection, which can be observed in other Countries where feudalism existed, as for example in Japan ... In general, such is to be found in all social orders where there exists a hierarchy; and such hierarchy ceases to be spontaneous, and comes to be imposed exclusively, or predominately, by force, only when it is about to disappear and to give place to another." Pareto justly recalls the part which the principle of "fidelity" plays in traditional systems. Swearing "fidelity" was equivalent to a sacrament, thus making "martyrs of those who sacrificed their own lives to maintain it, and accursed those who violated it." Various interesting quotations are to be reported in this respect.

Pareto's realism issues from the following passage (§ 2183): "All Governments use force and all aver to have their foundation in reason.

---

322 Tacitus (56-120) was a paramount Roman historian and senator, writer of the *Annals* and the *Histories*.

323 From the Ancient Greek ὁμοίιος, meaning "like in mind" or "at one with." For the Greeks a peer was one whose will and mindset was similar to one's own.

In truth, with or without universal suffrage, it is always an oligarchy which governs, which knows how to give to the 'popular will' the expression that it desires ... from the votes of the majority in an assembly variously elected, to the plebiscite which gave the empire to Napoleon III[324] and so forth, up to a wisely guided universal suffrage, which is bought and manipulated by our politicos. Who is this new god that bears the name 'universal suffrage'? He is not better defined, nor any less mysterious and less foreign to the reality of things than so many other divinities: nor is his theology, as others, lacking in patent contradictions."

Regarding the new hypocrisies, Pareto observes (§ 1462): "In barbaric times a people brought war on another, it sacked its lands, it fleeced it of its money, without too many speeches; in our times the same thing is still done, but one says one acts only in the name of 'vital interests,' and this is supposed to represent an immense progress." In a not dissimilar way, he puts his hand on ideals, on moral values, on the "right" to mask one's various ends. He cites the case of the Boxer Rebellion[325] in China at the beginning of the century—a war really fought by the Europeans in order to impose the opium trade. However

---

324 Louis-Napoléon Bonaparte (1808-1873), nephew and heir of Napoleon Bonaparte. He molded his republic into an empire following a bid to establish his popular precedents through a national plebiscite (1851), in which the voters agreed, in better than a ten to one proportion, to give Napoleon extraordinary powers to produce a new constitution. Napoleon took the results of this plebiscite as a mandate. Many commentators at the time, including Victor Hugo, questioned the legitimacy of the vote. It was followed by an even more incredible vote in 1852, in which 96.9% of voters approved Napoleon's becoming emperor.

325 Reference to the 1899 uprising of the Chinese against the imperial presence of the Europeans, and especially the British. The "Boxers" were so called by the British for their athleticism; they were trained in the martial arts and they practiced a spiritual discipline which rendered them (as they believed) invulnerable to foreign weapons. The Boxers were put down in 1901, and the consequence was a forcible opening of Chinese borders to "trade" with the West.

there is no doubt as to the way in which Pareto would have judged yet more perspicuous cases—such as that label "Crusades in Europe" which was applied by the Americans (and in fact by Eisenhower)[326] to their intervention in the Second World War, or the macabre farce of the Nuremberg Trials,[327] which was celebrated in the name of "humanity" and "civilization." How much better was the crude frankness of him who limited himself to declaring: *Vae victis!*[328]

Pareto goes so far as to fly into a temper when he hears talk of the so-called "popular will" or detects the servile demagogic adulation of the "people." He says, for example (§ 1713), that in other times even kings could be harshly attacked by their very nobles or by the Popes, "while today no one is spirited enough to censure the 'people' and less

---

326 Dwight D. Eisenhower (1890-1969) was president of the United States from 1953-1961. His very memoir, the personal recounting of his role in World War II, is entitled *Crusade in Europe*.

327 The Nuremberg Trials, named for the city in which they were conducted, were military tribunals organized by the victorious Allies at the close of World War II against the higher echelons of the Nazi command for their "war crimes." They have received numerous trenchant criticisms, among the most serious of which are these: that the charge of "war crimes" was a *post hoc* invention of the victors, thus essentially creating a crime and then retroactively applying it to past actions; that the Tribunal established arbitrary and unconventional rules of evidence, admitting as evidence much that in a normal trial would be precluded by any number of fundamental juridical principles; that an unusually high percentage of the judges, whose selection could not be appealed by the accused, were Jewish; and that torture was used before the trial in several high-ranking cases to elicit confession.

328 Latin: "Woe to the vanquished!" The phrase is actually attributed to a non-Latin, one Brennus, chieftain of the Gallic Senones. Brennus led to the sack of Rome 390 BCE, after which devastating event the captured Romans attempted to purchase their release. A balance was brought to measure out the gold that had been agreed upon, but the weights of the Senones were heavier than those of the Romans. When the Romans disputed this fact, Brennus cast his sword upon the scales, with the cry "*Vae victis!*"

still to openly resist it; the which does not exclude that one turns it round, one deceives it, one exploits it, as once upon a time sycophants and demagogues exploited the *demos* of Athens, and as the courtiers in times not so distant to us really worked on behalf of their patrons." It is obvious that all of this might be truer in yet greater measure for the most recent, sacrosanct taboo constituted by the 'working class.'

Pareto observes also that the famous "freedom of thought" of "progressive times" is in reality so understood that one claims such freedom only for oneself while negating it to one's enemies. This, not only on the social plane but also on the religious: in the name liberty the orthodox and traditionalists are supposed to tolerate the heretics and revolutionaries, but these last do not think at all of recognizing to the first the freedom to think as they wish and to defend their tradition: *they* do not have the right, because they are "obscurantists" (§ 1852). And in the same vein one can speak of the intolerance of the "free democracy"; it is observed that few societies are so fanatical as those which proclaim precisely liberty (see, for example, the United Sates). One might add to this the case of recent events, in which "liberty" has been imposed on peoples who did not ask for it at all. It is superfluous to remember the intrigues and the armed interventions of the communist powers to "liberate" other nations. As in a new Manicheaism,[329] humanitarianism and pacifism are associated with democracy as angels of light, which save and defend wretched humanity from the chicaneries of various "backward" entities.

Pareto observes that the grip which humanitarianism has on the soul is usually sign of the weakening of those impulses which tend toward the conservation of the individual, of society, and of the State. "The windbags imagine that their declarations can be substituted for

---

329 A prominent religious current of the Sasanian Empire in Persia, Manicheaism originated with the prophet Mani in the third century. It is best known for its moralistic dualism: it conceives of the world as being starkly divided between the forces of good (light, spirit) and evil (darkness, matter).

the sentiments which really maintain the social and political equilibrium" (§ 2741). For which Pareto continuously affirmed the necessity
of a strong State acting on the plane of reality, rather than on fictions
whose true underpinnings remain invisible. In consequence, he recognized the significance of the Prussian State, and he could not help but
sympathize with fascism.

In this way he combated the anti-German myth, as well as that
of an adulterated "Latinity." Against those sectarian Catholics who
wish to see in Latin Catholicism the principle of every order and every
discipline, and in Protestantism the matrix of every anarchy (Guido
Manacorda and Francesco Orestano,[330] for example, later amused
themselves with like antitheses), Pareto observed (§ 1856) that, though
Italy is Catholic, "sentiments of discipline there are much less potent
than in Prussia"; also in Germany considerably more concrete and efficacious impulses reigned—that is, "the monarchical faith, the military
spirit, the submission to authority—all exceedingly weak in Italy."

Precisely in a comparison with the attitude that predominated in
Germany, Pareto makes certain observations fully applicable to today's
Italy: "One presumes that if the revolutionary forces or even only the
popular forces collide with the forces of order, the first have every right,
the second every duty—and principally, the duty to submit to everything before making use of arms. Affronts, blows, stones—everything
is excused if it comes from the people; while the public force must
possess an inexhaustible patience. Struck upon one cheek, it has to offer the other. The soldiers [referring to the period in which the military

---

330 Manacorda (1879-1965) was an Italian intellectual, philologist, editor of the
   journal *Biblioteca Sansoniana straniera*, and a decorated soldier during World
   War I. He converted to Catholicism in 1927, and became a prominent figure in
   the Catholic milieu, even acting as a mediator between Hitler and the Vatican
   in 1936 and 1937. He remained a strong adherent of the Church until his death.
   Orestano (1873-1945) was an Italian thinker and the author of various works of
   philosophy.

was employed in periods of disorder] have to be so many ascetic saints; one does not understand why one puts into their hands a rifle or a dagger rather than a rosary of Saint Progress." Pareto counterposes the Prussian view to this, that every true State should look after its own, or that "to react against insults and blows is not only permitted but even imposed on the forces of order; an official is dishonored if he lets himself be grazed with impunity by the lightest blow" (§ 2147).

Pareto was also an anti-conformist precursor in the domain of sex.

He wrote a book, which issued first in French, *Le virtuisme*, in which he stigmatized sexophobic puritanism. He highlighted the fact that modern sexual "virtuism" finds no comparison to any of the great civilizations of the past. Ancient Rome was ignorant of it; Rome above all sought dignity and measure. Pareto relates two examples of the famous Cato the Censor.[331] Cato was present at the *Floralia*,[332] a Roman festival in which at a certain moment a girl would appear on the scenes completely undressed. The stage direction, becoming aware of the presence of Cato amongst the public, hesitated to offer this scene. Cato therefore departed, so as not to deprive the public of their amusement. Another time Cato saw one of his young disciples leaving from a bordello. He said nothing. Only when the affair was repeated

---

331 More commonly known as Cato the Elder (234-149 BCE), he is not to be confused with his son Cato the Younger. Cato the *Younger* was renowned for his stoical and incorruptible virtue, which some interpreted as a punctilious moralism, and for his opposition to Caesar. Cato the *Elder* came to be known as "Censor" due to his zealous attempt to keep Hellenistic influences out of Rome, which desire he manifested most strongly in his discharge of his duties as official censor. Either Evola or Pareto is in error here, for the anecdote regarding the Floralia refers, not to Cato the *Elder*, but to Cato the *Younger*. (See Valerius Maximus, *Factorum et Dictorum Memorabilium*, Book II, Part 10, Section 8.)

332 Ancient Roman festival held in honor of the goddess Flora in springtide. It is perhaps not superfluous to note that the temple for this fertility goddess was built on recommendation of the Sibylline Books (see Chapter 9 above).

several times, did he remark that there was nothing wrong in those visits, if only the boy did not confound the brothel with his home.

Here is a spirited quip from Pareto (§ 1890): "If one is seized by this protective mania, why occupy oneself only with the seduction of women, and neglect that of men? Why not invent some other expression, like that of 'white female slave trade,' which counts equally for 'white males'?"[333]

And again: "Amongst the dogmas of the present sexual religion (the bourgeois 'virtuism') is one which holds prostitution to be an 'absolute evil,' and one is not to dispute this ... just as one is not to dispute any religious dogma. Yet from an experimental point of view it is still to be seen if prostitution is or is not the profession best suited to the temperament of certain women, so that it, more than any other profession which they might attain, appears welcome to them; and moreover if prostitution is or is not, within certain limits, useful to society as a whole" (§ 1382). And he emphasizes the "honest" character of the prostitute who at bottom makes trade of that which belongs to her, her body, compared to the censurable prostitution of so many political men of today, who unworthily trade the collective goods of others, betraying that trust which they have obtained by seducing the masses...

---

333 The original is impossible to render in English, playing as it does on an Italian phrase together with Italian's gendered nouns: *Perché non si inventa qualche altra espressione, come quella di "tratta delle bianche" che valga pure per i "bianchi"?* Here "*tratta delle bianche*" means "trade of whites" where "whites" is feminine.

31. JOSEPH DE MAISTRE

A new edition of Joseph de Maistre's *St. Petersburg Dialogues*, edited by Alfredo Cattabiani, has recently been published. This is Maistre's best known work; in it, however, Maistre's political references, for which Maistre counts as a "reactionary," are scarcer than in others of his writings. Indeed here we find above all considerations on moral and religious problems, and the very subtitle of the book, "Discussions on the Temporal Government of Providence" indicates this line of thought, which for us does not generate any great interest. Presupposing precisely the existence of a Providence conceived in moralizing terms, Maistre confronts the problem of reconciling this Providence with the spectacle that the world and history in their reality present us: wickedness which goes unpunished, virtue which has no recompense, and so on.

One cannot say that the solutions which Maistre proposes to this problem are entirely convincing. However Maistre is not brought to a redimensioning or an amplification of his concept of divinity in the terms we have indicated in our previous essay on the Left-Hand Path. The idea of a divine justice which would procrastinate only in its sanctions seems to us somewhat makeshift. (As its basis, Maistre translated a tract of Plutarch in the appendix of his book, a tract entitled precisely *De sera numinis vindicta*[334]). However the same Maistre offers a freer

334 Latin: "On the Delays of Divine Justice," Plutarch's investigation into the problem of Providence, given the fact that the unjust are not immediately punished, nor sometimes even during the course of this lifetime.

and more satisfying view when he compares the evils and the contingencies which rain on the entire human race to bullets which strike
an army in war, and which make no distinction between the good and
the wicked. One must believe that a being, acquiring the human state
of existence (wanting it, either thoughtlessly, or out of temerity, as has
been said in a hermetic tract), cannot help but find itself exposed to the
contingencies proper to such a state. One might naturally be brought
to search for transcendent moral nexuses in either case, but this retains
ever the character of reckless hypothesis.

But leaving this order of problems aside, we move on to mention certain ideas of Maistre which are interesting from the traditional point of view. In the first place, we might indicate the idea of
a Primordial Tradition. It may be that Maistre owes this to Claude de
Saint-Martin,[335] whom he knew, and who was an exponent of esoteric
doctrines (ever in the framework of Masonry, which at that time was
much different than now, so much so that even Maistre participated in
it). We might also indicate Maistre's thesis that the natural originating
state of humanity was not a barbaric state. On the contrary, it was a
state of light and of knowledge, while the wild man, the presumed
"primitive," was only "the descendant of a man detached from the
great tree of civilization, following a malfeasance which cannot be
repeated." But in other respects man finds himself feeling the effects of
a malfeasance and of a consequent degradation, caused not only by his
spiritual and intellectual, but also by his physical, vulnerability. Such
an idea is evidently similar to that of the "original sin" of the Christian
mythology, though the framework is wider and more acceptable. As
for the aforementioned thesis on the true nature of the "primitives," it

---

335 Louis Claude de Saint-Martin (1743-1803) was a French philosopher who published under the pseudonym *le philosophe inconnu*, "the unknown philosopher."
He had influence particularly in mystical and Kabbalistic circles, and his follow-
ers became known as Martinists.

has the potential of carrying ethnologic research to a higher level, and preserving the same research from many blunders.

Maistre indicts the savants, scientists and their like who, as if in conspiracy, do not admit that one may know more than them, or in a different way than they do. "One judges a time in which men saw effects in causes by the mentality of a time in which men struggle to rise from effects to causes, or in which one says it is useless to occupy oneself with causes, or in which one almost does not even know what a cause is." He adds: "One hears endless rubbish about the ignorance of the ancients who saw spirits everywhere: to me it seems that we are much more foolish than they, because we do not see spirits anywhere. We hear talk always of physical causes. But what, in the end, is a physical cause?" For him the axiom that "no physical event regarding man can have a higher cause" is inauspicious, and promotes a fundamental superficiality.

Maistre negates the idea of progress. Regression appears considerably more plausible to him. He observes that myriad traditions attest that "men have commenced with science, but with a different science than our own, superior to it, because it departed from the heights, which rendered it at the same time very dangerous. And this explains why science, in its beginnings, was ever mysterious, and remained closed in the sphere of the temples, where in the end it was extinguished, when this flame no longer served for anything other than to burn."

Maistre strongly emphasized prayer and its power. He wrote in the end, "No one can prove that a nation which prays is not fulfilled"—but it is really the opposite which one must demonstrate, and this is not easy. One finds oneself standing before the antithesis between prayer and the virtue that one attributes to it on the one hand, and the immutability of the laws of nature on the other—antithesis which Maistre seeks to get to the bottom of, in a way which is, however, little convincing. He holds that if prayers are not granted, this is owed only to a higher divine wisdom.

Maistre's apologia of the executioner as instrument of God is often cited as though it were scandalous, and also his conception of the divine character of war.[336] Unfortunately in this last connection he does not consider that war might bring about heroism and super-individual actions, but he sees it in the gloomy terms of an expiation which strikes a fundamentally guilty and degraded humanity. The difference between just war and unjust war, between a war of defense and a war of conquest, between a victorious war and a lost war, is not considered. These are views which little accord with a positively "reactionary" orientation.

In another of his works, *Considérations sur la France*, Maistre, while declaring himself for a restoration, enunciates an important concept by saying that the counterrevolution must not be a "contrary revolution" but rather "the contrary of revolution." To him one owes a kind of theology of revolution; he brings to light the "demonic" aspect which generally conceals itself in the revolutionary phenomenon. Such an aspect is observable also in the fact that revolution sweeps its artificers away, rather than letting itself be truly guided by them, and often crushes them in the process. Only in the modern epoch do we

---

336 Maistre's stances on both of these questions are explicated most famously in the same *St. Petersburg Dialogues* that Evola here considers. His notorious statement on the executioner is put into the mouth of the Count, who says in the First Dialogue, "And yet all grandeur, all power, all subordination rests on the executioner: he is the horror and the bond of human association. Remove this incomprehensible agent from the world, and at that very moment order gives way to chaos, thrones topple, and society disappears."

For the question of war, see the Seventh Dialogue of the the same work, where the Senator says, "War is thus divine in itself, since it is a law of the world. War is divine through its consequences of a supernatural nature which are as much general as particular, consequences little known because they are little sought but which are nonetheless indisputable. Who could doubt the benefits that death in war brings? And who could believe that the victims of this dreadful judgment have shed their blood in vain?"

find the phenomenon of a more or less institutionalized "permanent revolution," with its technicians and its lucid manipulators.

In *St. Petersburg Dialogues*, leaving apart certain disquisitions (for example Maistre's prolix analysis of Locke), the reader might glean many other interesting points. We shall not resist the temptation to relate Maistre's comment on woman: "Woman cannot be superior save as a woman; but from the moment she emulates man, she becomes naught but a monkey." This is pure truth, whether or not it pleases various contemporaneous "feminine movements."

32. PAPINI

We intentionally withheld these notes on Papini[337] in the period immediately following his death. His demise has naturally provoked many commemorative articles, of the sort which one is accustomed to writing on occasions of this kind.

After expressing this due reservation, however, it would be amiss of us if we did not sort some things out in the case of Papini, by looking at these matters from a different perspective than the literary viewpoint of the literary critics. Papini was a very brilliant and lively writer, and may his value in the literary field remain here unprejudiced. A very different problem, however, is constituted by Papini's significance in the whole of his Italian intellectual life, and above all in relation with the spiritual crisis of an entire generation. That which the many have written on him in this connection is little enough apt. Papini might be esteemed by our conformist "right-thinking" bourgeois, especially that part of it oriented toward the Democratic Christians; the same cannot be said however for whomever feels the crisis of thought and of modern society to its depths.

---

337 Giovanni Papini (1881-1956) was an influential Italian writer, poet, and essayist who was particularly active in the period preceding the First World War, during which he became a central and very influential figure in Italian cultural life. He maintained solidarity with the fascists throughout the Fascist Period, but distanced himself discreetly from the Nazis, in particular from their racial theories. He made quite a stir when he converted to Catholicism in 1921; Evola speaks of this event later in the present chapter.

Let us premise our remarks by noting that we have followed Papini's work from the beginning. As adolescents, there was a time in which Papini was truly our model. This was the period of the only *Sturm und Drang*[338] which Italy ever knew—the urgency of those forces which had become intolerant of the suffocating climate of Italy's petty bourgeois in the first decades of the twentieth century. This was the period of "Leonardo" and of "Lacerba."[339] Papini had real significance only in that period, by his decisive inversion of the judgement of that time. He was as an opener of the breach. We owe it to him and to his group that the most interesting foreign currents of thought and art of the *avant-garde* came to be known here in Italy, renovating and amplifying our horizons. We are not referring only to the journals just cited, but also

---

338 German: "storm and stress." This refers to the German literary movement of the late 18th century which included such luminary figures as Goethe and Schiller. It takes many of its philosophical roots from the thought of the French philosopher Rousseau, and it is characterized by an insistency on passions and individuality *à la* Romanticism—the subsequent artistic movement which it decidedly prepared.

339 Reference to two famous journals of that period: the *Leonardo*, published from 1903-1907 with a total of 25 editions, and the *Lacerba*, founded in 1913 and interrupted with Italy's entry into the First World War in 1915. The *Leonardo* published articles of philosophy and ideas and reveled in particular in polemicals. It featured numerous debates, and was responsible for bringing the work of many foreigners into Italian intellectual currents, such as for example Henri Bergson (see note 124 to Chapter 12 above). Its founder was none other than Papini, who contributed to it under the pseudonym Gian Falco. The *Lacerba* takes its title from a poem of the heretical Medieval poet Cecco d'Ascoli, "*L'Acerba*," meaning "Bitterness," and it posted a line from the poem on its title page: "*Qui non si canta al modo delle rane*," ("Here we do not sing in the way of the frogs.") It, too, was founded by Papini, in collaboration with Arengo Soffici. In its mission statement, one finds the following line, which might be taken in a way as the essence of the entire project: *Tutto è nulla, nel mondo, tranne il genio.* ("Everything is nothing in this world, except for the genius.")

to initiatives such as the "Culture of the Soul"[340] collection which was directed by Papini, and which brought to the conscience of the young of that time a series of particularly significant ancient and modern writings. But during that time the paradoxical, polemical, iconoclastic, anti-conformist, revolutionary Papini interested us yet more: because we believed that, despite his brilliant scandal-mongering façade, he was really in earnest. In the attack against the official academic culture, against intellectual servility, against those who were famous merely for being famous, against the values of society and the bourgeois morality, we were enthusiastically on his side, even if we were troubled by a certain neo-realist style[341] *avant la lettre* and a certain Florentine rascality transposed onto the intellectual plane. And here, as an aside—since it is accounted to Papini's merit that he "spoke badly of Croce"—it is appropriate to make an observation: if Papini attacked and demolished Croce,[342] he did not do the same thing with Gentile, merely because Gentile at that time was almost nonexistent culturally, was a mere disciple of Croce. Papini's later attitude toward Gentile would have been the same, the doses would have been even doubled, if Papini were still what he had before been, in the period when Gentile came to the foreground.

---

340 Papini was responsible for conceiving a series of scholarly titles which were subsequently published by Rocco Carabba from 1909 to 1938. The series was known as *Cultura dell'anima*, the "Culture of the Soul," and it published a total of 163 titles, which are still available in Italian from Rocco Carabba.

341 For Neo-Realism, see note 27 to Chapter 2 above. As for the reference in this sentence to "Florentine rascality"—Papini was born in Florence, city known to this day in Italy for the irreverent and impish sense of humor of its citizens.

342 Reference in particular to a notorious 1913 speech that Papini gave at the Costanzi Theater of Rome, entitled "Against Rome and Against Benedetto Croce," in which Papini endorsed the Futurist movement, accused Rome of being antiquarian and counter innovation, and launched a scathing attack against Croce as the representative of this intellectual current. He said of Croce that he was a "*grand'uomo per volontà propria e per grazie della generale pecoraggine ed asinaggine,*" that is, "a great man by his own will, and thanks to the general sheep-like and donkey-like quality of the public."

Matters grew murkier for us upon the emergence of Papini's interventionism and his association with the Futurists, which was due in part to this same interventionism. We were young then: besides, we did not understand how anyone might take seriously these hackneyed "Latin" and anti-Germanic commonplaces sufficiently to carry Italy into a war which, in our opinion, ought to have been fought, if at all, in fidelity with the Triple Alliance, or at the least by affirming a will to empire equal to that of Germany's, rather than on the basis of some kind of banal and sentimental irredentism. I understood why Marinetti[343] (to whom I said these things when I encountered him on the front) declared that I was "farther from him than an Eskimo." I did not understand however how Papini, anti-comformistic intellectual that he was, could have ended up toeing this jingoist line. Naturally, the matter will present itself differently to certain current viewpoints of a generic nationalism, devoid of true principles, and for them all of this might even convert to a patriotic title for Papini.

On the cultural plane, the first serious cold shower to our enthusiasm was Papini's autobiographical *A Finished Man*.[344] This was not the

---

343 Filippo Tommaso Marinetti (1876-1944) was an Italian poet and playwright, and is known as the founder of the Futurist movement. His works (which were often written, not in Italian, but in French) provoked a scandal in Italy for their overt and sometimes outrageous sexuality. He enlisted voluntarily in the First World War, in which he was injured, and he was an early adherent of the fascists, though later he distanced himself from them. He believed fervently in war, if one may put it that way, and even participated in the Russian front of World War II at the age of sixty-six, which utterly exhausted his physical resources. He died of a heart attack near the end of the war in the Hotel Excelsior of Bellagio. Evola speaks here surely of the front in World War I, during which he, too, served as an officer. This experience evidently prepared Evola for a kind of spiritual awakening, which came to him upon his reentry into Rome as he was reading a Buddhistic text. (See *The Path of Cinnabar*, "Personal Background and Early Experiences," in which chapter he also mentions this meeting with Marinetti.)

344 *Un uomo finito*—written however in 1913, when Papini was only thirty years old.

balance sheet of a spiritual failure, but worse yet: for this failure was
exploited and almost commercialized, as an exhibitionist would use it,
to extract a brilliant book from his failure. The initial Papinian position, certainly, could not help but bring us to a "ground zero of all values." This was the experience anticipated by Nietzsche and Stirner,[345] it
was that which would present itself anew with the "burnt generation,"
with the early Jünger, and with a certain kind of existentialism. We
understood the idea of the "finished man"; but the man who is really
finished stops writing and has done with intellectualism; he does as
Rimbaud[346] did: he burns all his bridges, he essentially changes plane.
Perhaps he kills himself.

---

345 Nietzsche, perhaps the first philosopher to look nihilism sternly in the face,
wrote in one of the most important sections of *Beyond Good and Evil* (Book 3,
Section 56), "Whoever has endeavored with some enigmatic longing, as I have,
to think pessimism through to its depths...; whoever has really...looked down
into the most world-denying of all possible ways of thinking...may just thereby,
without really meaning to do so, have opened his eyes to the opposite ideal..."
(translator Walter Kaufmann). Max Stirner (born Johann Caspar Schmidt,
1806-1856) was a German philosopher, known almost exclusively for his 1845
work *The Ego and its Own*, which has been variously interpreted as a work of
amoral nihilism, a proto-anarchical tract, and an early form of existentialism.
This work was as notorious as it was influential, and for the former quality the
latter has often been kept hush; most of those who have taken inspiration form
Stirner have said little or nothing about this influence in their public works.
Among these men are Carl Schmitt, Jürgen Habermas, Albert Camus, and possibly also Edmund Husserl and Friedrich Nietzsche. (Some have gone so far
as to accuse Nietzsche of plagiarism on this score—the which is absurd, but
suggestive of Stirner's impressive subterranean influence.)

346 Arthur Rimbaud (1854-1891) was a French poet best known for his 1873 prose
poem *Une Saison en Enfer* (A Season in Hell). He was involved in a stormy
affair with the poet Paul Verlaine (1844-1896), which culminated in Verlaine's
attempting to shoot Rimbaud, thus landing the older man in prison. Rimbaud
was precocious both in his beginnings (he was published already at the age of
16) and in his endings (he abruptly stopped writing at the age of thirty-one, and
dedicated the remainder of his life to travelling and working).

The definitive confirmation of our doubts was not long in the coming. We speak of Papini's "conversion" to Catholicism.[347] Let us understand each other: if a socialistic anticlerical or an atheist passes over to Catholicism, we cannot do other than praise him, and it remains unquestionable for us that the humblest regularly ordained priest stands at a considerably higher rank than any university professor and any pseudo-intellectual. But for Papini matters stood otherwise. His cultural experiences did not restrict themselves to the sphere of profane culture. As he was part of the Florentine coterie of the "Philosophical Library,"[348] currents of high mysticism and even of initiation were not unknown to him; indeed, on the recommendation of a Florentine savant of esoteric studies of uncommon stature, one Arturo Reghini,[349] he had even attempted transcendent experiences in a retreat (frivolously described in *A Finished Man* as an attempt to "become a god"). Now, if despite these precedents he ended up a Catholic, one must imagine that there was nothing serious in all those past experiences.

Our most immediate impression was effectively that Papini, who no longer knew how to scandalize, followed the counsel of Chesterton,[350] and chose the most fitting expedient for putting himself

---

347 Papini converted in 1921 with his usual flamboyancy, announcing the fact with his publication of his *Story of Christ*. The event was of some importance of the cultural milieu of the day, bringing the praise of some and the condemnation of others.

348 The *Biblioteca filosofica* was a center of philosophical, religious, and spiritual studies founded in Florence in 1906 by Papini and others, who published their work in numerous volumes.

349 Reghini (1878-1946) was an Italian mathematician and esotericist who was involved for a time with the *Lacerba* journal and also, together with Evola, the *Ur* group, though the two later had a falling out, evidently having to do with Evola's stance regarding Masonry. (For more on this stance, see Chapter 10 above.)

350 G.K. Chesterton (1874-1936), English writer and lay theologian who is well known for his defense of Christianity and particularly of Catholicism. The counsel in question might be reference to the reflections included in Chesterton's essay "Why I Am A Catholic."

paradoxically on the line of conformist normality. Only much later did we read the *Life of Christ*, while we were in hospital. Enough; we were dumbfounded by the fact that a book of the kind might have been "successful"—and, yet more, that the Church might have so esteemed and recommended it. It seemed to us to constitute the most evident proof that there was no true, profound spiritual crisis at the bottom of Papini's "conversion," that at most an interior renunciation might have acted out, the need to pacify himself and to render things easier for himself by drawing out of a fixed body of beliefs those certainties that he could no longer find in the wake of his iconoclastic phase. For in this book there is nothing transfiguring and nothing transfigured; one perceives not even the least mutation of the human substance. The style is the same, nothing is garnered and given as a deeper dimension of Catholicism and of its myths: it is a banal apologetic based on the most exterior, catechist and sentimental aspects of Christianity. It absolutely leaves us speechless that Del Massa[351] could associate Papini with the "origins of a path which might be defined as properly Italian, on account of its tradition"—provided that one intends here tradition in the higher sense, rather than some hackneyed traditionalism.

Now, if it is from that moment—from the period of his "conversion"—that Papini has obtained ever more recognition and has acquired fame, it is also from that moment that he he has truly become for us the "finished man," and has ceased to have any meaning at all in the most vital problems of those who keep themselves spiritually in the breach. He is the symbol not of a conquest, but of an abdication. He remains a brilliant, interesting writer who from the start felt the need to scribe articles and aphorisms.

There is nothing wrong in attributing to Papini all due recognition—the same recognition which (politics apart) one will not fail

---

351 Aniceto Del Massa (1898-1975), Italian writer and esotericist, was a friend and collaborator of Evola's.

to concede, upon their death, to Malaparte, to Baldini, to Soffici, to Moravia,[352] and to many other exponents of that which we might call our "well written intelligent stupidity." But we would do well nonetheless not to confound the issue. One limits oneself to what is humanly due to those who finally come to the end of their earthly itinerary.

---

352 Curzio Malaparte (born Kurt Erich Suckert, 1898-1957) was an Italian journalist, dramatist, and novelist, who chose his surname (Malaparte, meaning "the bad side" or "the wrong side") in deliberate contrast to Napoleon Bonaparte ("good or right side"). He began as a supporter of Mussolini but somehow or other ended up a communist. Antonio Baldini (1889-1962) was an Italian journalist, writer, and essayist. Ardengo Soffici (1879-1964) was an Italian writer, essayist, poet, and painter. He was one of the founders of *Lacerba*, but, as many of its contributors, broke off to fight in the war against German *Kultur*. He was a fascist, though he liked to distance himself from Mussolini. Alberto Moravia (born Alberto Pincherle, 1907-1990) is considered one of the most important Italian writers of the twentieth century. He was a continual critic of the fascist regime, often veiling his attacks in allegorical and surreal writings, or concealing his work by means of a pseudonym.

33. CARLO MICHELSTAEDTER

Carlo Michelstaedter[353] is one of those writers of the modern epoch who affirm the individual's need to rise up to *being*, to an absolute value, by putting an end to all those compromises which mask an ἄβιος βίος,[354] a life that is not life. Through this one brings oneself to that which man fears more than every other thing: facing oneself, measuring oneself in relation to "being." Michelstaedter calls the state of being "persuasion," and defines it essentially as a negation of correlations. When the *I* places the principle of its very consisting not in itself, but in the "other," when its life is conditioned by things and by relations, where there is subjection to dependencies and to need—in this kind of existence, there can be no "persuasion," but rather only the privation of value. Value is only an existing in oneself, not asking another for the ultimate principle and the sense of life itself: it is "autarchy" in

---

353 Michelstaedter (1887-1910) was a Jewish Italian writer, philosopher, and man of letters who was remarkably productive in the short span of his life. He was a student of the classic philosophers, especially Plato and Aristotle, and his work bears a decidedly classical stamp of rare purity. He attempted, as the classical philosophers, to extract himself from a tragic existence by becoming internally complete. His life runs in intriguing parallel to that of the Jewish Austrian Otto Weininger (see note 178 to Chapter 15 above). Michelstaedter's most important work is thought to be his *Persuasion and Rhetoric*. All quotes in the following chapter, unless otherwise noted, come from that work.

354 Ancient Greek: "lifeless life."

the Hellenic sense.[355] Thus not only the whole of an existence made of needs, of affects, of "sociality," of intellectualistic adornment and the like is included in the sphere of non-value, but also the corporal organism and the system of nature itself (the experience of which is understood as generated, in its indefinite spatio-temporal development, by the incessant gravitation with which deficiency pursues being; however, insofar as being is sought outside of itself, deficiency will never succeed in possessing it).

The *I* which believes itself to be insofar as it *persists*, that is insofar as it ignores the fullness of an actual possession and carries its "persuasion" back to a subsequent moment, on which, moreover, it makes itself dependent; the *I* which in every present flees itself; the *I* which one does *not have* but seeks, and *desires*; the *I* which however in no future can ever be, since the future is the very symbol of its privation, the shadow that runs alongside the one that flees, at a given distance from the body of its reality, which at every point maintains itself unchanged—such an *I* is, for Michelstaedter, the meaning of daily life, but also of "non-value," of the "must-not-be." Against such a situation, "persuasion" postulates rather consisting, resisting existential deficiency with all one's own life and at every point, never ceding to the life that is lacking to itself by searching beyond or in the future. It postulates not asking, but grasping "being" in one's very fist: not to "go" but to endure. While existential deficiency accelerates time in its continuous anxiety for the future, and barters a present emptiness on a future one, the stability of the individual pre-occupies infinite time in the now, and arrests time. Its firmness is a dizzying slipstream for those who are still in the current. "Every one of the instants of such a man is a century of the life of the others—so long as he makes of himself

---

355 Autarchy comes from the Ancient Greek αὐτάρκεια, meaning literally "self-rule," but coming thus to mean to the Hellenic mindset total self-sufficiency, perfect independence.

a flame and reaches a consisting in the ultimate present."[356] To clarify this point, it is important to comprehend the nature of correlation which is contained in its premises: given that the world is understood as generated away from the right direction and toward deficiency, of which it is almost the tangible incarnation, it is an illusion to think that "persuasion" might be realized through an abstract and subjective consisting in that value (as in Stoicism) which has being (experienced nature) against it, such that, though it has no value, it is. He who tends toward absolute persuasion must arise instead to a cosmic responsibility. That is: I must not flee from my deficiency—which is mirrored by the world—but take it onto me, adjust myself to its weight and redeem it. For which Michelstaedter states: "You cannot call yourself persuaded as long as something is, that is not persuaded," and he hints at persuasion as being "at the extreme consciousness of him who is one with things, who has all things in himself: ἒ ουνεχές."[357]

To clarify Michelstaedter's central problem, one can relate the concept of insufficiency to the Aristotelian concept of the imperfect act.[358] The imperfect or "impure" act is an act of potencies that do not arrive in themselves (κάθ αὐτο)[359] to the act, and for this have need of an *other*. This is the case, for instance, of sensory perception, whose potency of perceiving is not sufficient in and of itself: by itself this potency does not produce perception, but has need of some correlated object. Now, the fundamental point which connects this to Michelstaedter's position is the following: in the transcendental realm the imperfect act resolves the privation of the *I* only apparently; in reality, it reconfirms it. To formulate an example through comparison, the *I* is thirsty. As long as

---

356 [Evola's note.]Taken from Michealstaedter's *Il dialogo della salute*. [*The Dialogue on Health*, yet to be translated into English. -Trans.]

357 ἒ ουνεχές is Ancient Greek, meaning "really or truly being ones own self" or "really and truly possessing one's own self."

358 That is, an act which requires something external to itself for its realization.

359 Ancient Greek: "just as the self" or "according to the self."

it drinks it confirms the state of him who is not sufficient in his own life but who, in order to live, has need of "other"; water and the rest are naught but the symbols of his deficiency. (On this point one must fix one's attention: one does not desire because there is a privation of being, but there is a privation of being because one desires—and, in the second place: there is not a desire, for example that of drinking, because there are determinate things, for example water, but the desired things, just as the privation of being which urges toward them, are created at one and the same point from out of the relative desire. Desire is, therefore, the *prius*[360] which creates the correlation as its two ends, namely privation and corresponding object, or in our example thirst and water.) And insofar as one feeds of it and *asks* one's life of it, the *I* feeds only of its own privation and endures in this privation, fleeing from that "pure" or perfect act, from that eternal water, of which speak the very words of Christ,[361] and wherein every thirst, and likewise every other privation, would be forever conquered. This yearning, this dark emesis,[362] which carries the *I* toward the external—toward the "other"—is that which generates in experience the system of finite and contingent reality. Persuasion, which burns such emesis in the state of absolute consisting, of the pure being-in-itself, has therefore also the sense of "consummation" of the world that reveals itself to me.

The sense of such a consummation is clarified by arriving at consequences which Michelstaedter has not completely succeeded in bringing out.

Before all, to say that I must not flee from my deficiency signifies, among other things, that I must recognize myself as the creative function of an experienced world. The justification of so-called transcen-

---

360 Latin: "first or primary thing, the prior thing."

361 [Evola's note.] John 4:14. "But whosoever drinketh of the water that I shall give him shall never thirst; but the water that I shall give him shall be in him a well of water springing up into everlasting life."

362 Italian: *conato oscuro.*

dental idealism (that is the philosophical system according to which the world is posited by the *I*) might follow from this, *based on a moral imperative.* But according to this premise the world is considered as a negation of value. A second point thus proceeds from the general postulate of redeeming the world, of taking on its deficiency—a second point which is as much a practical postulate as a moral one: the very negation of value itself must be recognized, in a certain way, as a value. This is important. Indeed, if I consider the impulse which has generated the world as a pure, irrational *datum*, it is evident that persuasion, insofar as it is conceived as the negation of that datum, comes to depend on it, and so is not absolutely sufficient to itself but depends on the "other," on the negation which permits it to affirm itself. In such a case, that is, in the case in which the same yearning is not reclaimed as the affirmation of value but remains entirely a datum, persuasion would therefore not at all be persuasion—the initiatory mystery would inevitably reduce perfection to an illusion. For which it is necessary to admit as a moral postulate that the same antithesis participates, in a certain way, in value. But in what way? Such a problem carries us to admit a certain dynamism in the concept of persuasion. Indeed it is obvious that if persuasion is not reduced to a pure, unrelated sufficiency (that is, to a *state*), but if it is rather sufficiency insofar as it is negation of an insufficiency (that is, an *act*, a relation), the antithesis certainly has value and is explained: the *I* at first *must* pose privation, non-value, if only under the condition that it is posed precisely so that it might be negated, because this act of negation, and it alone, generates the value of persuasion. But what does it mean to negate the antithesis—which in this context is equivalent to saying, nature? One recalls that for Michelstaedter nature is a non-value insofar as it is symbol and incarnation of the flight of the *I* from actual possession of itself, insofar as it is correlative to an imperfect or "impure" act in the sense mentioned above. One does not treat therefore of negating this or that determination of the existent, because with such negation one would strike only at the effect, the consequence, not the transcendental root, of non-value; nor even of eliminating in general every action, because the antithesis is not the action in general, but rather the action insofar as it is flight from oneself, insofar as it is "going"—and it is not a given that every action necessarily has such a sense. What must be resolved is rather the passive, heteronomous, extroverted mode of action. Now negation in such a mode is constituted by the action sufficient to itself, which is also potency. To live every act in perfect possession and so to transfigure the whole of the forms until these do not express anything but the very body of an infinite *potestas*[363]—let us say, of the absolute Individual made of potency—this is therefore the sense of cosmic and, (at the same time), existential redemption. Just as the concretization of "rhetoric" is the development of the world of dependency and of necessity, so the concretization of persuasion is the development of a world of autarchy and of dominion, and the point of pure negation is only the neutral point between the two phases.

The development of Michelstaedter's views on that which one might call a "magical idealism" appears therefore to proceed according to a logical continuity. Michelstaedter in a certain way however remained fixed in an indeterminate negation, and this, in great part, because he did not consider sufficiently that the finite and the infinite should not be referred to a particular object or action, but that they are two modes of living any object or action. The true Lord does not in general have need of negating (in the sense of nullifying) nor, under the pretext of rendering it absolute, of reducing life to an undifferentiated unity, almost, if you please, in a species of lightning flash: the act of potency—the which is not an act of desire or of violence—rather than destroying perfect possession, attests it and confirms it. But Michelstaedter, for the very intensity in which he lived the need of absolute value, did not know how to give this value a concrete body

---

363 Latin: "power, ability, potency."

and simultaneously to develop it in the doctrine of potency; the which perhaps is related to the tragic end of his mortal existence.[364]

However Michelstaedter himself affirmed that "we do not want to know in relation to what things a man is determined, but rather we want to know *how* he is determined," which is to say, beyond the act, one treats of the *form* or *value* according to which the individual is to be seen. In fact every logical relation is in a certain way indeterminate, and value is a higher dimension in which it is specified. One of Michelstaedter's merits is his reaffirmation of the importance of value in the metaphysical order: indeed "rhetoric" and the "path of persuasion" are distinguishable not from a purely logical point of view, but rather by the point of view of value alone. It is very important here that Michelstaedter in a certain way recognizes that there are two paths. This duplicity is itself a value: because the affirmation of persuasion cannot count as affirmation of liberty when one does not have the awareness of the possibility of affirmation as a value of non-value itself, a kind of indifference: for only the "Lord of Yes and No" is free and infinite (on this problem, cf. our *Theory of the Absolute Individual*, I, §§ 1-5). The other justification of the antithesis, introduced above, evidently takes as its presupposition the positive option for "persuasion."

---

364 On October 17, 1910, the very day that he finished the appendices of his *Persuasion and Rhetoric*, and following an argument with his mother, Michelstaedter took his own life. Evola's speculation that this might have had something to do with Michelstaedter's failure to bring his own ideas to necessary conclusion, his remaining on the plane of mere negation, is certainly an intriguing one. It is made all the more intriguing by the fact that thoughts of suicide were not altogether foreign to Evola. Indeed, in a kind of spiritual crisis following the First World War, Evola was almost carried away by such an urge. (See note 343 to Chapter 32 above; also, *The Path of Cinnabar*, "Personal Background and Early Experiences.")

34. THE CASE OF GIOVANNI GENTILE

In those circles which are defined neo-fascist, one hears frequent reference to Giovanni Gentile[365]—references which exalt his figure and proclaim him to be the "philosopher of fascism." It is true that all this reduces in general to vague references, and that certainly no one has bothered to read Gentile's books of philosophy, nor to deeply investigate his ideas. This gives rise nonetheless to misunderstandings, and two formulae which are commonly disinterred from Gentile— that of the "ethical State" and that of "humanism of work"—indicate where we are going and where we will end up on account of our lack of discernment. Whatever might have been the factual rapport between Gentile and fascism, whatever important posts he occupied in the Fascist Period (the which, moreover, gave him the means of affirming his philosophy often in disagreeable ways), this does not alter the fact that a true Right can have really very little to do with Gentile.

The critique of Gentile's purely philosophical thought, his so-called "actualism," which we have already submitted in another place, cannot interest us here. Only in the field of practical and political applications can his work be of any interest. Gentile's personal and social equation is, in this last respect, determinant. Gentile came of a certain intellectual bourgeoisie of jingoist and simultaneously Enlightenment hue—which means also of anti-traditionalist hue. Not for nothing did he exalt "the Prophets [sic] of the Risorgimento," and in his last book

---

365 For biographical information on Gentile, see notes 6 and 12 to Chapter 1 above.

Genesis and Structure of Society he professed the same theses of historiography which are professed not only by Enlightenment-Masonry but even by the Marxists. Thus we read: "The humanism of culture, which was the glorious stage [!] of the liberation of man [!!], is followed today, or will be followed tomorrow, by the humanism of work." This is precisely the thesis of "progressivist" Marxist historiography: first the liberal bourgeois anti-traditional revolution, then the socialist revolution. "There is no doubt," continues Gentile, "that the social movements and the parallel socialist movements of the twentieth century have created a new humanism; and it is the task of our century to see to the introduction of this as a politically concrete and present-day movement." He is alluding again to the so-called "humanism of work." And again, in the *Speech to the Italians* (1943): "Whoever speaks of communism in Italy today, is but a corporatist impatient with the delays necessary for the development of his idea." Two strictly observant Gentilians, Arnaldo Volpicelli and Ugo Spirito, had already previously proclaimed the theory of "integral corporatism," a mix between totalitarian statism and radical collectivizing syndicalism. And today Ugo Spirito, evidently taking it for granted that "delays are necessary for the development of his idea," has declared himself communist—indeed, to all appearances, has gone so far as to declare himself Maoist.[366] This is verily a curious end for the creator of the "Spirit as a pure act" and "Absolute Subject"—and it is an end exalted surely by smoky "idealistic" Gentilian philosophy.

But beyond indicting these decided left-leaning perspectives from the historiography of the "philosopher of fascism," it is against Gentile's very "historicism" that one must take a stand. It is necessary to ap-

---

366 That is, a student or admirer of Mao Zedong (1896-1976), one of the principle figures of the communist revolution in China, and Chairman of the subsequent Communist Party from 1949-1976. Zedong is responsible for the deaths of more human beings than any other person in history (some 40,000,000 by the most modest estimates).

proach this matter from a distance, from the theory of knowledge, or the gnoseology,[367] of so-called "absolute idealism." We limit ourselves to an exceedingly fleeting gesture in this direction. The point of departure here is Berkeley's principle of *esse est percipi*,[368] which holds that I can concretely speak only of the being that I perceive, think, and experience. Schopenhauer, integrating this thesis, spoke of the "world as (my) representation."[369] The post-Hegelian idealistic philosophers, like Gentile, did not stop here, but affirmed that the world is "posited" by the *I*, that it would not exist save in the act wherein it is posited by the *I*. But here arises the tedious difficulty, that if I can really say that what is perceived or represented does not exist beyond the act of my perceiving it or representing it to myself (the which is almost

---

367 A term derived from the Ancient Greek γνῶσις ("knowledge") and λόγος (reason, word, discourse, speech). It emerged as a theory of knowledge in 18th century aesthetics, and is connected to Eastern Orthodox Christian theology.

368 Reference to the immaterialist theory of the Irish philosopher George Berkeley (1685-1753). *Esse est percipi* is from Berkeley's famous 1710 work *A Treatise Concerning the Principles of Human Knowledge*, Part I, Section III (in the original, "*Esse* is *Percipi.*") The term is Latin, meaning "to be is to be perceived." Thus, objects have their being, not in their "materiality" or in some other quality pertaining to them as such and separate from all observers, but rather through the very act of their being observed. For these ideas, Berkeley is often (but not altogether justly) associated with the concept of solipsism.

369 Arthur Schopenhauer (1788-1860) was a German philosopher, famous for the work which Evola references here, *The World as Will and Representation*, in which he developed Kantian metaphysics by positing a metaphysical will at the root of all phenomenon. The main sources of inspiration for his philosophy were Kant, Plato, and the ancient Hindu Upanishads. He was a notorious opponent of Hegel at the very peak of Hegel's fame and influence, calling Hegel's philosophy "a colossal piece of mystification." He had an important influence on a noteworthy number of thinkers and artists, perhaps most importantly and famously on Nietzsche, but also on figures as diverse as Gustav Mahler, Leo Tolstoy, Thomas Mann, Richard Wagner, and Jorge Luis Borges.

Lapalissadian[370]), so far as to say that that which I perceive I have also freely and voluntarily "posited" (outside of the exceedingly restricted limits of certain mental and intellectual domains), to that extent the *I* is made almost into a god-creator of the contents of experience. But this is evidently another question entirely.

Gentile muddled through these difficulties with the theory of the so-called "concrete will" and of the "historicism of spirit," the which is an authentic mystification. In the face of everything which happens, but which I neither will nor desire in the least, and of which I am not at all the author, Gentile states that it is only as "empirical subject" and "abstract will" that one did not want all this—but that one wants it perfectly as "I-pure-act," in whose "concrete will" and "historicity" the real and the desired, the act and the fact, reality and rationality, become a single thing.

And I as "empirical subject" (that is, as that which I truly am) must conform myself to this daydream called the *I*. The result is this: that to be able to "immanentize," that is to be able to redirect the content of all that which is experienced to a hypothetical transcendental *I*, I am condemned to recognize as "mine" and "wanted by me" also that which I least want and which I simply suffer. Thus the unique ethics coherently deducible from such a philosophy is one which is ready to sanction every interior capitulation, every conformism, every acceptation of the accomplished fact—and with an equal readiness to accord the same recognition to an opposite *fait accompli* tomorrow, suppos-

---

370 Meaning that it is almost tautological, a mere truism. This is a reference to Jacques de La Palisse, a French nobleman and military officer who enjoys the curious privilege of being remembered almost exclusively for his tombstone. That stone bears the epithet *"Ci-gît le Seigneur de La Palice: s'il n'était pas mort, il ferait encore envie"* ("Here lies the Seigneur de La Palisse: if he were not dead, he would yet be envied.") easily misinterpreted as *"...s'il n'était pas mort, il serait encore en vie"*: that is, "if he were not dead, *he would still be alive.*" The ambiguity here quite naturally erupted in innumerable Gallic jollities.

ing it is able to undermine that of today. This is, in the last analysis, the origin and the essence of "historicism." *De rigueur* it is the philosophy of the spineless, in opposition to those who assert themselves and who truly make history.

One must ascribe to Gentile's merit however the fact that he remained fascist even when "history" evidently was rendering fascism "anti-historical," insofar as history was making anti-fascism become real—and thus just, true and rational—with the help of the Allies. This demonstration of character and of civil courage, which entailed moreover doctrinal incoherence, cost Gentile his life.[371]

Given the premises just now indicated, it might be surprising that Gentile advocated for authoritarianism. This is another fount of misunderstanding, as is the Gentilian conception of the "ethical State" which, as has been said, is being advocated for today. The fact is that there are different types of authority, and here yet again Gentile's personal equation makes itself felt, beginning already from his education. One must keep in mind that the strong and traditional States recognize hierarchical, heroic and spiritual values, not "ethical" values, and still less moralizing preoccupations. Not a moral canon but the natural prestige of masters and sovereigns, of superior natures (the which often left much to be desired from the moralistic and "virtuistic" point of view) constituted its basis. But in the "ethical State" morality is instead set at the zenith of the State; one hopes thereby to guarantee it a higher dignity than that granted to the agnostic, neutral and juridical conception of the public thing.[372]

Nothing but a deplorable authoritarianism (that which Croce called the "governmental morality") and totalitarianism can derive from all of this. One can compare totalitarianism in the robes of the "ethical State" to pedagogy with the whip in hand, a force which med-

---

371 See note 12 to Chapter 1 above.

372 Italian: *la cosa pubblica*, reference to the etymological root of our word republic: *res publica*, Latin for "public thing."

dles in everything, for it is persuaded that it has not only the right but
the duty to "educate" and "perfect" individuals, treating them almost
as children, without any respect for their liberty and personality. The
dean of a high school with paternalistic-authoritarian velleities (here in
particular Gentile's "personal equation" betrays itself[373]), or a sergeant
instructor, might yearn for such a political ideal. Such a State more
than any other might be called "officious," because it does not know
limits to its petulant interference in the public and the private, nor to
its intolerable "virtuistic" and reformatory control. The fanciful dream
that people might become other than they are and fundamentally
always have been, here plays an essential role. Unfortunately disagreeable aspects of this kind were present also in fascism, and they were
sanctioned by Gentilian theory.

It is barely worth speaking about the opposition between the
Ethical State and the organic and aristocratic ideal of the State. In the
second kind of State one is not dealing with pedagogical relationships
like those of a religious school, but rather of spontaneous and natural
relations of inferior to superior. One is not dealing with conformity
to abstract "moral" values which are made valuable by authority, but
of obeying the masters who posit themselves as the center of relations
of loyalty and of fidelity—relations which leave large margins to autonomy, for they desire that everyone and every group develop its own
natural way of being. They take care that everything harmonizes in
a species of synergy, and they intervene—with energetic admonitory
interventions—only in cases of emergency or of manifest malfeasance.
And even in such circumstances they make their natural authority
appear as the counterpart of absolute power. This signifies true human
respect, as opposed to that degradation of the State into a school-bar-
racks, which is proper to the theory of the totalitarian "Ethical State."
In a singular reversal, the man who commenced from the premise of

---

373 Gentile was a university professor toward the beginning of his life.

strict obedience to an internal law (the *societas sive status in interiore hominis*,[374] the State which, according to the Gentialian conception, is "interior" and which, like everything else, does not exist if I do not "posit" it for myself, even if I have done so only after having come to terms with "historicism")—this same man ends up playing the part of nothing more than a schoolboy, or at most of the "head of the class." He lives in expectation that the pedagogic-ethical phase will pass to the yet more luminous phase of factory-like disciplining. Apart from vestiges of jingoism, and apart from his mere words, this is the true conclusion of late Gentilian thought, that of the "humanism of work" and of the "ethicality of the new workers' State." And here another dialectic manipulation permits Gentile to give a philosophical anointment to "sociality." Nearly forgetting the theorized pure absolute act, Gentile discovers the law by force of which the *I*, to have consciousness of itself, must "posit" the other from out of itself (other individuals) and then recognize itself in these others: whence its intrinsically "social" structure...

With this we can conclude. Apart from the fact that in Gentile's obscure philosophy, which has reduced the thought of the previous classic transcendental idealism to the absurd, one would seek in vain anything inspired by a higher plane—certainly nothing of spirituality, but neither anything of austere speculation. In the political conception of the philosopher of Castelvetrano[375] there is nothing which might be of worth to a true orientation of the Right. The communist epilogue written by the Gentilian Ugo Spirito indicates the immanent tendency in all this.[376]

Our "nostalgic" contemporaries, who do not limit themselves to rendering homage to the man Gentile for his comportment after

---

374 Latin: "society, or the state within man." I have not been able to find the source of this reference.

375 The Sicilian town where Gentile was born.

376 Evola offers quotations from this work in Chapter 1 of the present volume.

25 July,[377] but who wish to propose once more, in the framework of a reconstructive movement, the fundamental Gentilian conceptions hereabove analyzed and criticized, demonstrate a lack of capacity for discrimination—the which, moreover, is unfortunately often detectable also in other aspects of their recollections.

---

377 *Venticinque Luglio*, the 25 of July, 1943. This was the day that Mussolini was dismissed from power, which led directly to the fall of the fascist party, and to Mussolini's arrest and subsequent assassination. After this watershed event, Gentile maintained his support for Mussolini and for fascism even unto his own murder in 1944. (See note 12 to Chapter 1 above.)

35. RENÉ GUÉNON AND "INTEGRAL TRADITIONALISM"

We have observed in another place (*La Destra*, May 1972[378]) the necessary relation of the concept of an authentic and non-improvised Right with the concept of Tradition. References to authors of traditional orientation might therefore be useful to us in our confrontation of a complex set of problems. At present, we wish to give a survey of the ideas of René Guénon[379] (1886—1951), who is considered to be the promulgator of "integral Traditionalism."

Guénon is already well enough known even in Italy. His books were translated before the war. Others have been republished recently, and in Turin there is a Guénonian group whose journal is a facsimile of the French *Études Traditionnelles*, of which Guénon was the *pars magna*.[380] This journal is issued even now under the care of a group of strictly observant Guénonians. Today Guénon is considered as a master and the founder of a school, and in France he has been accepted even by the official and academic culture, if with various reservations.

---

378 *La Destra* ("The Right") was a monthly journal published in Rome from 1971 to 1976. Evola was one of its collaborators.

379 See note 1 to Chapter 1 above.

380 *Études Traditionnelles* ("Traditionalist Studies"), previously the *Voile d'Isis* ("The Veil of Isis"), was a journal founded by Guénon in 1935 for the furtherance of studies in metaphysics and spirituality. It continued in print until 1992. *Pars magna* is Latin, literally "the great part," referring to a person of central importance, for good or bad, in a given context, attempt, or event.

The work of Guénon is complex, but also organic. His work should be considered before all as a radical critique of the modern world, differentiating itself from that of various authors of yesterday and of today for its positive point of reference, namely, the "world of the Tradition"—world to which the modern world stands as antithesis. By "Traditional" one describes a universal type of civilization which, in various but homologous forms, has been realized more or less completely both in the Orient and in the Occident.

Traditional civilization—as Guénon affirms—has metaphysical points of reference. It is characterized by recognition of an order which is superior to everything human and contingent, as well as by the presence and the authority of elites who draw from this transcendent plane the principles and the values necessary to found a well-articulated social organization. Thus they clear the way for a superior consciousness, toward the end of conferring true significance to life. At the opposite pole stands modern civilization, characterized by widespread desacralization; by the systematic will to *not* recognize that which is superior to man, as individual and as collective; by materialism; by the impulse toward entirely profane and temporal realizations; by an insane activism. Guénon's two books *La crise du monde moderne* and *Le règne de la quantité et les signes des temps*[381] contain the essence of this critique, and in them the themes which have already been indicated by various authors of yesterday and today acquire a peculiar edge and a stabler foundation. This critique appears also in the book *Orient et Occident*,[382] but there it is associated with assumptions which in the meantime have become impugnable. Indeed, although Guénon recognizes—and he cannot help but recognize—that civilizations of the traditional type have existed both in the Orient as well as in

---

381 *La crise du monde moderne* (1927) has been translated into English as *The Crisis of the Modern World*. *Le règne de la quantité et les signes des temps* (1945) has been translated into English as *The Reign of Quantity and the Signs of the Times*.

382 Guénon's 1924 work, translated into English as *East and West*.

the Occident, in *Orient et Occident* he affirms that they can be now found solely in Orient (above all in India), so that reference to the Orient might be efficacious for a reintegration of the West. Now, this thesis might be valid at most for the Oriental Wisdom Tradition,[383] not certainly for the present reality of the Orient. Guénon was convinced of the survival of Oriental groups entrusted with the Tradition to this day. He had direct practical relations with the Islamic world, where initiatic veins (as Sufi and Isma'ili)[384] exist even now alongside the exoteric (that is to say religious) tradition. And he "Islamicized" to the extreme. He settled in Egypt, and he received the name of *sheikh* ʿAbd al-Wāḥid Yaḥyá, as well as Egyptian citizenship. In his second marriage, he married an Arab.

Guénon makes no mystery of the fact that after various disillusioning experiences in "occultistic" French spheres, he was able, thanks to exponents of the Orient, to find the right way, that of "initiatic or "metaphysical knowledge."

Such knowledge was the declared or implicit foundation of the doctrines expounded by Guénon in various books, notably in *Le symbolisme de la Croix*, *Les états multiples de l'être* and *L'homme et son de venir selon le Vedânta*.[385] A reservation here imposes itself: that which Guénon presents as a "metaphysics" in a special transcendent sense, apart from his terminology, is often at bottom little different from

---

383 The Wisdom Tradition refers to the idea that there is a hidden and identical core to the great diversity of religious and spiritual traditions which unite their esoteric meaning beneath a variety of particular façades.

384 The Sufi Orders are practitioners of a kind of Islamic mysticism connected with various forms of asceticism. The Isma'ili are practitioners of Isma'ilism, a branch of Shia Islam. They are so named for their belief that Isma'il ibn Jafar (719-762) was the legitimate seventh Imam, or spiritual successor to Muhammad himself. They are known for their esoteric interpretation of the Quran.

385 Translated into English as *Symbolism of the Cross*, *The Multiple States of the Being*, and *The Man and his Becoming according to the Vedânta* respectively, these works were published in 1931, 1932, and 1925.

that which bears the same name in the history of profane Occidental philosophy, and frequently his work in this connection exhausts itself in rather tedious abstractions—as for example in the case of all the dissertations on "Universal Possibility" and the like. Nevertheless what Guénon affirms remains valid: namely, that the rational is not the extreme noetic limit of man, and that the normal human condition can be removed, because man "does not represent, in reality, anything but a transitory and contingent manifestation of true being." Thus, as a matter of principle, it would be possible to tend toward a higher plane, in which knowing a thing signifies being the thing known, and the individual transforms himself through knowing and integrates himself. This is analogous to the ancient conception of the "gnosi."[386] Initiation would be the most direct and regular path to such a realization. Guénon distinguishes it totally from simple mysticism.

The tradition, in a primary sense, concerns the whole of this knowledge of "metaphysical" and not merely human order. It admits a variety of forms, even while remaining singular in its essence. In relation to this unity Guénon speaks also of the "Primordial Tradition." A conception of the kind had been formulated before him. One finds indications of it in Maistre himself, in Fabre d'Olivet,[387] and in a certain sense it was adopted recently also by the Catholic Father Schmidt[388] in his powerful book on the "idea of God." Properly speaking, however, one must distinguish the metaphysical aspect from the historical aspect of this conception. Regarding the first aspect, it is necessary

---

386 See note 19 to Chapter 1 above.

387 Antoine Fabre d'Olivet (1767-1825) was a French author, poet, and composer who interested himself in hermeneutics and occult studies.

388 Father Wilhelm Schmidt (1868-1954) was an Austrian Catholic priest, as well as an ethnologist and linguist. From 1912 to 1952 he wrote a twelve-volume work entitled *The Origin of the Idea of God*, which studied among other things primitive forms of religion and attempted to demonstrate that these forms were almost entirely monotheistic.

to refer to forms whose affinities do not derive from material and historically ascertainable transmissions; one and the same law can give place to distinct but corresponding and homologous forms, as in various points in a stream distinct whirlpools might arise, having one and the same form as the effect of one and the same law in one and the same situation. Regarding the second aspect, one must refer to the concrete common origin which precedes a complex of traditions, for which Guénon accepts the idea of a "Hyperborean tradition"[389] situated at the beginning of the present cycle of civilization (notably of the civilizations of the Indo-european race). Such an idea had already been affirmed by other authors of esoteric orientation (but also in the profane sphere: Herman Wirth[390] in his large and uneven work, *Der Aufgang der Menschheit*, had sought to establish such an idea). All this carries us to the thesis of a "transcendent unity of the traditional forms" (Guénon's disciple F. Schuon[391] in particular has written on the "transcendent forms of the religions"). One of the capacities attributed to him who has arisen to the higher knowledge of which we have spoken recently, is that of descrying such a unity; also, conversely, of expressing any given content in the terms of one or the other tradition, even as one can express a concept with a word in one or another language. (Symbolically, this would be the "gift of tongues,"

---

389 For the Hyperboreans, see note 99 to Chapter 9 above.

390 Wirth (1885-1981) was a Dutch-German historian who dedicated many of his studies to ancient religions and their symbols, as well as to racial studies particularly surrounding the Nordic races. Although he received a degree of early acclaim from the Nazis and even from Hitler himself, his attempt to interpret Christianity in the light of a Nordic faith led to his falling out of favor when the neo-pagan strands of Nazi thought began to rise to prominence. His 1928 work *Der Aufgang der Menschheit* (The Accession of Mankind) has yet to be translated into English.

391 Frithjof Schuon (1907-1998) was a Swiss metaphysician who began his spiritualism with his studies of the Hindu scriptures. At an early age he met Guénon, who convinced him to move to Paris and to begin to study Arabic.

as well as the foundation of an essential "ecumenism," which is much different from that squalid and vacillating ecumenism which appears in the post-conciliar Catholic climate[392]). Guénon has given concrete proof of possessing that capacity, quite beyond what one might have expected from mere erudition.

Guénon likewise uses traditional ideas for his critique of the modern world. He has no doubt that today we find ourselves near the end of a cycle, in the *Kali-yuga* or "dark age" prophesied in ancient Hindu doctrines but foreseen also in other traditions (for example, in the Hesiodian "iron age"[393]). He represents the negation, therefore, of every progressivist fancy. Beyond the material sphere (wherein, moreover, progress often extracts another price), progress for Guénon is nothing but one of Western man's superstitions. Guénon is one of those authors who have interpreted the course of history in an inverted and decidedly anti-Marxist sense, indicating precisely its significance in terms of the so-called "regression of the castes." The point of reference here is the traditional articulation of society in four castes or "functional classes": at the summit, the exponents of spiritual and sacral authority, then the warrior aristocracy, then the bourgeois, and finally the working mass. A society borne by the first caste has receded by now into almost mythic distances. The successive reign of the second caste closes with the decline of the great monarchies. The reign of the Third Estate takes its place—of the bourgeois, of industrialism and of capitalism. Finally comes the emergence of the fourth caste and its struggle for dominion of the world, in the form of Marxism and communism. Every interpretation of the right, every anti-Marxist interpretation of

---

392 That is, the climate in the Church after Vatican II. See note 158 to Chapter 14 above.

393 For Hesiod, see note 193 to Chapter 17 above. Hesiod's *Works and Days* outlines five successive and descending ages of man. The Iron Age is the last and worst of these, characterized by toil, the fragmentation of family bonds, and a proliferation of shameless immoralism.

the course of history, should take precisely this scheme as essential, as we ourselves have argued on multiple occasions.

One of Guénon's theses is that a normal, that is traditional, civilization is characterized by the primacy of contemplation, and of pure knowledge over action; this is also one of the foundations of his critique of the modern Western world, in which he ascertains the opposite principle, that is the preeminence of action. This is however precisely the point at which it is necessary to advance certain reservations. Our objection might commence from the indication of the elective nature of power which stood at the summit or at the center of traditional civilization. It is inexact to say that it was kept by elites who cultivated "contemplation" or "pure knowledge" in more or less priestly terms. Historically, such does not appear even in India, because, although it had a predominately Brahminic civilization,[394] India also possessed regal dynasties and exponents of the warrior cast in possession of traditional knowledge. In reality, the aforementioned summit is characterized rather by an undivided unity of sacrality and of regality, of spiritual authority and temporal power. Apart from ancient China and an entire series of other ancient civilizations, Japan has almost up to today maintained such a level, and it is significant sign of Guénon's idiosyncrasies that he never once referred to Japan and to its specific "tradionality," because it did not correspond with his scheme.

The awareness of the completely desacralized and deviant character of the modern West has not impeded Guénon from considering the problem of its possible rectification, its possible *redressement*.[395] Departing from the conviction that if the West has ever had a tradition, it was a tradition corresponding to Catholicism, he saw the "traditional" integration of Catholicism itself as point of departure, though he did not exclude the possibility of contact also with Oriental elements.

---

394 That is, a civilization in which the Brahmin or priestly caste was given responsibility for administering state affairs.

395 French: "recovery."

But even before the recent post-conciliar orientations of Catholicism clarified the state of affairs (and here it is well to observe that the irresolute "ecumenism" of this post-conciliar Catholicism has nothing in common with the views of "integral traditionalism"), Guénon did not suffer from too many illusions here; he declared as much also in a letter that he wrote us, confessing that in principle he felt it his duty not to exclude certain possibilities, without however expecting any results therefrom. Catholicism has remained insensitive to any petition of the kind, as it was insensitive as well to that petition which, albeit a much lower level, the Abbé Constant (alias Éliphas Lévi)[396] had in his time advanced. The sole result is that various Catholics arrived, precisely through Guénon, at penetrating the deepest sense of Catholicism, of its symbols and its dogmas. Unfortunately, these are not persons who have weight in the official hierarchy and who therefore might exercise a relevant influence. On the other hand a Catholic theologian would probably notice certain incompatibilities between orthodox truths and that which derives from the "metaphysics" which Guénon takes as his inspiration, and would be led to oppose *une fin de non recevoir*[397] to "integral traditionalism."

Guénon was allergic to the whole of the political in the strict sense, for he held that there was no current political movement to which he might have adhered (he consented, however, exceptionally, to publish extracts of his writings, with his signature, as articles in a special cultural page, unique of its kind, which we organized in the "Diorama" of *Il Regime*

---

396 Constant (1810-1875) was a French occultist and practitioner of magic, and the writer of numerous important works on the same, including *Dogme et Rituel de la Haute Magie*, (*Transcendental Magic, its Doctrine and Ritual*, 1854–1856) and *Histoire de la magie*, (*The History of Magic*, 1860). The "petition" to which Evola refers was probably Constant's attempt to open Catholicism to an occult understanding and esoteric interpretations.

397 French: lit. "an end of non-reception," meaning a categorical refusal.

Fascista of Cremona, 1934-1943[398]). However, he pertained by every right to the culture of the Right. In Guénon one finds radical negation of the entirety of corrosive democracy, socialism and individualism. He goes beyond all this, however; he carries us to domains barely touched by the present awareness of the Right; he opposes traditional knowledge and the "traditional sciences" to modern science and to scientism; he is not afraid of revalorizing the former after having revealed their true sense, indicating not only the limits of profane scientific knowledge but also the devastation deriving inevitably from the corresponding vision of the world and from its applications. A lapidary phrase of Guénon summarizes the sense of this modern adventure over to which Western man has given himself, as it commenced from the Renaissance: "[Man] severed himself from the heavens with the excuse of conquering the earth." And here one might cite a saying of the Far East: "The net of Heaven has a wide mesh, but no one may pass through it," when Guénon indicates the game of concordant actions and reactions which has brought us to the present "dark age" (dark, despite its "putrescent splendors," as H. Miller says).

Apart from the possibilities he perceived in an "integrated" Catholicism, Guénon hoped for a rectifying action such as the *élites intellectuelles* might exercise. It is possible that he had in mind here the sort of action already exercised—however in an opposite, subversive sense—by the so-called *societés de pensée*,[399] since the time

---

398 *Il Regime Fascista* was a fascist newspaper active from 1943-1945, which included a weekly page called the *Diorama filosofico* which was edited by Evola himself. The *Diorama* was subtitled "*Problemi dello spirito nell'etica fascista*," or "Problems of the spirit of the fascist ethic," and it took as its primary subject the philosophical and the spiritual basis of the idea of fascism.

399 French: "societies of thought." As identified in the work of the French historian Augustin Cochin (1878-1916), these were secret circles whose members were steeped in revolutionary Enlightenment doctrines. The adherents to these societies were prepared by these meetings to put their doctrines to practice. This came in a movement parallel to—but perhaps also disconnected from—Masonry as such.

of the French Revolution and more marginally Masonry. But even if Guénon's term "intellectual" does not have its present sense, and even if Guénon does not refer to the intellectuals of today, but rather to an intellectuality of conservative and "traditional" stamp, yet still that concept in present conditions is not in the least abstract. If ever, the conception of a kind of *Order* would seem to us more adequate—an Order reuniting personalities faithful to determinate principles, rooted in traditional spirituality but also in a more direct contact and confrontation with reality and with historical currents. Moreover, this Order would constitute the spine of a true Right, and if its members might refrain from flaunting their quality, and thus might succeed little by little in occupying certain key positions in contemporary society and culture, a rectifying action could become possible.

All of this is a question of principle, because the milieu and the men of today are such who leave scarce possibilities for initiatives of such a kind. There is yet a way out in something more or less like what Guénon had in view: namely the formation of centers of a traditional intellectuality whose action would realistically be limited solely to the cultural domain. Even such an action should not be underestimated. Today it is rather in vogue to speak of a "culture of the Right," without however being clear as to what this might be and without being able to avoid the sensation that it is something improvised. However there seems to be a favorable soil now, and various editorial initiatives confirm these appearances. In this context, Guénon should be employed (in a way which is not slavishly derivative). Given the variety and the multiplicity of the subjects he treated, it is well however to leave apart those subjects which have a particular relation with esotericism, "metaphysics" and initiation. Although these are for Guénon the final foundation of all the rest, yet given their unusualness, they might well alarm and even ostracize a certain circle of readers, if they are brought to the fore.

Certainly, even apart from the intellectual side of the question, there is also its existential side. As has been said, traditional knowledge, rigorously speaking, means also its realization. The Nietzschean axiom: "Man is something that must be overcome,"[400] is also the postulate of the superior consciousness and—as has been observed—commences from the idea that the human state of existence should not be hypostasized, that it is only one of multiple states of being. Only that one must indicate all that is necessary to prevent every distortion, every erroneous or risky application of this idea.

This is not the best place for a particular consideration of the domain of this realization, through an examination of Guénon's book *Aperçus sur l'initiation*.[401] We note only that there are certain reservations to be made about that possibility which Guénon considers almost to the exclusion of all others. He is insistent about the necessity of a connection with a given "chain," with a given "regular organization," as transmitter of a spiritual influence. To clarify this, an analogy might be offered in the ordination of a priest by a bishop, as administrator of the spiritual influence of which the Church holds itself to be the depository. In Guénon's case, that connection must principally be realized—as we have said—by Islamic "chains." But Guénon offers little

---

400 In the original German: *Der Mensch ist Etwas, das überwunden werden soll*. This is the message that is brought down from the mountain by Zarathustra in *Thus Spoke Zarathustra* (Section 3 of the First Speech of Part I). In the same passage Nietzsche introduces the notorious concept of the *Übermensch*, the overman, or the man of the future toward which the present human being must work ceaselessly, even at risk of his own self-sacrifice or "going under." The counterpart to this high vision of the human future was the almost equally famous Last Man, that man who no longer comprehends what is high and noble in the human being, to say nothing of those exceptionally elevated forms which might come in the future; he hears the old words, like "nobility, honor, duty," and "he blinks." Such a man might be brought back to Evola's analysis of the Fourth Estate; see Chapter 3 above.

401 Guénon's 1946 work, translated into English as *Perspectives on Initiation*.

enough to whomever is not up for entrusting himself to Muslims and Orientals. Whoever has read the extracts of our correspondence with Guénon in *La Destra* (March 1972) will recall that we have not been able to follow Guénon in the idea that present-day Masonry, despite its degeneracy (which he admits), remains in principle an organization for the dispensing of real initiation, rather than being merely symbolic and ritualistic. There are personalities in the West who have certainly held the rank of Masters, as for example Gurdjieff[402] and, on the so-called "Left-Hand Path," Aleister Crowley.[403] Or else one needs must seek some surviving branch of operative Kabbalism, which again cannot be considered a Western tradition. Naturally, the sects and the

---

402 G. I. Gurdjieff (?-1949) was an enigmatic figure, an Armenian mystic and composer who traveled widely in the West and wrote numerous spiritual works. He was the proponent of a spiritual discipline which he called "the Work" (also the "Fourth Way," meaning the fourth alternative to the methods of the fakir, the monk, or the yogi) which he intended to be Oriental teachings translated into a form appropriate for the West. His method might be distilled to the principle that we are all of us asleep in a kind of continual somnambulism, that it is possible for us to awaken, to rise to ever higher levels of consciousness. Though his disciples and pupils are famous for insisting on the necessity of working in groups to attain spiritual improvement, the problem that Evola identifies in this paragraph finds a gesture toward an intriguing possible resolution in three of Gurdjieff's books: *Beelzebub's Tales to His Grandson*; *Life is Real Only Then, When 'I' Am*; and *Meetings with Remarkable Men* (known comprehensively as the *All and Everything* trilogy). This trilogy was written in part to lead its readers toward awakening—work which, as all reading, must be eminently *private* and *individual*.

403 Crowley (1875-1947) was an infamous English occultist, magician, and practitioner of the Dark Arts, remembered most widely for his outrageous and continuous flouting of social mores. His drug use and his free sexuality were much noted during his life, particularly as that was a time of comparative moralism. He was deported from Italy by Mussolini himself in 1923 for his reprehensible activities. Crowley, ever a courter of notoriety, happily adopted many of the postures which the press attributed to him—pretending to be, among other things, a Satanist and a devotee of human sacrifice.

occultistic, theosophic, pseudo-Rosicrucian conventicles[404] and the like, which pullulate in our days, represent something spurious and inauthentic, and cannot in any way enter this question. The situation is thus a difficult one, and the problem must remain open for most, and perhaps must be reformulated in terms other than those indicated by Guénon.

However the theme of "integral traditionalism" can be detached from such problems, and can be used toward the formation of a culture of the Right.

---

404 Reference to Theosophy and Rosicrucianism, respectively. Theosophy was the doctrine propagated by the very popular Theosophical Society of Madam Blavatsky (1831-1891), which proposed an eclectic mixture of multiple occultist traditions. Rosicrucianism was originally a European movement of the 17th century which freely employed features of the Kabbalah, Hermeticism, and Christianity.

36. CULTURE AND LIBERTY

There has been some recent discussion about the "liberty of culture"—an argument of some importance, but one which requires certain clarifications.

In the first place, one must clarify precisely what one really means by "culture." Some have opportunely recalled that in antiquity the term "culture" signified predominately the formation of self and also the development of one's own possibility, analogous to the aim of every "cultivation."[405] This is obviously something very different from "forming one's culture" or having culture, for in these latter instances one might speak of a merely intellectualistic fact which has no existential effect. So far as the formation of the self goes, the model for it was almost always tied to a given kind of civilization, to a tradition, perhaps even to a doctrine. In this case there is but a small margin of liberty in

---

405 Culture indeed comes from the Latin *cultura*, meaning originally agriculture, the tilling of and care for the soil. Consider for instance one of the earliest mentions of culture by Cicero in his *Tusculanae Disputationes*, where he speaks of *cultura animi*, the "tilling and care of the soul." (See *Tusc. Disp.*, Book 2, Section 13: *Cultura autem animi philosophia est*, "Philosophy moreover is a culture of the soul." Translation mine.) The current use of this word, indicating any kind of human group joined by any kind of common activities or customs, is frankly a stark corruption of its original roots and meaning.

the sense of *arbitrium*.[406] Matters stood thus in the type or the ideal, for instance, of the *civis romanus*, of the ancient sage (especially the Stoic sage), of the Samurai, of the medieval knight, of the Prussian Junker and, if you please, of the English gentleman.[407] In all these cases the formation of the self has had a well determined direction.

Passing on to consider culture in its current sense and to examine the "liberty of culture," it is necessary to take up once more the well-known distinction between liberty *"from* something" and liberty *"for* something."[408] The first is a negative liberty and it presupposes, in general, the existence of coercion or limitation. For instance, one might

---

406 Latin: "will, choice, power to decide," hence also "mastery, authority." *Arbitrium* is a term used in many legal and humanistic contexts. It has been of abiding importance in post-Christian philosophy, ever since the early Christians introduced the concept of free will (*liberum arbitrium*), meaning will unconstrained by necessity. This has been the core of a vital dispute in philosophy from then up to the present. Evola here means to say that the traditional idea of culture left but little room to arbitrary human will.

407 *Civis Romanus* is Latin for "Roman citizen," or a man born of Roman parents, and of good standing, who thus enjoyed the special prerogatives of the Roman state. (In certain specific cases, also persons of non-Roman birth could be made citizens.) The sage understood classically was that man who had attained wisdom, meaning that man who had progressed from the stage of the philosopher, the lover of wisdom, to being the possessor of wisdom. The Stoics held that the sage was an ideal one should aim for, but which never could be reached. The sage was thought by the Stoics to be the only happy human beings, because he was the only human being who had completed virtue. (For more on the Stoics see note 241 to Chapter 21 above.) For the Samurai see note 232 to Chapter 19. Evola wrote extensively on the question of knighthood; see *Revolt Against the Modern World*, Chapter 13, "The Soul of Knighthood," as well as his work *Mystery of the Grail*. The Prussian Junkers were broadly speaking members of the nobility, Junker being an honorific title. The term came to mean simply the landed ruling gentry, which was connected explicitly to the military; hence the militaristic overtones of the term. "Gentleman" is in English in Evola's original.

408 This idea traces its origin to the English utilitarian John Stuart Mill (1806-1873). Mill explicated it in his 1859 work *On Liberty*.

advance, through protests, the needs of a free culture in a totalitarian State. One must recognize however that such a State wholly has the right to defend itself. Indeed this reservation might be extended further yet. In the climate of democracy everything is, in principle, licit; there is no authority which condemns or combats culture, which might be free to act even in a disgraceful and destructive way. Of course, this does not mean wishing for a regime of censure in the face of this. Rather, it means deploring a state of affairs in which even such a regime as that might in certain cases be opportune, despite all—provided only that such a regime is adopted with intelligence, with measure and with discernment.

It is of utmost importance however to oppose the atmosphere of a civilization of an *organic* type to the atmosphere of democracy. In a remarkable work entitled *Das Reich und die Krankheit der europ-dischen Kultur* (*The Reich and the Sickness of the European Culture*), a German author, Christoph Steding,[409] has thoroughly indicated the process of degenerescence which results when particular domains, previously joined in a unitary order, or all reflecting a unique impulse, are autonomized disassociatively, becoming, so to speak, so many "neutral" zones. In this connection, Steding was able to speak of a species of "Switzerization" of Europe and of its culture. It is fundamental to observe the current nonexistence of any center to which the idea of "empire" (Reich) might also correspond, even if it be understood, not in a political and material sense, but in terms of a center of animation and gravitation in a given historical reality—as happened, to a certain degree, in the Medieval Western ecumene.[410]

Whenever such an organic system exists, the liberty of culture would take on a peculiar character: namely, the character, above indicated, of "liberty *for* something." One can even agree in part with what the

---

409 Steding (1903-1938) was a German historian. The work here mentioned was published in 1938, and has not been translated into English.

410 For the concept of the "ecumene," see note 258 to Chapter 23 above.

Marxist Lukács[411] says, when he stigmatizes a superficial, inconsistent, "spineless" culture, a culture made for the use and the consumption of the good bourgeoisie, little more than a pastime which serves also to "dignify" this bourgeoisie and to render it "distinct." One does not have to be a Marxist to formulate a similar indictment. Even a man of the Right may formulate such indictments, and it is an idiocy to insist that one can be "occupied" with culture only in the squalid and trivial sense of Marxism, that one cannot also be so occupied in the opposite sense.

Now, culture, in this alternate perspective, should be free in creative and organic terms. It should, that is, assume and develop the contents of an organic civilization, naturally and without any extrinsic determination, meaning without any determination apart from that almost imperceptibly owed to a general syntony. As a comparison, one might refer to a process of growth in which nothing is arbitrary. We have grown too accustomed to confounding that which is free with that which is arbitrary in an individualistic sense—with that which is deprived of profound roots. Modern mentality is all too inclined to such deprecable confusions, the which, moreover, are brought about by the very general situation in which we find ourselves in today's day. For the opposite standpoint, one should presuppose a human type which knows "culture" above all in the sense indicated at the beginning—that is in the sense of self-formation, of discipline: for it is only in him that liberty can acquire a positive character.

---

411 György Lukács (1885-1971) was a well-known Hungarian Marxist, responsible for a very influential attempt to rework Marxist doctrine in the West in light of the rise of the USSR. He was particularly influential in the field of art criticism, into which he imported a form of Marxism, the influences of which are still reverberating in the humanities to this day. Far from limiting himself to theory, he was actively involved in the communist movement in Hungary from 1918-1919, even serving as commissar in the Hungarian Red Army (during which time he was responsible for executing a number of his own men). Nonetheless, it is as an intellectual that he has had his principle effect. The present references are probably to his 1947 work *Literature and Democracy* (Chapter 4, part 2).

An anarchically free culture can be the origin of almost as many calamities as has been the ill-famed "freedom of the press," with its invasive, impertinent, instigating, partisan journalism, which is capable of anything. Naturally, here one must make distinctions between various sectors. It is evident that in the sector of fiction and non-fiction the problem does not present itself if not in the practical field: which is to say, it appears not in the sector of composition, but in that of publication, because, as one knows, in criticism and in the publishing industry there exist well organized and powerful gangs, capable of rendering the famous authorial freedom ephemeral, by blocking its manifestation, its expression and its diffusion. Moreover, one can observe that consumer culture has as much liberty as it wants to have, and that it takes ever more, recognizing neither valid limits nor conventions. Thus our culture at bottom does not even merit the name. There is also a culture of informative character, the which serves, as one likes to say, to "enrich the mind," and there is a culture of specialist character, which, naturally, must not be obliged to anyone or anything. For the first, one might nevertheless pose the problem of what is truly worth knowing, as well as the problem of what it is dangerous to know. If we recall rightly, it is Maistre who (though referring to a different context) spoke of "withdrawing" certain knowledge, insofar as it acquires, for the majority, the character of a fire which serves better to burn than to illuminate.[412] But today the strange superstition prevails that humanity has "grown up," so that everything must be accessible to everyone; while if one but thinks of the power that advertising, slogans, watchwords have in our world, it appears evident that our contemporaries demonstrate a noteworthy passivity, that they have an exceedingly scarce capacity of discrimination and of true reaction. It is not necessary even to specify to what end this kind of "liberty" might carry us, even in the intellectual and cultural field.

---

412 A fuller quotation is provided in Chapter 31 above.

The conclusion of these brief considerations returns us to what we said at the beginning: the problem ought to be drawn in much wider terms, in its relation to a given kind of civilization and society—a kind that today unfortunately is nearly nonexistent, because what reigns or predominates today is the massified, not the organic and differentiated with an internal form in the living Goethian sense.[413] And since everything is interconnected, such a state of affairs inevitably has implications also for the problem of liberty and for the liberty of culture. As can be easily understood, we hold that when a "system" exists (or when one permits it to exist), any sporadic affirmations of liberty, despite a certain demonstrative moral value they might possess, remain inconclusive; and beyond that there is the danger that they might be dictated only by the mania for standing out, and by the self-valorization of certain individualities, which origin deprives these affirmations of every serious significance. We believe that this is the case for certain anti-conformistic branches of Soviet "intellectuals" and literati, to whom we do not feel like granting too much importance, as is generally done in the "free" Western world. We will add that there is even something hysterical in these manifestations of intolerance. They have but a peripheral character. One ought to give the word rather to an action of the whole on the plane of the real.

---

413 For Goethe, see note 56 of Chapter 7 above. The present is reference to Goethe's very influential scientific investigations into the vital principle, which can be found most particularly in his 1788 *Metamorphosis of Plants*, but also in his 1810 *Theory of Colors*. (Also to a lesser extent in his 1809 novel *Elective Affinities*, which attempted artistically to apply the laws of chemical affinity to the relations between human beings.) *Metamorphosis of Plants* presented a view of organic life as a resilient and mobile adoption of ever new forms, in dynamic interaction with the environment around them. This is a view which seems to have had some importance for Evola's vision of the world. Goethe's *Metamorphosis* introduced, for instance, the concept of "homology" *avante la lettre*, which idea Evola takes up in the final chapter of the present volume.

Were a revolution to change the spiritual and intellectual situation—though such is presently unforeseeable—then even those problems which we have here brought to attention would present themselves in a very different way, and there would be no doubt as to what might assume a character of normalcy, in what pertains to culture—normalcy, naturally, understood in a higher sense.

37. THE RIGHT AND CULTURE

Today there is often talk of a "culture of the Right," so much so that the alarm has to some degree sounded in the opposite camp. On the other hand, there are authors who act and speak as if this culture were something that they themselves had today fabricated or invented. Now we would not know how to conceive of a true culture of the Right without some reference to a tradition, and at an opportune distance from individualism. It is precisely the habit of the man of the left, of the revolutionary and the "progressivist," to valorize the new, without any continuity or organic connection.

If one does not perceive this point clearly, there is danger that this culture of the Right, of which there is so much talk today in Italy, will reduce itself at least in part to simple formulae. For this reason some have held that the phenomenon of a "culture of the Right" has been overestimated and that the apprehensions displayed by the predominant culture, which is left-leaning and which has at its disposal precise enough an ideology, are unjustified. Now, setting aside those authors who today envisage things almost as if the culture of the Right were their own invention tossed into the market of ideas, it is not easy to perform the task of giving a *positive* content to this culture. We have said "positive," because a definition based only on spurning, on critique and opposition, cannot suffice.

Moreover, this task and this difficulty appear equally with respect not only to the "culture" of the Right, but also to the Right in general as a political formation and a vision of the world. (The economic Right must obviously be set aside: in the present context it has no interest for us.) Indeed, what can one call the antecedent of the political Right in Italy? Certainly, the so-called "historical Right" has existed: but while one must justly bestow recognition on the figure and the activity of a Crispi, a Di Rodinò,[414] and other surely worthy personalities of the time, one must also agree that, on account of the very atmosphere of post-Risorgimento Italy, this Right is not at all to be compared in any way with what the conservative Right has been, for example, in central Europe, where it could relate itself to precise traditions and to equally precise social articulations, given that the ideological influences deriving from the French Revolution had taken little enough hold in such countries. Even today in Italy, the presuppositions for an integral and traditional Right are sadly lacking. Indeed neither democracy nor republic can form the congenial soil for such a Right. It is difficult enough for us to conceive of a true Right without a monarchy and an integral aristocracy as a political class. A Right which reduces itself to generic nationalism and to the defense of those values proper to a bourgeois society—Catholic or otherwise—is naught but a very approximate Right.

---

414 Francesco Crispi (1818-1901) was an Italian statesman of the Risorgimento period, and one of the major figures behind the Italian unification of 1860. He was admired by Mussolini, and for this his name was resurrected to a considerable extent during the Fascist Period. For the same reason, Crispi was reviled by the anti-fascists as being a kind of proto-fascist, the figurehead of a sort of warlike imperialism. Though I am not altogether certain, I believe the second reference is to Giulio Rodinò di Miglione (1875-1946), an Italian politician and one of the founders of the *Partito Popolare Italiano* (The Italian Popular Party), which brought many Catholics into Italy's political life, and supported a conservative outlook of the modern style. Evola's point here is surely at least partially this: that these "conservative" figures to a great degree adopted precisely the revolutionary Enlightenment movement toward republicanism which has brought us to our present straits.

Even the *culture* of the Right cannot help but be touched by the general cultural, political and social situation. To ward off the accusation or the insinuation that the "culture" of the Right today is but a phenomenon owing to circumstances alone, it would be necessary to indicate its antecedents; but these are sporadic. It will seem natural, for some, to refer to the Fascist period. But then one needs must make certain distinctions, because it remains to be seen to what measure fascism, *on the whole*, can be considered as a pure movement of the Right; on this point, we might redirect the reader to the contribution we have afforded in our study of fascism, entitled *Fascism Viewed from the Right*, published by Volpe. If we seek some antecedent in the culture of the precedent period, we might consider, for example, the historian Gioacchino Volpe, and Vilfredo Pareto[415] ever remains a figure of the very highest anti-conformist and antidemocratic sphere. We would rather set aside the Corradinian current,[416] as its predominant trait is political nationalism (a certain kind of nationalism might even be the antithesis of the Right). In the field of journalism, rather precise positions were most recently defended by G.A. Fanelli.[417] Fanelli is a

---

415 Volpe (1876-1971), beyond being an historian, was also a politician of the interwar period. He was a nationalist who supported the rise of fascism, to the extent of seeing in it *the* historical aim of all previous Italian development. He distanced himself from the regime, however, when it fell under the sway of Hitler, and in consequence he lost his teaching post and dedicated himself to the life of a scholar. His son Giovanni (to whom Evola makes reference in the preceding sentence) became an editor. For Pareto, see Chapter 30 above.

416 Reference to Enrico Corradini (1865-1931), an Italian writer and politician who was a primary exponent of Italian nationalism. Evola furthers his critique of nationalism in the following chapters of the present volume.

417 Giuseppe Attilio Fanelli (1899-1985) was an Italian journalist and editor of the weekly periodical "*Il secolo fascista*" ("The Fascist Age"), which was dedicated to consideration of fascist thought. It ran from 1934-1935. The book which Evola here cites (in English, *Cowardice in the Twentieth Century*) has not been translated into English.

lively monarchical and traditionalist writer, director of a journal and author of a book of the title *Vigliaccherie del secolo XX*. A small and fairly well-knit group formed around him, in which Nino Serventi and Nino Guglielmi[418] played a role, among many others. We must also reluctantly mention our own activity of the same period (our book *Revolt Against the Modern World*, decidedly a work of the Right, issued in first edition in 1933). The group of collaborators in the *Il Regime Fascista's* special page, entitled "Diorama," was certainly formed by exponents of a true and proper culture of the Right, and it is worth highlighting that foreign collaborators of the same orientation united with them. Today Giuseppe Prezzolini[419] has sought to valorize his past as a conservative, and has also recently published a little volume wherein he has enunciated his theses on conservatism; but in all sincerity we do not feel like taking him very seriously. Many other references to an authentic cultural tradition of the Right could however be indicated.

So far as the present period goes, it would be opportune to take a close look at the "credentials" of those who are generally considered as the exponents of the culture of the Right, for it is always easy to apply labels without very carefully examining the contents. As is known, whenever there is the sense that something is gaining ground, many gather around it and even convert to it with growing frequency. As a perspicuous example we recall what occurred at the moment of the

---

418 I have been unable to find much information on these men. Both of them opposed themselves to the populist aspects of fascism. Gaetano Nino Serventi seems to have written several books, including one on European democracy and another on the infamous Lucrezia Borgia, daughter of the Renaissance Pope Alexander VI. Nino Guglielmi was a contributor to the periodical *Roma Fascista*, and evidently wore a monocle.

419 Prezzolini (1882-1982) was an Italian literary critic, journalist, and editor who became a naturalized American citizen in 1940. He was an admirer of Benedetto Croce (see note 10 to Chapter 1). His attempts to align himself with the Right are certainly compromised by the *petit fait* that he spent the better part of the Fascist Period teaching in the United States.

"racist" fascist revolution: an entire series of publicists unexpectedly realized, from one day to the next, that they too were "racist." And the beauty of it is that these same gentlemen today find themselves amongst the democrats and the antifascists.

An intellectual still needs a certain courage to proclaim himself for the Right today. It is just for us to recognize such courage, but this does not touch the specific, objective question of merit. For we should then ask if this intellectual commences from a general and precisely characterized vision, a vision of life and of history itself, proceeding to all the rest only consequentially. One cannot always observe this in the alleged culture of the Right today, while, as has been noted, the connections of this Right with any antecedents are nigh nonexistent. The accusation is often made that this entire Right in the last analysis is fabricated and improvised, and, given certain attitudes in the Right, one cannot help but recognize that this critique does not appear entirely unjustified. It is only an extenuating circumstance that the prevalent cultural climate in Italy has not been such as to furnish consistent footholds for such a culture. There is in reality a vast field of work: having a right and serious orientation, shunning improvisations—these will be the decisive factors.

38. PERSPECTIVES OF THE CULTURE OF THE RIGHT

It is quite in vogue today to speak of a "culture of the Right." One cannot easily however banish the suspicion that all of this can be reduced to a "phenomenon of circumstance." Given the advancement that the Right has enjoyed in the political field, one evidently wishes to put up some kind of cultural counterpart to that advancement. Yet this gives rise to various problems.

As a preliminary observation, the introduction of a political concept, like that of the Right, into the cultural field, does not seem very apropos. One should rather seek to move on the more concrete and objective terrain of a morphology of culture, by defining the orientation and the tasks proper to a given kind of culture. This all the moreso, as it would be difficult for Italy to take inspiration from any tradition, and it is certainly not suitable to think that in the present republican and democratic climate the hoped-for culture might take on the characteristics of anything organically grown. Beyond all, it is necessary to come to terms with the concept of culture itself. Here one ought to distinguish three domains: that of spiritual formation, that of creativity (literature, novels, theater, in part film), and that of ideas and of doctrine. To which is added the problem of specifying the function of the culture that one has in mind, and its relations with sufficiently extensive strata of the population.

So far as the first domain goes, that is the creative domain,[420] it little tolerates formulae and recipes, since every authentic and valid production depends essentially on the existence of a corresponding atmosphere. The inconsistency of any "on-demand," commanded artistic creativity, was visible, for example, in the nullity of production in the so-called "Marxist" or "socialist realism" framework. One might always encourage, however, a certain production with an intrinsic character of protest. And thus the signs are inverted: while until now protest has been predominately the prerogative of the left, today it ought to be conducted by the Right. Nor should one forget—as today one does forget—the great aristocratic protesters of yesterday, beginning with Friedrich Nietzsche, in those ideas of his which remain valid.

Classically, "culture" (see Cicero or Seneca) had the sense neither of erudition nor of intellectualism, but of spiritual and characterial formation of the person. In order to renew this meaning for a culture of the Right, the task arises of indicating models and human ideals in a formulation which assures them a normative value and a real suggestive force. Today there is truly a great need for people who do not chatter, nor "write," nor argue, but who begin with *being*. Their authority and their prestige would come as a natural consequence, and the effects of this can otherwise be reached only with difficulty.

In the second domain—that of ideas and doctrines—it is both necessary and possible to specify, sector by sector, the content of a culture of the Right. Apart from this circumstantial appellation—"of the Right"—this means in essence making reference to intellectual orientations and preexisting criticisms which could be taken up again

---

420 This would appear to be an error, insofar as Evola initially characterized the *second* domain as "that of creativity." The same thing applies to the paragraph below which begins "In the second domain": originally this was the "third domain." Rather than second-guessing Evola here, I have not corrected this discrepancy. I leave it to the judgement of the reader to determine whether this was an oversight on his part or in some way intentional.

and developed further. The attack against Marxism is an obvious example, but to a certain degree it can be taken for granted. Those who yet hold to the threadbare dogmas of Marxism are rare: and if Marxism today constitutes a danger, it is not a danger on the cultural plane but essentially on the plane of practical politics, where not polemics but resolute action are needed to fight it. However the existence of a species of Marxian underworld cannot be ignored; it must be decisively unmasked and denounced.

A critique of science and scientism might partake of a culture of the Right, since the collusions between such views and Marxism are well known. The "demythification" of science is a very important task, and in a wider perspective it would be necessary to juxtapose, on the one hand, the positive contribution of science in the material sphere, and on the other the spiritual destruction derived from the scientific vision of the world.

One of the most important fields for the work of a culture of the Right is historiography. It is a fact that we of the Right have almost without exception written historiography in the anti-traditional, Masonic-liberal and more or less "progressivist" key. The so-called "fatherland history,"[421] and not only its most stereotypical form, is characterized by its emphasizing and exalting as "our" history all that which in the past had a predominately anti-traditional character,

---

421 Italian: *storia patria*. That is, the historiography (generally pedagogical) which understands the past as leading inexorably to the liberal-democratic present. One does not hear much about this any longer in Italy, but in the past this "*storia patria*" extolled the Risorgimento as a kind of historical peak toward which the entire Italian past had been working. (For the Risorgimento, see note 110 to Chapter 10 above.)

departing from the very revolt of the Commons[422] against imperial authority, up to those aspects of the Risorgimento which had undeniable relations with the ideas of '89,[423] and, finally, to Italy's intervention in the First World War. Something of the kind must be said, not only for "fatherland history," but also for history more generally.

Here unfortunately we are lacking our own tradition, our own antecedents to take up once more and to develop. It is useless for us to strain ourselves in looking for them. Some have uttered the names

---

422 Italian: *rivolta dei Comuni*, where *comune* means today "city hall," or "district," and in the past referred to a local governmental authority as opposed to the larger imperial authorities. I am not entirely sure to what historical event Evola is referring in particular. There was a *rivòlta dei comuneros* around 1520 in Spain which was a kind of rebellion of cities and towns against what were perceived as the unfair fiscal practices of Charles V. It may be that Evola is referring instead to the dissolution of the Medieval *Regnum Italiae* into a number of much smaller regions, almost parallel to the city-states of Ancient Greece. During this period, the *Comuni*, which is to say the local authorities of the cities, sought greater autonomy and freedom from the imperial authority which had been established by Charlemagne in 774. This movement in many ways prepared the way for the Renaissance. Nonetheless, the historical movement indicated by this paragraph, as well as its reference in Chapter 39 below, would seem to suggest that this "*rivolta dei Comuni*" was a more recent event. It may also be a reference to the initial proto-democratic stirrings in Italy which led subsequently to the Risorgimento.

423 Reference to the watershed year 1789 which sparked off the French Revolution. Key events of that year were the Storming of the Bastille, the Abolition of Feudalism, and the Declaration of the Rights of Man, all of which followed a rapid decomposition of the French monarchy in the first half of 1789.

Machiavelli and Vico,[424] whom we cannot imagine bringing into this context, since they treated of diverse and limited material. From Vico one might infer at most the interpretation of history in a regressive sense, the descent of civilizations from their once proper level, to the level of what he called the "heroic peoples," and thence toward barbarism. But in Vico this is connected with the theory of cycles and historical "occurrences and recurrences." Something analogous counts also for the more up-to-date theories of Oswald Spengler, with his "twilight of the West."

We really do not know what one might possibly take from Machiavelli for a historiography of the Right. And historiography aside, we must advance precise reservations against those who would like generally to bring Machiavelli back into "our fold," as one of the thinkers of the right. Not by chance did Machiavelli lend his name to "Machiavellism," and even leaving aside the more trivial aspects of this notion—namely the unscrupulous use of means toward reaching a given end—we will take this occasion to say that we do not feel at all like defining, as a piece of the Right, the mere "strong style" of a power which trenchantly affirms itself, when this power is formless, devoid of any higher anointment or superior legitimization. Otherwise we risk having to include not a few regimes from behind the Iron Curtain in our assessment of what belongs to the Right. Here one should consider, for instance, the phenomenon of a plenipotentiary dictatorship. In this respect Ancient Rome's point of view seems to us the just one,

---

424 Niccolò Machiavelli (1469-1527) was an Italian philosopher and dramatist who had a remarkable influence on modern thought. He is best known for his 1513 work *Il Principe* (The Prince), but his most important work was probably his *Discourses on Livy*, written between the years of 1513 and 1519. His name is associated with the development of a kind of political realism which some (for example, the twentieth-century philosopher Leo Strauss) have seen as the seeds of all subsequent modern political thought. The commonplace that "the end justifies the means," which Evola subsequently references, traces its philosophical genealogy to him. For Giambattista Vico, see note 140 to Chapter 13 above.

which considered dictatorship only for situations of emergency rather than as a permanent institution: for otherwise Rome would have confounded itself with the tyrants of Magna Graecia.[425] With reference to current events, we might think analogously of the "strong regimes," the authoritarian regimes of Spain and Greece, while fully recognizing their contingent *raison d'être*.

For the Right's consideration of history in general (apart from indications to be found in a Burke, in a Butler, in a Tocqueville and in a Maistre[426]—indications which, however, one must develop in view of a changed world) the unique valid contribution known to us is the book of L. de Poncins and E. Malynski, entitled *The Occult War*[427] and translated also into Italian. It is illuminating in its indication of the the processes, often unfolding behind the scenes of history, which have led to the dismemberment of the traditional European world. Unfortunately its exposition stops with the advent of Bolshevism. There remains however a lengthy period standing between then and today—a period moreover which is particularly dense in events; this analysis ought to be continued through that period with the same conservative, traditional, Rightist spirit displayed by those two authors.

---

425 Latin: "Greater Greece." This is actually a reference to the southern part of Italy, which was colonized by the Greeks already from the time of the Trojan War. Sicily in particular was famed for its tyrants. One gets a sense of their quality from the fact that the Brazen Bull, the terrible torture device to which Evola alludes in Chapter 21, was first developed by an Athenian for the use of a Sicilian tyrant.

426 Edmund Burke (1729-1797) was an Irish politician whose books, but even more whose influential speeches, have provided a great deal of the groundwork of contemporary conservatism, particularly in the United States and Britain. Burke was a noted opponent of the French Revolution. For his historiography, see in particular his 1757 work *The Abridgement of the History of England*. I have been unable to trace the reference to Butler. For Tocqueville, see note 300 to Chapter 28 above; for Maistre, see note 36 to Chapter 3 and also Chapter 31 in its entirety.

427 See note 290 in Chapter 27 for more on this work.

Sociology too offers an important field of work to the thought of the Right. Indeed this discipline, even when it is not carried out in an openly Marxist key, ever contains a perverting component—namely, the reduction of the higher to the lower—and the sociological currents from Overseas give us paramount examples of this tendency. Anthropology itself, in the sense of a general theory of the human being, has its worthy place as an important further object of these efforts. For instance, one should study here the unfortunately rather diffuse orientation, accepted a-critically, which is proper to psychoanalysis, in order to observe and ascertain the mutilated and distorted conception of man which constitutes its fundament.[428]

We can consider two further fields. In the first place, an adequate consideration of the world of prehistory and protohistory is in order, of the ancient and "mythical" world, sans the prejudices and the incomprehension of the greater part of our academic culture. It is here that Vico, in part, can indicate the way. The Swiss J.J. Bachofen,[429] however, has given an infinitely more valid contribution in the last century, with his studies on ancient religions and primordial symbols. Bachofen's studies have a particular importance, because they consider also the connections of the social and political world with the sacred and with mythology (another contribution in the same direction is

---

428 Evola develops this idea in Chapter 2 above.

429 Johann Jakob Bachofen (1815-1887) was a Swiss jurist, philologist, and anthropologist. Evola in note 69 to Chapter 9 above recommends his work *Der Mythus von Orient und Occident* which has yet to be translated into English. Also of interest is surely Bachofen's critique of what he calls the "myth of matriarchal prehistory." A selection of his writings have been offered in English in the volume *Myth, Religion, and Mother Right*.

the well-known work of Fustel de Coulanges, *La Cité Antique*[430]). A comparative study of religions and civilizations might frame research of this kind, and in this respect the so-called "integral tradition" of the school of René Guénon[431] could also form a valid basis.

In the second place, we might mention a field related to that which we have just now considered. One must take a stand against those who, out of a badly understood exigency toward realism and clarity, lash out against the entirety of esotericism, symbol and myth, making of every molehill a mountain and winding up in a species of flat and jejune Enlightenmentism or rationalism. Evidently their restriction of purview and of horizons impedes them from recognizing the existence also of a super-rational clarity. They do not perceive that there is the possibility of undressing symbols and myths so as to make their real contents appear—contents indeed of a higher order. They believe they are clearing the field, when instead they only create deprecable confusions with the discredit that they cast on certain lines of thought. Whoever follows them seriously, will find himself in the squalor proper to a world devoid of the third dimension—that is, the dimension of profundity.

Let us come to the other of the points hereabove mentioned, namely the position that the culture of the Right—whatever might be its primary definition—ought to assume before a vast public and the representatives of the same. It has been asserted that this culture ought to open itself to the widest strata of the population, and ought not to be exclusivist and "aristocratic." In our opinion, this is an absurdity,

---

430 Numa Denis Fustel de Coulanges (1830-1889) was a French historian, whose best known work, also his first, is that mentioned here by Evola. It has been translated into English as *The Ancient City*, and it treats of the centrality of religion as a binding factor in the ancient Greek and Roman civilizations, so much so that the decline of the old cults led to a corresponding decline of society as such.

431 For Guénon, see Chapter 35 above.

almost a contradiction in terms. We do not have in mind any artificial closure, but we exclude all concessions which implicate a descent in level. "Social" preoccupations must be extraneous to a true culture of the Right, the which does not at all mean closing oneself off in individualism of the *fin de siècle*[432] type. Certain positions must be maintained, in the sense of "presences" and of bearing witness. Their possible influence does not depend on the one who defends them—it does not depend on these persons "keeping themselves busy"—but it depends rather on those who receive them. Just as with the function which Julien Benda[433] attributed to the *clercs* before their "betrayal," one is dealing here essentially with the problem of establishing distances, even be they distances like those of the "Feast with a Stone."[434] The first distance is that between "being" and "well being," and also between culture in the characterial and existential sense heretofore indicated on the one hand, and living day to day, scattered, at the mercy of suggestions, of politico-social ideologies of the moment and of the alienating conditionings of the general milieu on the other. We must make this contrast apparent through the position of a superior order of values,

---

432 French: "end of the century." This is a reference in particular to the end of the nineteenth century, and to the general atmosphere of malaise and ennui which characterized it.

433 See Chapter 14 above.

434 Reference to the legend of Don Juan. The 1631 comedy of the Spaniard Tirso de Molina, entitled *The Deceiver of Seville and the Feast with the Stone*, was the first to introduce this idea, and the 1665 play of the French comic playwright Molière (1622-1673) was likewise entitled *Dom* [sic] *Juan or the Feast with the Stone*. The same Don Juan was the inspiration for Mozart's famous opera *Don Giovanni*. In the legend, Don Juan finds himself eating dinner with a statue of the man he has killed. The Italian phrase *convitato di pietra* thus comes to mean the oppressive presence of a person who is in fact absent.

much different from those which Marcuse[435] proposed—Marcuse who took his inspiration heavily from Freud and Freud's critique of the ruling system.

What follows this is none of our affair. It depends on the sensibility and the capacity for a positive reaction of which the widest stratum of the public might yet be capable, or which might reawaken within it. One effect might be the perception of the distance between that which "is" and that which has the right to be; if nothing else this will impede one, not only from adhering to today's reality, but of making apologia for it, of considering it as what "must be." If then, commencing from this awareness—we could also say, commencing from this awakening—one reacts, the opening to whatever can be offered from a culture of the Right in its other various aspects will come automatically. The action of this "anagogic" action[436] will be natural, and it will differ from that direct action of him who adopts the formula of "commitment" in an exterior, social sense, and who thus ends up remaining on the democratic plane. It will not bring any impairment of the dignity of the exponents of the culture in question.

---

435 Herbert Marcuse (1898-1979) was a German Jewish intellectual of decided Marxist hues, and one of the foremost figures of the Frankfurt School. His best known work is perhaps *One-Dimensional Man* (1964). He became a naturalized citizen in the United States in 1940. The "values" which he proposed are those which would lead to the transcendence of social oppression. His Marxian views here come to the forefront; he conceived of culture and indeed art as completing itself in political revolution—revolution, naturally, which was meant to encourage the revolt of the proletariat. The inspiration he took from Sigmund Freud (the seminal Jewish father of psychoanalysis, who lived from 1856-1939) was primarily from what many consider to be Freud's most important work, *Civilization and its Discontents* (1931), which posited a fundamental conflict between the individual and society, leading naturally to ever greater constraint on the one by the other. This tension was conceived of as the origin of a great many of the most important psychological features of the human being.

436 See note 181 to Chapter 15.

It is not easy to conceive of all this in the present milieu. One can await only a gradual change—a change which will not be for one's own benefit, but for the benefit of others.

Finally, and not without a certain relation to this, we must once more contest the character of "individualism" which is often here attributed to an "aristocratic" position—designation which however does not affright us in the least. Here we are not speaking of the field of letters and of the arts, in which, moreover, "hermeticism" apart, individualism has been more creative than any pseudo-social orientation. In the field now in question "aristocraticality" has nothing to do with individualism; it is based instead on personality in the highest forms of its realization and explication. It is curious that such a confusion seems to have arisen also with respect to our ideas, and the sole excuse for this might be an inappropriate reference to the problems and the terminology of our works on "gnoseology" which are by now distant enough, and which had a rather technical and specialized character.[437] But if one considers the entire part of those works which might reasonably enter into question in the present context, it is evident that that part itself was given over to the ideas of authority and hierarchy, and that it places itself beyond all individualism.

---

437 The titles in question would be those relating to Evola's theory of the "absolute individual," namely, *Teoria dell'individuo assoluto* (1927) and *Fenomenologia dell'individuo assoluto* (1930). For gnoseology, see note 367 to Chapter 34 above.

39. THE HISTORIOGRAPHY OF THE RIGHT

A noted German historian, Carl Schmitt,[438] once observed that while the left had systematically elaborated and perfected its historiography as the general background for its destructive action, nothing of the like had appeared in the opposite camp, in that of the Right. Schmitt made this observation while expounding certain considerations on the European significance that one might attribute to Donoso Cortés, that most interesting political man and Spanish thinker, who developed his activity in the period of the first revolutionary and socialist European movements. And Schmitt noted that the historiographical work of the Right at that time could be reduced to a few sporadic essays which were in no way comparable, in their coherency, radicalism and breadth of horizons, to that which Marxism and the left have long possessed in this sphere.

In large part, Schmitt is correct. In fact, if one sets aside all history of Marxist intonation, the only history known to most, the only history which matters, is essentially of liberal, Enlightenment, and Masonic derivation and origin. It takes its inspiration from those ideologies of the Third Estate which have served only to prepare the ground for the radicalist movements of the left; and these themselves stand of course on an essentially anti-traditionalist foundation. A historiography of the Right has yet to be written, and this constitutes one of our titles to

---

438 For Schmitt, see note 306 to Chapter 28 above. For more on Donoso Cortés, mentioned in this same paragraph, see Chapter 28.

inferiority with respect to the ideologies and the agitating action of the left. Not even the so-called "fatherland history" can compensate for this lacuna, because, apart from its possible national coloratura and its touching commemorations of heroic incidents and figures, it itself is effected in large measure by the suggestions of thought which does not belong to the true Right. Above all, it cannot bear competition, in terms of the breadth of its horizons, with the historiography of the left.

This is the fundamental point. Indeed, one must recognize that the historiography of the left has known how to cast its glance to the essential dimensions of history. Beyond conflicts and episodic political revolutions, beyond the history of the nations, it has known how to glimpse that general and essential process which has been realizing itself in these last centuries, as transition from one type of civilization and society to another. That the basis of its interpretation has been in this connection economic and classist subtracts nothing from the breadth of framework of its whole historiography. It indicates to us the essential reality in the course of history, beyond all contingent and particular reality—specifically, in the end of the feudal and aristocratic civilization, the advent of the bourgeois, liberal, capitalistic and industrial, and, after this, the annunciation and the incipient realization of a socialist, Marxist and finally communist civilization. Here the revolutions of the Third and Fourth Estates are recognized in their natural causal and tactical concatenation. It contemplates the idea of an over-ordered process, served by forces which had no desire to serve it and did not know they were serving it—by the more or less "sacred" egoisms of the peoples, and by the rivalries and the ambitions of those who believed they were "making history," without ever departing the field of the particular. It studies precisely the transformations of the whole of that social structure and civilization which are the direct effect of the game of historical forces, and justly relegates the history of nations to the simple "bourgeois" phase of the general development.

(In fact, "nations" did not emerge as historical subjects save out of the revolution of the Third Estate, as its consequence.)

Measured against the historiography of the left, the historiography of other viewpoints thus appears superficial, episodic, two-dimensional, sometimes even frivolous. An historiography of the Right needs to embrace the same horizons of the Marxist historiography, with the will to glean the real and the essential in the historical process unfolding in the latest centuries, all myths, superstructures and the flat chronicling of events aside. It would accomplish this, naturally, by inverting the signs and perspectives of the left, since in the essential and convergent processes of latest history, we have witnessed, not the phases of a political and social process, but rather that of a general subversion. As is logical, even the economic-materialistic premise should be eliminated by recognizing that *"homo oeconomicus"*[439] and the presumed inexorable determinism of the various systems of production are mere fictions.

Much vaster, profounder, and more complex forces have been, and are, in action in history. And, so far as particulars go, one ought to reject even the myth of the so-called "primordial communism"; this ought to be counterposed to the idea of organizations based predominately on a principle of spiritual, sacral, and traditional authority in the civilizations that preceded those of the feudal and aristocratic type. But this aside, to say it again, a historiography of the Right will recognize, no less than the historiography of the left, the succession and the concatenation of distinct general, supernatural phases, the which have regressively led us to the current disorder and subversions: and this will be, in itself, the basis of an interpretation of single facts and revolutions, which never loses sight of the effect that these produce in the entire framework.

---

439 Latin: "economic man." Clearly a play on scientific nomenclature.

It is impossible to indicate here, even through particular examples, the great fecundity of such a method, the unsuspected light that it would cast on a quantity of events. The politico-religious conflicts of the imperial Medieval period; the constant schismatic action of France; the relations between England and Europe; the true sense of the "conquests" of the French Revolution; and so on, up to episodes which interest us particularly, such as the effective face of the revolt of the Commons; the twin faces of the Risorgimento as a national movement, activated however by the ideologies of the Third Estate; the significance of the Holy Alliance and of the efforts of Metternich, that last great European;[440] the significance also of the First World War with the rebound-action of its ideologies; a discrimination between the positive and the negative in the national revolutions which yesterday arose in Italy and in Germany; and so forth and so on, to reach finally a vision of the naked reality of those true forces today in battle for the control of the world—here is but a choice of suggestive arguments, among the great many to which the historiography of the Right could apply itself, acting in an enlightening way and revolutionizing the views that the many are accustomed to holding on all these matters, thanks to the historiography of the opposite orientation.

If it is true that, owing to irreversible objective processes, alliances are ever more frequent today which do not limit themselves to ethnic unities nor particular political and closed communities, then a historiography thus formulated, a historiography aiming at universal principles, would really be up to the height of the times. Yet, unfortunately, it is from this very hoped-for historiography alone that such growth of consciousness might come. Given the present state of affairs, one can hardly expect practical efficacy from such historiography, toward the end of trenchant action, or of a global and inexorable battle against the

---

440 For the "rivolt of the Commons," see note 422 to Chapter 38 above. For the question of the Risorgimento, see Chapter 10. For Metternich, see Chapter 27.

forces which stand on the brink of crushing the little that yet remains of the true European tradition. Indeed, toward such an end as that we would require also the existence of an international organization[441] of the Right, organized and armed with power like that of the communists. However one unfortunately knows that, for the dearth of men of high caliber and of sufficient authority, for the prevalence of interests *ex parte* and of small ambitions, for the lack of true principles, and last but not least for the lack of intellectual courage—for all of this, it has not been possible up to now to build a unitary formation of the Right, not even here in our Italy. It has only been recently that certain initiatives of this kind have been announced.

---

441 That is, an international organization like to the Communist International, or Comintern. Though the Comintern was formed in Russia during the Russian Civil War, it later came to develop a sophisticated network of affiliated agents and representatives throughout the entire world (hence the name), putting up a great many front organizations to push its agenda clandestinely. These front organizations would often recruit non-communists who agreed with communism on certain discrete points, thereafter seeking to indoctrinate these into deeper communist principles. Evola's point here—which he makes in other forms elsewhere throughout this book—is that the Right, if it is to compete with the international left, has need of an equally international logic, rather than any form of reasoning which rests content with nationalism.

40. THE RIGHT AND THE TRADITION

The idea of the Right today is awakening interest in wide and various spheres. Given the political and cultural marasmus of present-day Italy, this is certainly a positive sign. However, whenever an idea begins to resonate, it happens that it increasingly loses its exactitude, and the formula comes to count for more than specific content. The same can be said also for the idea of the Right, especially insofar as it is referred to planes beyond its origin (that is, the political), and comes to be taken as a general attitude.

In this context, the problem of the relation between the concept of the Right and that of Tradition might acquire a special interest. It is necessary to bring attention to this point if one wishes to give a positive content to the Right, rather than a merely polemical or oppositional one.

The merely polemic content of the Right was implicit in its origins. Indeed one recalls that the Right was so named in relation to the place occupied by those assembly members who had aligned themselves against the revolutionary elements; while the revolutionary elements were for this same reason characterized as the "Left."[442] In the assemblies of the *anciens régimes*, however, this opposition was not between elements of comparable force. Indeed in general those regimes were

---

442 This in the days preceding French Revolution; the supporters of the *ancien régime* placed themselves at the right of the parliamentary president, and those agitating for revolution at his left.

monarchical, and the Right did not act on its own behalf, but assumed the defense of the superior principles of authority and of order eminently seated at the very zenith of the State. Moreover, in its origin even the so-called "opposition" had a functional character, because loyalty and cooperativism was presupposed in its representatives—an idea which is characteristically expressed in the English formula: His Majesty's most loyal opposition.[443] Only at the appearance of ideologies and revolutionary movements did one come to define the Right and the Left as entirely counterposed formations. In such a situation, it was naturally proper to the Right to assume a conservative orientation.

With this we have already delineated some essential concepts for the entire problem that we intend to consider. With the twilight of the "*ancien régime*," a higher *positive* principle of reference partially failed, or became uncertain. It is easier to specify what the Right does not want and what it combats on the political plane, than that which it wants and wants to defend; and in this respect divergences of some importance might arise.

Even when one speaks by extension of a cultural orientation and of a life-vision of the Right, the purely negative definition is the most manageable, though it be evidently incomplete. The introduction of positive principles is necessary to give force to any true antithesis between Right and Left—principles which at the end of the day cannot have anything but a "traditional" character. Yet one must specify exactly how to take inspiration from the concept of a particular and eminent tradition; and thus it has become common, for more than merely rhetorical reasons, to write the word Tradition in the uppercase when outlining a corresponding current of thought.

---

443 "His Majesty's most loyal opposition" is in English in the original. This formula in fact dates back to a relatively recent period, the early nineteenth century, and was originally meant in a classically dry English jest. It was later gladly adopted by those to whom it had been applied, and quite in the spirit that Evola here indicates.

Indeed, a generic traditionalism of empirical or merely historical character does not suffice. But often the political Right can offer nothing else. We have indicated that this Right is naturally "conservative," and therefore also "traditional," taking its inspiration, that is, from a given system of principles and institutions that one wishes to maintain or to safeguard. On this level one remains evidently in the field of factuality and also of relativity, for one refers case by case to that which one has simply inherited. It is for this trait of inheritance alone that one attributes value to it, its quality as a thing to conserve and to preserve.

But a broader and more elevated conception is possible, which takes its reference from constant values of universal nature. *Such values can furnish the positive content of a true Right.* In this acceptation the concept of Tradition is applied to a system in which "all activities are ordered, as a matter of principle, from the heights and toward the heights."

In consequence, the natural and fundamental presupposition for a "traditional" Right appears to be the admission of the reality of a superior order, which has also a deontological, that is to say a normative, character. In antiquity, one could speak of an over-world opposed to the world of becoming and contingency. Religion therefore could form its basis. Here, however, the existence of a positive institutionalized religion a Church might appear as a limiting condition: the practical danger arises that this Church might then monopolize spiritual authority (this is the orientation which historically provoked the Ghibelline "dispute"[444]). Thus it is preferable to keep oneself to a more neutral plane, to express only subordinate references of a strictly religious character and to employ instead the concept of "transcendence." Transcendence, that is, with respect to whatever is simply human, physical, naturalistic and materialistic, but which is not for this reason detached and abstract, so that, almost paradoxically, one might speak

---

444 For the Ghibellines, see note 149 to Chapter 13 above.

of an "immanent transcendence"; for one must relate oneself also to a real formative, energizing and organizing force, a force precisely "from the heights" and toward the heights. In this one might indicate the final point of reference of the traditional orientation, lying beyond every one of its particular expressions and concretizations.

Consequently, the background for any true Right which also has "traditional" content, the background for every corresponding vision of the world and of life, should analogously be a spiritual background. Only by keeping oneself to this plane can one thereby furnish a foundation and higher legitimization to every particular position of a traditional Right. This Right cannot be other than hierarchical and aristocratic. It can do no other than pose well differentiated hierarchies of values, and affirm the principle of authority; it can do no other than oppose itself to the world of quantity, of the masses, of democracy, of sovereign economy; it can do no other than emphasize that which truly merits commitment, that to which it is truly worth absolutely subordinating one's own particular interest, so that one might have an anagogic virtue—that is, a virtue which directs toward the heights ("toward the heights" as counterpart to "from the heights"). And this precisely on the basis of an anchorage in the "other," in super-ordered reality. It has been justly observed that personality in the eminent sense does not exist when it is not open to the super-personal; this corresponds precisely to the spirit and the climate of the Tradition.

Certainly, for the formation of such a Right, which will in any case not exhaust itself in mere politico-social positions (these ought to be defined and to matter only in consequence), a great work of demolition would be required, and vocations and qualifications would become necessary which today are not easy to find. Courage would be also necessary, in some cases not merely of the intellectual kind. In this connection a paradoxical convergence might appear between traditionalism and revolution. But "conservative revolution" is not a new term: it was even the designation of an interesting politico-cultural current of pre-Nazi Germany. Conservation in this sense refers to nothing present, but rather to basic ideas of a perennial currency (Möller van den Bruck).[445] With respect to today's modern civilization and society, one can effectively say that nothing has a revolutionary character like the Tradition; one is speaking here, in good Hegelianism, of a "negation of the negation"—the second negation being that which we owe to "progress," which has brought us to where we today find ourselves, by desecrating everything, by subverting every normal order. This is the negation to be negated. Thus another watchword might be meet for the traditional Right: "revolution from the heights"—the opposite of all these protesting anarchoid velleities of the day, which culminate in vain or insane agitation because they lack a positive counterpart. Their exponents are indeed incapable of so much as conceiving of such a counterpart—even when they do not find themselves, openly or unconsciously, in the orbit of the ideologies of the left, or when they are not being exploited by the same.

If one casts one's glance to what is or has been designated as Right, a few clarifications are necessary on the basis of what we have said. The Right has been characterized in terms of economic forms associated more or less with capitalism, the which have served as a convenient target for Marxism and for the other forces of subversion. A disgraceful descent in level is evident here, even if one must recognize that in this very material sphere there are structures which should be conserved and defended. Speaking more generally, there is a Right defined

---

445 Arthur Möller van den Bruck (1876-1925) was a German cultural historian and one of the dominant figures of the *Konservative Revolution*, to which Evola here alludes. Möller van den Bruck was a forerunner of many of the nationalistic and racialist theories which later actuated the rise of the Nazis. *Konservative Revolution* refers in particular to the opposition to the materialistic, democratic world of quantity which was then arising in the Weimar republic. The movement was associated with Nietzsche (Thomas Mann even used the term to apply to Nietzsche in particular).

by a predominately conservative orientation in the bourgeois middle class—which has been the case particularly in Italy. The points of reference in other nations, on the other hand, bring us back, in part, to the higher level before indicated. The traditional French Right has been essentially Catholic and monarchic, even if reservations might arise with respect to a certain genre of Catholicism *a là* Charles Maurras,[446] and in particular when such a religion comes to be considered as more than a merely political background of the Right.

A species of monarchical mysticism is implicit in the Right of the Anglo-Saxon Countries. These countries have not been constrained to Catholicism, but Protestantism has likewise been able to make itself felt as a point of reference. The Protestant Bismarck was no less paramount an exponent of the true Right than the Catholic Metternich, or the Catholics Maistre and Donoso Cortés.[447] A certain secular retrogression must be observed in Prussianism, however, for its references to the transcendent are veiled. One finds rather in the first place a species of autonomous ethics, a traditional, congenital characterical formation which apparently has a force of its own, but which at bottom—in the emphasis it gives to what is super-personal—would not know how to truly justify itself if it were not, so to speak, the derivative of a precedent orientation which possessed a spiritual background (one might recall that Prussianism with its

---

446 Maurras (1868-1952) was a French author, poet, and critic, known for his attempt to wed nationalism with Catholicism. Evola's reservations toward him here are most telling, as in many ways Maurras seems superficially to represent precisely the kind of figure that Evola should have praised: he was an anti-modernist, a devotee of the old orders, a monarchist, a critic of the French Revolution and of the entirety of the Enlightenment, an admirer of the Roman Empire. The locus of Evola's critique seems to be in Maurras' desire to establish the Catholic Church as a political power and a state religion.

447 For the last three figures, see Chapters 27, 31, and 28, respectively.

ethics was born as a secularization of the Order of the Teutonic
Knights[448]).

One sometimes speaks of the Right also in reference to political
systems of the "fascist" type. Here however one must formulate some
reservations. It has been observed, most fittingly in a group of essays
dedicated to the European Right *(The European Right* edited by H.
Rogger and E. Weber, University of California Press, 1966),[449] that
these systems cannot be called "Right" in the ancient and traditional
sense of the term, that they are rather characterized by a mixture of
the Right with the Left; for if on the one hand they have defended the
principle of authority, on the other they were based on mass parties,
and they incorporated the "social" and revolutionary demands proper
to the Left—demands against which the men of a true Right would
certainly have taken a stand. More generally, it is a distortion to attribute the character of the Right to dictatorship, for dictatorship as such
has no tradition, being as it is a formless constellation of the potency
in a given individuality (dictatorship here understood as a type of constitution, not as something transitory imposed in situations of crisis

---

448 The Teutonic Order was a Catholic religious order founded around 1190 in
Acre. It proved a remarkably long-lasting and resilient organization, officially
dissolved only by Napoleon in 1809. In the course of their many centuries of
existence the Teutonic Knights assumed numerous manifestations and roles
throughout many territories in Europe. For more on their meaning and their
organization, Evola himself wrote on them in Chapter 13 of *Revolt Against the
Modern World*, and more extensively in his work *The Mystery of the Grail*. The
Teutonic Knights indeed were conquerors of the entire Prussian region, and
their influence on the budding Prussian state is not to be passed off lightly. As a
merest indication of this influence—the Prussian flag is taken directly from the
arms of the Teutonic Order.

449 Hans Rogger (1923-2002) was an American historian who specialized in imperial Russia. Eugen Weber (1925-2007) was a Romanian who moved to the
United States for his university studies in history. He specialized in the Western
Tradition. The two men co-edited and contributed to a compilation of essays on
the European right post World War I.

or of emergency). Machiavelli's *Prince* incarnates nothing that one can call Right; rather, we find in him an inversion of relations, since if the Machiavellian leader might take inspiration from spiritual or religious values, he does this only by adopting them as simple expedients for his government, without any intrinsic recognition of their worth. The same argument could be extended to those principles, possibly of a superior order, which in the framework of dictatorial totalitarianism might nevertheless fall under the species of simple "myths"—that is, having in view exclusively formulations apt to cause or canalize the irrational forces of the masses. It is not necessary to underline that the Right and demagogy are irreconcilable.

All these observations confirm the importance of the connections, indicated in the preceding, between a true Right and the Tradition.

After all that has been said, if one must conceive of a "culture of the Right," one ought to recognize as one of its paramount tasks highlighting the values of the Tradition, and distancing itself, in the meantime, from every merely "traditionalistic," that is to say conformistic, orientation. The field of the culture of the Right is potentially quite vast. The historiography and the morphology of civilizations could play an important part in it, because, rejecting every historiography of liberal, Marxist, and progressivist tendency, it would be necessary to systematically highlight everything which in previous periods incarnated traditional principles, so as to make its paradigmatic character evident. Valid contributions have already been furnished above all by that current which takes as its head René Guénon,[450] the true master of modern times. Within the limits of our possibilities, we have dedicated ourselves to a not dissimilar task, insofar as we have sketched, on the basis of comparative research, a species of "doctrine of the categories" of the "World of the Tradition" in the first part of our work *Revolt Against the Modern World* (1934; 3rd ed. 1969).

---

450 See Chapter 35 for more on Guénon.

Once strong points of axiological reference have been fixed, it would become the task of a culture of the Right to study also their possible applications to the current state of affairs. The danger of a sclerotic conservatism should be overcome by adopting the principle of *homology*.[451] Homology does not signify identity but correspondence—not exact reproduction but transposition and reaffirmation of the same formal principles from one level to another, from one situational complex to another. If we wish to employ an image, consider a stream, wherein a whirlpool which has disappeared at one given point returns to form itself at another point, in obedience to one and the same law: it is identical but at the same time different, precisely because it is in a fluid medium—like time, like history—that these whirlpools take shape.

This general methodological indication might be concretized in the consideration of the various fields of problems which a culture of the Right ought to confront, so as to build schemata valid also in praxis. It is here important to hold the line, not ceding to the temptation of accommodating positions, such as might assure a wider, but less select, resonance. We must remember that we do not work only for today but also and above all for tomorrow. Here we might make reference to Hegel's words: "The idea has no haste."

These considerations are not superfluous, because the idea of the Right today seems to have achieved, as we observed at the beginning, a certain vogue; and this has often brought one to label very different and even spurious attitudes as belonging to the Right. This attests in any case the absence of a rigorous and coherent line of thought. Yet such a line is mandatory if one is to speak of something more than

---

451 Homology is the study (usually in biology, but here extended by Evola to a much wider field) of similarities or developments in two different places which issue from a common origin. See note 413 to Chapter 36 above. In Evola's use, it is evident that this "origin" is not necessarily historical, but might also indicate a spiritual origin at a higher level of being.

mere improvisations, and also if one is not to limit oneself to political positions—if one wants, that is, to define also an existential and general cultural orientation.

INDEX

OTHER BOOKS PUBLISHED BY ARKTOS

OTHER BOOKS PUBLISHED BY ARKTOS

OTHER BOOKS PUBLISHED BY ARKTOS

	William's House (vol. 1–4)
RAIDO	*A Handbook of Traditional Living*
STEVEN J. ROSEN	*The Agni and the Ecstasy*
	The Jedi in the Lotus
RICHARD RUDGLEY	*Barbarians*
	Essential Substances
	Wildest Dreams
ERNST VON SALOMON	*It Cannot Be Stormed*
	The Outlaws
SRI SRI RAVI SHANKAR	*Celebrating Silence*
	Know Your Child
	Management Mantras
	Patanjali Yoga Sutras
	Secrets of Relationships
TROY SOUTHGATE	*Tradition & Revolution*
OSWALD SPENGLER	*Man and Technics*
TOMISLAV SUNIC	*Against Democracy and Equality*
	Postmortem Report
	Titans are in Town
HANS-JÜRGEN SYBERBERG	*On the Fortunes and Misfortunes of Art in Post-War Germany*
ABIR TAHA	*Defining Terrorism: The End of Double Standards*
	The Epic of Arya (Second edition)
	Nietzsche's Coming God, or the Redemption of the Divine
	Verses of Light
BAL GANGADHAR TILAK	*The Arctic Home in the Vedas*
DOMINIQUE VENNER	*The Shock of History*
	For a Positive Critique
MARKUS WILLINGER	*A Europe of Nations*
	Generation Identity
DAVID J. WINGFIELD (ED.)	*The Initiate: Journal of Traditional Studies*

41487793R00203